Desktop Publishing
With Word
for Windows

THROUGH VERSION 6

Second Edition

Tom Lichty

VENTANA
PRESS

Desktop Publishing With Word for Windows Through Version 6, Second Edition
Copyright © 1994 by Tom Lichty

Library of Congress Cataloging-in-Publication Data

Lichty, Tom.
      Desktop publishing with Word for Windows through version 6 / Tom Lichty. -- 2nd ed.
                p.   cm.
      Rev. ed. of: Desktop publishing with Word for Windows for version 2. c1992.
      Includes index.
      ISBN 1-56604-074-4
      1. Microsoft Word for Windows. 2. Word processing. 3. Desktop publishing. I. Title.
Z52.5.M523L53 1994
686.2'2544536--dc20   93-43450
                                     CIP

Book design: Marcia Webb, Karen Wysocki
Cover design: *Series Concept:* Holly Russel; *adaptation:* Marcia Webb
Index service: Dianne Bertsch
Technical review: Cyndi Bishop
Editorial staff: Charles Hutchinson, Diana Merelman, Pam Richardson
Production staff: Midgard Productions, Terri March, Marcia Webb
Proofreader: Eric Edstam

First Edition 9 8 7 6 5 4 3 2 1
Printed in the United States of America

Ventana Press, Inc.
P.O. Box 2468
Chapel Hill, NC 27515
919/942-0220
FAX 919/942-1140

Limits of Liability and Disclaimer of Warranty

TRADEMARKS

ABOUT THE AUTHOR

Tom Lichty is an author/lecturer/farmer living in Oregon, where he is senior instructor at the University of Oregon's microcomputer program in Portland. His book *Design Principles for Desktop Publishers* (published by Scott Foresman Professional Books) received the Computer Press Association's Best How-To Book of 1988 Award. He also wrote *The Official America Online Membership Kit & Tour Guide* (Mac, Windows and PC Editions) and *Mac, Word & Excel Desktop Companion* (both published by Ventana Press).

Dedication

for Victoria

Contents

8 FONTS & PRINTERS 237

Introduction

I'm an old-timer. I've been in the desktop-publishing business since 1986 and in the business of publishing for 12 years before that. I'm picky: I demand quality design, quality typography, quality graphics and quality printing. So, when Ventana Press suggested I write about desktop publishing with a *word processor*, I suspected their equanimity.

Word processors, after all, are tools for text entry. A word processor roughs out text as a chain saw roughs out sculpture. Nobody uses a chain saw for refinement, just as nobody uses a word processor for page layout. Everybody knows that.

Well, *almost* everybody. Nobody told the people at Microsoft. In their enthusiasm and ignorance of the conventional role of the word processor, they developed Word for Windows Version 6, and aimed it directly at the desktop-publishing market. They made it easy to use, retained all its word-processing authority and embroidered it with more accessories than a 1973 Coupe de Ville.

They even made Word for Windows fun.

But did they succeed in producing word-processing-cum-desktop-publishing software? Can you use it for anything beyond roughing out text? If so, how?

You hold the answers in your hands.

WHO SHOULD READ THIS BOOK?

In the first chapter, I define the desktop publisher as a generalist. Desktop publishers often write, edit, design, produce and distribute their material. Few desktop publishers, however, are full-time practitioners. The words *desktop publisher* may not even appear in your job description; and if they do, you can be sure they don't appear at the top.

More often than not, desktop publishing is a supplementary task. You probably aren't a publications specialist, you have a thousand other things to do, and your desktop-publishing budget contains more digits to the right of the decimal point than to the left.

Budget or not, we all share a common goal: the adornment of the printed page. We acknowledge that the presentation of our material is nearly as vital as its content. The more professional looking and attractive the document, the more effective the message. And we know that getting the message across in this age of information-overload is not only a noble but an essential objective.

This book is for you if you own and use Word, but you're by no means a black belt. Most of the symbols on the Standard toolbar are babble to you and words like *fields* and *annotations* aren't even in your vocabulary. You know enough about the program to get by: to enter, edit and print a simple document.

However, simple documents aren't on your mind right now. You need to move to a new level and prepare pages that sparkle. Pages that attract your readers, flatter your subject and reflect your excellence. Because you aren't disposed to buy and learn another program, you wonder whether Word is up to the task. You need a better understanding of graphics, fonts and typography; but you're a semi-normal person and you fear you may never be able to relate to these kinds of anomalies.

WHAT'S IN THIS BOOK?

On one level, *Desktop Publishing With Word for Windows* guides you through the techniques of formatting and producing professional-looking, attractive documents. On another level, this book eggs you on, encourages you to unleash Word's considerable graphics power in the Windows environment.

And power it is: together with Windows, Word offers a wealth of features for the desktop publisher. Between Windows *Paintbrush* and Word, nearly all graphic file formats are supported. *WordArt* offers display-type fonts and a rich environment in which to prepare them. Microsoft *Graph* features over 70 formats for business graphics, 30 of which are three-dimensional. The *Equation Editor* makes mathematical equations almost fun; the grammar checker checks your spelling and grammar; the thesaurus suggests synonyms; and the zoom feature lets you view *and edit* your document in any size between 10 and 200 percent of the original. Macros, tables, columns, styles and a Help file round out the most feature-laden software package you can buy.

The opening chapter casts a harsh light on Word and asks, "Is Word *really* desktop-publishing software?" I define the term *desktop publishing* and compare Word feature-by-feature (and dollar-for-dollar) with PageMaker, Ventura Publisher and QuarkXPress. The comparison is qualitative, quantitative and merciless.

Chapters 2 and 3 address the typographic principles of properly formatted body text, examine Word's tools for fulfilling that responsibility and lament some of its omissions.

Chapters 4 and 5 do the same for display type. I remove the shrink wrap from some of Word's unusual utilities and apply them to the production of "cheap tricks": textual embellishments that give documents more personality, individuality and appeal.

Chapter 6 revels in Word's relevant and extensive use of styles. No single feature offers more potential for the desktop publisher, and no other program matches Word's fulfillment of that potential.

The seventh chapter probes the elusive realm of computer graphics. Nothing is more challenging to the desktop publisher, or offers as much potential, but graphics are, well, *elusive*. In an exhaustive study, I clarify the formats of computer graphics, examine those that Word imports and suggest how and when to use each.

In the eighth chapter, I unravel the conundrum of fonts and printers. We compare the merits of competing systems and weave them into Word's context.

The ninth chapter explores the newest additions to Word: AutoFormat, wizards and templates. There really isn't much of an opportunity for Microsoft to increase the number of features Word offers—after all, everything's here but the proverbial kitchen sink—so instead, they concentrated on making the program easier to use. AutoFormat, wizards and templates make the production of everyday documents nearly automatic. All you have to do is type. This chapter identifies these new features and explores their appropriate use.

All this information is voiced in a tenor of candor and equity. As I make clear in Chapter 1, I don't work for Microsoft. I'm not indebted to ulterior motives. I offer *Desktop Publishing With Word for Windows* in your interest and for your benefit.

THE HARDWARE YOU WILL NEED

There's a price attached to Word's power, and you will eventually pay it—if you haven't already—in the form of hardware. This book assumes that you have successfully installed Windows and Word, and that you have a Windows-compatible computer and printer.

A minimal-configuration system for the productive use of Windows and Word consists of the following:

✔ A 386-based system or better. Word's desktop-publishing features are practically intolerant of 286 or 386SX systems.

✔ Four megabytes of random-access memory (RAM) or more.

✔ At least 40 megabytes of free space available on a hard disk before Word or Windows are installed.

✔ A VGA or SVGA monitor, color or monochrome.

✔ A mouse and an operator who's willing to use it.

✔ A high-resolution printer, capable of at least 300 dots per inch.

You should have a pretty good idea of how to operate this system. You don't have to recite your WIN.INI file from memory, but you should be able to copy files, format disks and switch among programs. If your best Solitaire score exceeds 5,000, you are at a clear advantage.

WILL ROGERS RETURNS

You want help; someone who won't talk down to you; someone who appreciates Word but doesn't venerate it—an authority with humility, wisdom and a sense of humor. Will Rogers would be perfect, but he died in 1935 and wasn't much of an authority on Word anyway.

May I interest you in a good book? It may not be Will Rogers, but it's relevant, competent and *convenient*. After all, all you have to do is turn the page....

—Tom Lichty
Gresham, OR

1 Is This Really Desktop Publishing?

I want to say from the start, I don't work for Microsoft. I beta-test its products and in turn receive advance information that enables me to have my books on the shelves in a timely manner. True to form, Microsoft is supportive, cordial, even benevolent—but never despotic. It gives me access to its stuff and staff, then politely recedes. But it's chapters like this one that challenge Microsoft's equanimity. In this chapter, I offer a candid inquisition, Is Word *really* desktop-publishing software?

APPLYING SOFTWARE INAPPROPRIATELY

I don't want you to fall into the all-too-common trap of applying software inappropriately. Allow me a simile: looking for a change after 20 years of piloting drift boats down the rivers of the Northwest, I bought a canoe. After a couple of test runs, my friend and I took it to the Deschutes River in central Oregon. Though we had never run the river and knew it harbored a number of Class 4 rapids, we embarked confidently, secure in our years of wisdom and skill. Six hours into the three-day trip, we encountered a rapids three miles long, an interminable ferment of caldrons and whirlpools, punctuated with waterfalls and switchbacks. The expression "in over our heads" took on a literal significance. We finished the trip in six days—walking with a canoe on your shoulders is slow going—and relegated the canoe to placid lakes and shallow streams forevermore.

This situation happens in computing as well. Confronted with a complex task, our first inclination is to employ the software we already have and know; or if we're new to it all, buy the software that Fred down the hall said is Really Neat Stuff. Days later, mired in manuals and unreturned phone calls, we realize we've applied the wrong tool to the task. We're in over our heads and have no choice but to continue, even though the journey is going to take twice as long as we planned.

If this fear haunts you, read on.

THE CHEEKY ATTITUDE

With Word for Windows 6, Microsoft confronted the desktop-publishing market with, well, a *cheeky* attitude. This attitude is Microsoft's legacy. When CP/M dominated the operating-system arena, Microsoft countered with MS-DOS, a cheeky move if there ever was one. When Lotus showed signs of complacency, Microsoft wedged a niche with Excel. When Apple touted the Graphical User Interface as its exclusive domain, Microsoft introduced Windows 3.0. And now Microsoft impertinently positions a *word processor* as a desktop-publishing program.

This kind of temerity begs for inquisition. That's what this chapter is all about.

WHAT IS DESKTOP PUBLISHING?

What *is* desktop publishing? We can't begin our investigation until we define the term. Interestingly, though desktop publishing represents one of the three largest markets in U.S. software sales, it is nonetheless ill-defined. Perhaps we can correct the situation in the next few pages.

The History

The term's origin is really quite prosaic. When PageMaker was first introduced, it had no home. It most certainly wasn't word processing: it couldn't spell or even keep up with a competent typist. It wasn't a graphics program either: lines, circles and boxes comprised the extent of its graphical repertoire. It was a page-composition program, but how many people have heard of page composition? How many people have toiled over a light table with Chart Tape and X-Acto knives? Paul Brainerd, PageMaker's guru, needed a term that conveyed humility and familiarity. Thus, the phrase *desktop publishing* was born.

Historically, then, desktop publishing is page composition, or *paste up*, to use the vernacular.

The Generalist

Who said it first?
A 1985 issue of *Small Press* magazine attributes the origin of the term "desktop publishing" to literature from Datacopy Corporation published in 1982. This use would predate Aldus founder Paul Brainerd's use of the term by three years.

But it wasn't long before the crack in PageMaker's armor was spotted. Before material could be pasted up, it had to be written. Brainerd's strategy was to leave word processing to the word processors. Though PageMaker offered some text-entry potential, it was slow and its screens were hard to read. Text entry and editing was better left to word processors, and PageMaker imported formatted text from them all. Among desktop-publishing programs today, this attitude still prevails.

But the division between desktop publishing and word processing is unnatural. Brainerd saw the developing marketplace but didn't foresee that it would be made up of generalists, not specialists: writing, editing, pasting up, printing—even producing artwork—are all included in the desktop-publishing job description.

Ornate Formatting

Formatting is the most evident characteristic: desktop-published documents are invariably more elaborate than their word-processed counterparts. Multiple columns, typography, graphics, text wrap and color immediately come to mind.

The additional design responsibility is daunting and, some might say, rarely well met. But one thing's for sure: desktop publishing is never dull.

DOCUMENT ORGANIZATION

Now that we've defined the subject, let's see how Word goes about addressing it. Perhaps the most significant difference between Word and most page-composition programs is that of document organization. This difference is so conceptual that it often isn't readily apparent. Nonetheless, it's the most fundamental and significant difference of them all.

Object-Oriented Composition

PageMaker, for instance, organizes documents in three dimensions. Each element occupies its own layer, and the layers are stacked on top of one another. You can move any element about on its layer in a random fashion. Don't like that graphic in the corner? Move it to the other corner, or under that text on the left—any place you want.

Look at the random arrangement of elements in Figure 1-1. It's almost as if someone dropped a sack full of tiles and they landed helter-skelter on the page.

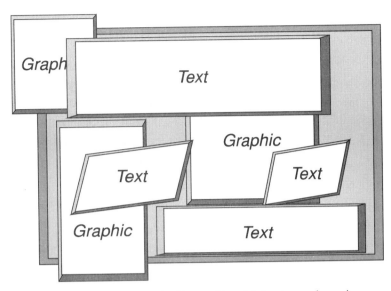

Figure 1-1: This illustration indicates PageMaker's random document construction strategy, which Word doesn't use.

An all-purpose adjunct

Figure 1-1 was created in CorelDRAW, a graphics program that uses object-oriented composition. You should consider this type of program first when expanding your desktop-publishing software library.

Indeed, this random document construction strategy is the founding concept underlying PageMaker. The program was designed to replicate the light-table environment where pieces of paper are manipulated like cards on a table.

PageMaker, like many other programs—graphics programs in particular—is object-oriented. Each element on the page is an independent object. (We'll discuss object-oriented programs in Chapter 7, "Graphics.")

With the object-oriented concept in mind, look at Figure 1-2. This figure illustrates the object-oriented, random-placement paradigm used to its best advantage. Only object-oriented programs are up to this kind of task. Faced with this assignment, Word would shrivel and die.

Figure 1-2: The random-object approach is well suited for documents that used to require hours of paste-up at the light table.

Linear Document Composition

Word documents, on the other hand, are two-dimensional. They never overlap. Each element follows every other, like cars in a freight train.

Figure 1-3 represents a schematic of a page in this book. Figure 1-4 is the same page, in a less abstract form. The left layout shows a parenthetical sidebar placed outside the margin and opposite the third paragraph on the page.

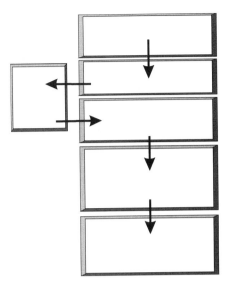

Figure 1-3: Word documents are linear: each element—text or graphic—follows another on a two-dimensional plane.

The advantage to the linear approach is that everything stays in order, even if you add or delete elements from the document.

The right layout in Figure 1-4 illustrates what happens when you add four lines of text to the second paragraph. If you were using the object-oriented approach, the sidebar would be an independent object and would remain stationary, regardless of whether you edited text in the column adjacent to it.

Figure 1-4: With linear-oriented composition, the sidebar remains locked to the adjacent paragraph, even after you add lines to the text column.

Frames do it all
A frame is the feature that allows elements to be placed outside of their normal locations. Frames are discussed in Chapter 7, "Graphics."

With the linear approach, however, the sidebar remains locked in place with the third paragraph. In fact, the sidebar *is* the third paragraph, and the paragraph to its right is the fourth (look again at the sequence of arrows in Figure 1-3). The sidebar is tagged with instructions that place it *beside* the paragraph "below" it. Once the sidebar is in position, Word closes the gap that remains between the second and fourth paragraphs.

Documents created in linear-oriented programs are better suited to formats containing elements placed relative to one another, such as the one shown in Figure 1-4. In Figure 1-2, the price of a gallon of milk stays put regardless of whether the headline is edited. The object containing the milk's price occupies its own layer and is independent of all other objects on the page, including the headline.

Neither one of these approaches to document organization is superior to the other. Each has its advantages and disadvantages, depending on the type of document you're creating.

Which is my point. One of the ways to determine whether Word is right for you is to ask, "Do the majority of my documents contain elements that should be placed independent of or relative to the others?" If your documents contain elements that must remain fixed on the page regardless of any editing that takes place, Word is not your best choice.

If, on the other hand, your documents contain captions that must stay associated with illustrations, or sideheads (heads to the side of paragraphs) that must move with body text or sidebars in the margin, then Word serves you well.

Hard-disk sales will soar

With all its graphics included, the Word file for this chapter measures almost two megabytes. If the graphics are stripped out of it, it measures less than 100 kilobytes—5 percent of the original and about the size of a Ventura file for the same chapter.

LONG DOCUMENTS/SHORT DOCUMENTS

Having long documents is probably the most touted argument when the subject of word processing versus desktop publishing is discussed. You hear it often: "Desktop publishing isn't well suited for long documents."

It's not true. In fact, Word is at something of a disadvantage for long documents containing a lot of graphics. Here's why: unless field codes are used, Word stores *everything* in a single file. If a 200-page document contains 75 graphics, Word stores all those graphics in the document's file (see Figure 1-5). If the graphics are rich in detail, the file's size could become astronomical. (See Chapter 7, "Graphics," for a discussion of high-resolution .EPS and .TIF graphics.)

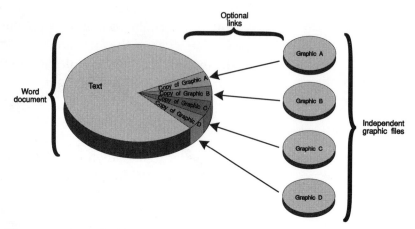

Figure 1-5: Word's file-management strategy involves embedding copies of supporting files within the Word file, which can result in large document files.

Field codes

I'm not being entirely fair here. Using field codes—the Include field in particular—you can coerce Word to combine multiple documents into one. Under these circumstances, the master document—the one with the field codes—can become quite efficient. On the other hand, field codes are lofty stuff, beyond the scope of this book and of most desktop publishers.

On the other hand, Ventura Publisher, along with most other dedicated desktop-publishing programs, stores graphics as separate files (see Figure 1-6). Its publication files are nothing more than a series of pointers that tell the program which files comprise the document and where they're to be placed. When a Ventura document is opened, it assembles these independent files into a completed publication.

Ventura's long-document files, therefore, are notably smaller than Word's. They load and save more quickly, require fewer computing resources and back up more conveniently.

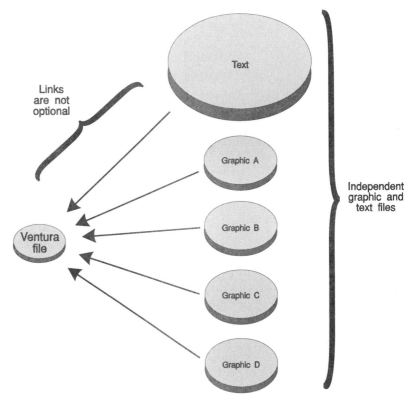

Figure 1-6: In Ventura Publisher, a "chapter" file lets the program know which supporting files to use and where to place them. Only one version of each supporting file is retained on the disk.

Linking is another advantage to the Ventura approach. Only one version of each supporting file resides on the disk; there's no second copy in the publication file. If you modify a supporting graphic, Ventura reflects that change the next time you open the publication. Ventura's supporting files are linked to the publication file, not stored within it. Therefore, everything remains current.

Though you can instruct Word to behave in the same way—it can link files and update them if they change—it nonetheless continues to store copies of supporting files in its documents. Updating links, in other words, involves updating the Word file. This process can be tedious, and though it can be configured to occur automatically, setting up an automatic link requires a comprehensive understanding of Word's file-management commands. (The automatic linking process is described in Chapter 7, "Graphics.")

Although Word's document-management strategy is inefficient, it *is* portable: because Word files are inclusive of all supporting material, you can conveniently transfer them to another machine (service bureaus and high-resolution imagesetters are covered in Chapter 8, "Fonts & Printers"). All you have to do is make a copy of the Word file, and you're ready for off-site printing.

The Ventura strategy requires scrupulous file management, especially if the document is to be transferred to another machine.

Let's wrap up this discussion: if your documents are long and contain a number of high-resolution graphics, Word's inefficient document-management strategy will place a demand on your resources and you too, if you must establish dynamic linking. On the other hand, if your documents are short (say, a 12-page newsletter), limited resources aren't a factor or you intend to do off-site printing, Word's single-document strategy will prove beneficial.

WORD'S WORD-PROCESSING TOOLS

In our discussion so far, Word has offered no specific advantage over dedicated desktop-publishing programs. Feature for feature, advantage versus disadvantage, our comparison has offered no winner.

That's about to change. Word is, after all, an industrial-grade word processor. Judged on its word-processing merits alone, few programs (some would say none) match Word's features and ease of use.

And more: section headers typically become heads and subheads. Heads and subheads communicate organization to the reader. They let the reader locate topics of particular interest and improve a document's appearance. Documents prepared with heads and subheads are more appealing than those that smother the reader with uninterrupted text.

Cheap tricks
The outliner's role in establishing heads and subheads is discussed in Chapter 5, "Cheap Tricks With Display Type."

Organization of Thought & Master Documents

No dedicated desktop-publishing program offers a feature that competes with Word's Outline utility. Briefly stated, an outliner provides an aerial view of your document (see Figure 1-7). From the outliner's lofty perspective, details converge into sections and give you an overall view of a document's organization. If you write as well as produce your material, an outliner is essential.

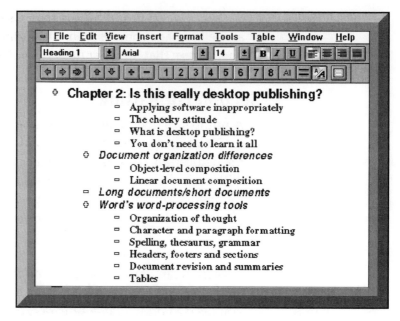

Figure 1-7: Practicing what I preach, the outline for this chapter reflects one stage of the chapter's development. It was an early stage: Chapter 1 became the Introduction and eventually this chapter became Chapter 1.

Behind the scenes

If you enjoy peeking behind the scenery, compare the outline pictured in Figure 1-7 with the final outline of this chapter. Observing the changes made along the way may help you appreciate the outliner's value.

There's more: you can add, delete and reorder sections even after the details are underway. If you move a completed section in Outline View, you move all its associated material—text and graphics—with it. Your document's organization is never static; it's as dynamic as you prefer.

And there's even more: *Master Documents* are documents that tie together several *subdocuments*. Think of this book: it's composed of a number of chapters, each of which is a separate Word document (the subdocuments). By creating a Master Document, we can view the outline for the entire book all at once. We can also make organizational changes by rearranging chapters, print all of the subdocuments (and renumber the pages, if necessary) with a single command, and even create a table of contents and index—all with Master Documents.

If your desktop-publishing responsibilities include writing as well as page composition, the outliner in Word is a compelling feature that no other desktop-publishing program offers.

Section Formatting

A number of documents require section formatting: a book, for instance, may contain front matter—the table of contents, the dedication, copyright information—placed in one column with equal left and right margins. This material may also be numbered independently, perhaps using lowercase roman numerals. The body of the book may contain unequal margins, and an index at the end may require a two-column layout (see Figure 1-8).

Word's sections not only accommodate changes in page numbering, margins and columns, but even page layout. If you need to print a table sideways on a page in the midst of a document, declare a section break (Insert menu, Break) and switch to landscape orientation (File menu, Page Setup).

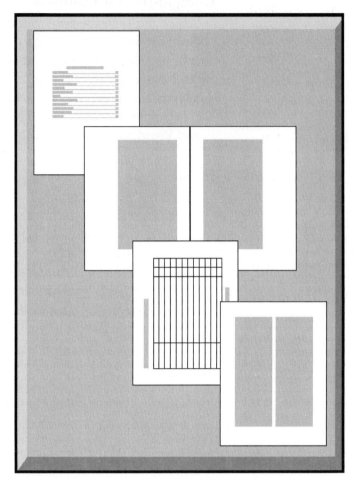

Figure 1-8: Word's section formatting can accommodate a one-column table of contents, body text with unequal margins, a horizontal table and a two-column index—all within a single document.

Although many dedicated desktop-publishing programs offer section formatting (most offer multiple "master pages" or multiple "underlying pages"), few match Word's section-formatting flexibility. If these features are significant, add another point to Word's score.

The Include field
Not only is section formatting supported, a Word section can actually be a separate document, inserted into a receiving document via Word's Include field. Thus, the table in Figure 1-8 could be an independent document included in other documents as well as the one pictured. Because only one version of the table exists, all documents that include the table (via the Include field) will reflect any changes made to it.

Unequal-Width Columns

While you're in the point-adding mood, give Word a big point for a brand-new feature that accommodates unequal column widths. Up until Version 6.0, you either had to use a table (very sloppy) or unequal-width margins (mind-bending) to simulate unequal-width columns. Now all you have to do is issue the appropriate command (Format menu, Columns) and Word complies instantly.

Jumps

This term is newspaper talk. A *jump* is a column that ends with a message like "Continued on page 4" and then continues on another page. Most desktop-publishing programs not only offer this feature, they automate it. Word neither automates nor offers it. While we acknowledge the omission, we won't hold it against the program. Jumps are used primarily in newspapers and magazines, two publications not often created in Word.

Templates

Templates allow numerous documents to share the same format. Section-, paragraph- and character-level formatting may be included in a template, as well as glossary entries, keystroke assignments, styles and macros. Changes you make to a template can be reflected in all documents that refer to that template, even after you've finished working on them.

Templates are especially valuable for periodicals, academic papers, correspondence, news releases—any series of documents in which formatting must be duplicated.

Word's templates are comprehensive and, once you understand them, easy to use. We will discuss templates in Chapter 9.

There's more
An especially valuable feature, templates are not unique to Word, but Word's interpretation of them is especially comprehensive. (We explore templates again in Chapter 6, "Styles," and once again in Chapter 9, "Templates.")

Character & Paragraph Formatting

You might hope that Word—being the ultimate word-processing program—offers all the character- and paragraph-formatting features that desktop publishing requires. Well, there is some good news, and there is some bad news. Let's take a look.

Kerning & Letter Spacing

Unfortunately, Word takes a tumble here. Two notable omissions in the program cripple it, almost fatally. Read carefully now: for some applications, we're about to disqualify Word as a desktop-publishing program.

In Chapter 3, "Setting Up Your Text," I lament Word's inability to properly manage letter spacing when justifying text. Though I'll spare the details for now, understand that Word justifies by adding space between words. This capability is hardly an improvement over typewriting. All dedicated desktop-publishing programs (and Word's biggest competitor, WordPerfect) justify by not only adding space, but also by removing it. Properly, desktop-publishing programs should add and remove space between *letters* as well as between words. Word's minimal approach results in justified text that's so inelegant as to be distracting (see Figure 1-9). Indeed, in Chapter 3, I simply recommend you avoid justifying text altogether when using Word.

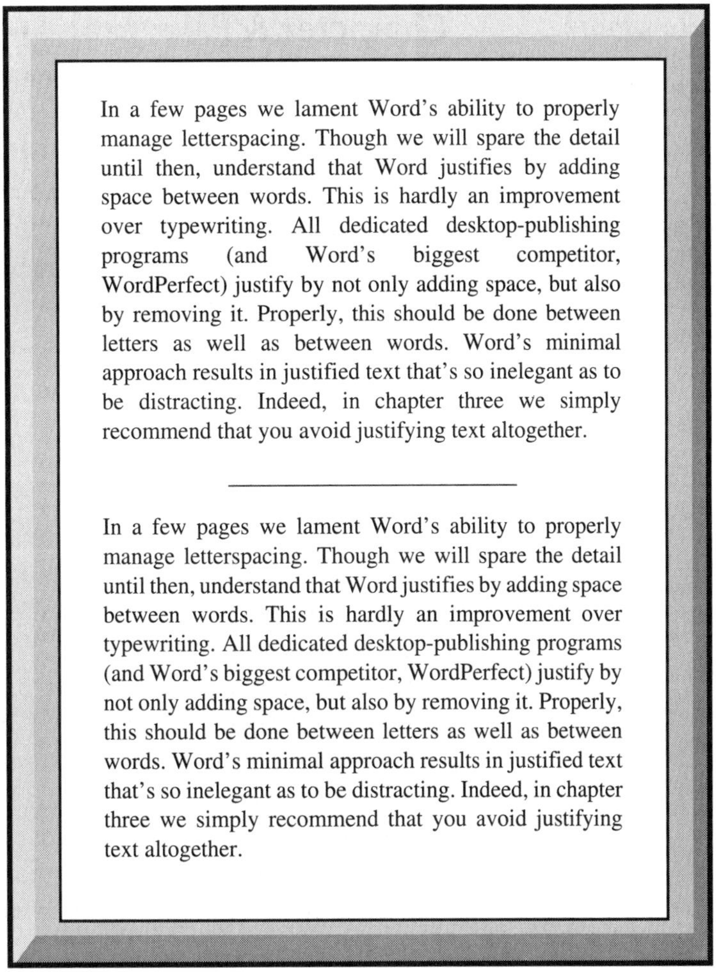

In a few pages we lament Word's ability to properly manage letterspacing. Though we will spare the detail until then, understand that Word justifies by adding space between words. This is hardly an improvement over typewriting. All dedicated desktop-publishing programs (and Word's biggest competitor, WordPerfect) justify by not only adding space, but also by removing it. Properly, this should be done between letters as well as between words. Word's minimal approach results in justified text that's so inelegant as to be distracting. Indeed, in chapter three we simply recommend that you avoid justifying text altogether.

In a few pages we lament Word's ability to properly manage letterspacing. Though we will spare the detail until then, understand that Word justifies by adding space between words. This is hardly an improvement over typewriting. All dedicated desktop-publishing programs (and Word's biggest competitor, WordPerfect) justify by not only adding space, but also by removing it. Properly, this should be done between letters as well as between words. Word's minimal approach results in justified text that's so inelegant as to be distracting. Indeed, in chapter three we simply recommend that you avoid justifying text altogether.

Figure 1-9: Word's add-space-only approach to justification (top) is a poor alternative to the typesetting approach used by dedicated desktop-publishing programs (bottom).

If the majority of your documents need to be justified (few do; see sidebar), Word is not for you. Subtract five points.

Although Word's letter-spacing controls are deplorable, its kerning controls are commendable. Letter spacing refers to spacing throughout a section of the document. Kerning refers to spacing between *pairs* of letters (kerning and letter spacing are discussed in Chapter 4, "Display Type"). Though the

Justifying justification

Let's say it right away: justification is overused. It began as testimony to the typesetter's mastery, an appropriate tribute when few had the skill. But it's no longer a tribute, it's a vestige. It invariably compromises texture and readability. There are few circumstances where it is, well, justified.

Windows system kerns automatically, Word gives you significant additional control (1584 points of control, to be exact, in 1/20 of a point increments). In other words, if you don't like the machine's idea of kerning, Word is prepared to remedy the situation.

That's one point against and one point in favor of the program. This one's a push.

Automatic Hyphenation

One reason desktop-publishing programs make second-rate word processors is that they hyphenate on the fly. In desktop-publishing software, hyphenation is not an independent process; it goes on all the time, without operator prompting. This makes sense: neglecting hyphenation can result in an excessive ragged-right margin when text is left-aligned, or hideous word spacing when the text is justified.

Unfortunately, automatic hyphenation can slow a program considerably. On some machines, automatic hyphenation slows the machine so much that it can't keep up with a fast typist. Hyphenation, after all, requires that the computer consult its dictionary to find syllable breaks for every word that falls within the hyphenation zone, and this search takes time.

In word processing, where speed is critical, the solution has usually been manual hyphenation. In most word-processing software, hyphenation is a separate command; the machine won't hyphenate until you tell it to. A burdensome task.

Word gives you your choice. If you want automatic hyphenation (and your machine is fast enough to support it), turn it on (Tools menu, Hyphenation). If you're willing to remember to do it yourself, leave it turned off (which is the default condition). The choice is yours, and for giving us the choice, Word gets another point.

Mirrored Page Layouts

Word wins a point here too. Few programs accommodate this need as well as Word, and it's a critical need if you format documents with mirrored page layouts.

Look at Figure 1-10: it features mirror images on pages that face one another. A wide outside margin on the left of left-facing pages is mirrored on the right of right facing pages.

Figure 1-10: This design incorporates mirrored left- and right-facing pages.

Word accommodates mirrored-page designs in its Page Setup dialog box (see Figure 1-11). Accessed from the File menu, this dialog box offers a Mirror Margins check box which, when activated, changes the margins to read "Inside" and "Outside," rather than "Left" and "Right."

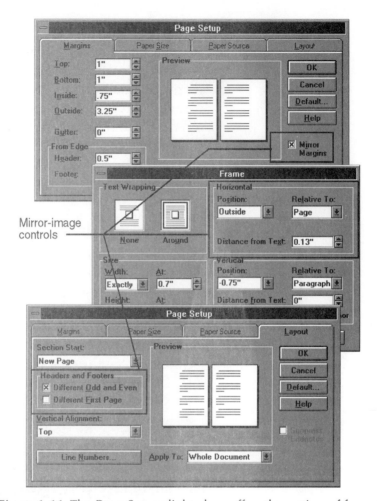

Figure 1-11: The Page Setup dialog box offers the option of formatting a document with mirrored margins.

Two other options complement this feature: 1) Word allows you to format even- and odd-page headers (and footers) independently; 2) You can place frames on the "outside" of pages. This feature allows you to place framed elements (graphics or text) on the right side of right-facing pages or the left side of left-facing pages *and cause them to swap places* if the text with which they are associated moves (due to editing) from a right-facing to a left-facing page. Word's capability to position frames relative to mirrored pages is particularly powerful. In addition to sidebars and graphics, illustrations and heads are often located this way. Surprisingly, even some dedicated desktop-publishing programs neglect to offer this feature.

Score a big plus for Word on this one. It accommodates mirrored page designs with aplomb.

Grammar

Admonishments & exhortations
Though the grammar checker offers paragraph, word and letter counts, you don't have to wade through the grammar checker's admonishments and exhortations to see them. For a quick summary of paragraph, word and letter counts, choose Summary Info from the File menu; then click on the Statistics button.

Though all dedicated desktop-publishing programs now offer spelling checkers, not all offer a thesaurus, and none offer grammar checking. When Microsoft set out to rebuild Word for Windows, it asked users, "Which features should we add to the program?" The number-one request was a grammar checker. Never one to skimp, Microsoft contracted with Houghton Mifflin to use its CorrecText Grammar Correction System.

CorrecText not only checks your grammar, it also provides statistics (see Figure 1-12). Although an appraisal such as this can be bruising to the ego, it will improve your writing.

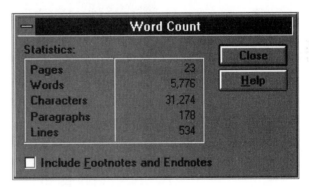

Figure 1-12: The grammar checker's statistics for this chapter of the book reflect counts.

If you're the writer as well as the editor and producer, Word's grammar checker and thesaurus are welcome—perhaps obligatory—features rarely found in competing programs.

Tables

Most of Word's table controls are now consolidated under a new Table menu item (see Figure 1-13). Because most changes in Word are the result of user feedback, the Table menu indicates the significance users put on tables. Tables have always been a little difficult to master, including those offered by Word versions previous to 2. Tables are now much easier to master.

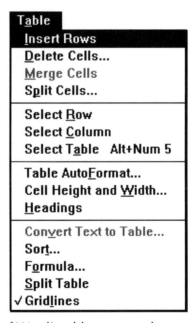

Figure 1-13: Most of Word's table commands are now grouped under a single menu.

With nearly every table command under the Table menu, Word's tables are almost—I hesitate to use the word—intuitive. All desktop publishers encounter the need for a table at one time or another, and Word obliges. That's more than we can say for most table editors, and it warrants another point in Word's favor.

Mail merge

The term *mail merge* refers to the merging of two or more documents into one, which is then printed as often as necessary. Typically, two documents are used: one, a database, contains names and addresses; the other contains a "form letter," into which the information from the database is merged. You can customize thousands of copies of the form letter for individual recipients and then print them. Word is great at merging. Ed McMahon probably uses it.

Macros

Word's macro language is more comprehensive than any word-processing or desktop-publishing program. The most significant advantage offered by a macro language is the ability to merge data from another file, database files in particular. With Word's extensive macro language, mail merging has almost infinite potential; and with Word's explicit merging dialog boxes (see Figure 1-14), this task is no longer the curse it used to be. If your applications require mail merging with desktop-published *élan*, there's no better program for the job than Word.

Give Word another point.

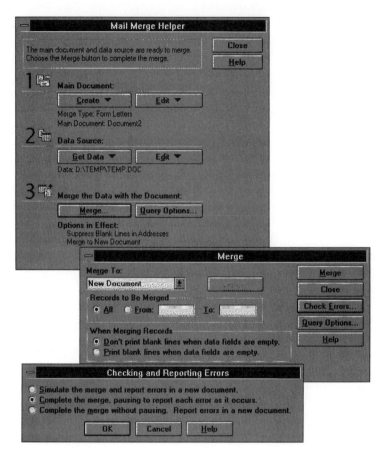

Figure 1-14: Word's mail merge commands make a once-grueling process almost fun.

Footnotes

As you would expect, Word automates footnotes, renumbering and relocating them as required. Footnotes can appear at the bottom of the page, at the end of a section or at the end of a document. They can be split over multiple pages, and can be either numbered or daggered. This feature is standard in a full-featured word processor, but not for desktop publishing. PageMaker, for instance, makes no provision for footnotes.

If your documents require footnotes or endnotes, give Word yet another point.

THE NEW TOYS

In an all-out effort to clobber the competition and win the lucrative Windows word-processing market, Microsoft embroidered Word with a bounty of utilities matched by no other software on the market. Taken collectively, Word and its utilities comprise a software library that serves the needs of many (if not most) casual desktop publishers without need for anything else: ample tools for text, layout and graphics are included in one box—a $495 box, mind you, about a fifth the cost of comparable stand-alone software.

Microsoft WordArt

Although body text is the stuff people read, display text is the stuff people see (see Chapters 4 and 5). But purchasing display fonts can be hard to justify, even though desktop publishers always covet fonts like Hobo and Bee's Knees—a futile aspiration, given the typical desktop-publishing budget.

Word's answer is *WordArt*, a display-text utility offering angled text, text along a curve, compressed and expanded text, and most important, 15 display fonts. WordArt provides captivating pull-quotes, decorative drop caps, lavish headlines and baroque bullets. Best of all, WordArt matches the desktop-publishing budget dollar-for-dollar: it's absolutely free. (WordArt is discussed in Chapters 4, 5 and 7.)

Figure 1-15: Using a font named, appropriately, Impact, WordArt provides a dazzling title page for a report on graphics software.

The Drawing Toolbar

In Chapter 7, "Graphics," I describe the two basic types of graphics: raster and vector. You already have a raster-graphics editing tool in the form of Windows Paintbrush, but how about vectors? Vector graphics programs are expensive—CorelDRAW and Micrografx Designer both cost over $500—and require sophisticated hardware. Although the Drawing toolbar isn't as feature-laden, it serves the casual desktop-publisher's needs adequately and meets the typical desktop-publisher's budget—you didn't pay a dime for it, after all. (For more on the Drawing toolbar and graphics in general, see Chapter 7.)

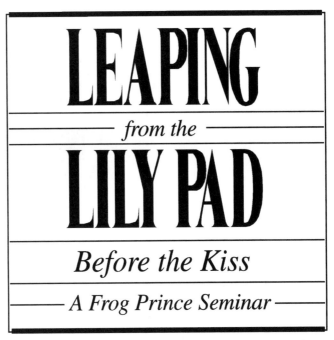

Figure 1-16: The Drawing toolbar assembles WordArt and system text, adds a few boxes and lines, and provides an appealing playbill design.

Microsoft Graph

At one time or another, every desktop publisher is called upon to provide a document or a presentation that includes business graphics. Even with the Drawing toolbar, the Word user would be hard-pressed to provide a graphic as exotic as, say, the three-dimensional bar graph in Figure 1-17.

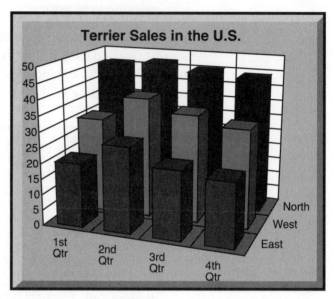

Figure 1-17: Microsoft Graph's three-dimensional business graphics are equaled by few stand-alone business-graphics programs.

Yet another Word utility, *Microsoft Graph* is in fact one-third of Microsoft's best-selling spreadsheet program, Excel. Graph features no less than 81 graphics formats, including 30 three-dimensional views. Each may be customized and many can be combined.

While Graph matches the clout of many expensive stand-alone business graphics programs (Harvard Graphics, for instance, which sells for $495), it is nonetheless included with Word absolutely free. (For more on Microsoft Graph, see Chapter 7.)

Microsoft Equation Editor

Although the spectrum of applications for Word's fourth utility, *Microsoft Equation Editor*, may not be as broad as that of Draw or Graph, the program is no less critical for those who need to include scientific equations in their documents (see Figure 1-18).

Documents containing equations typically require a number of them: they must be constructed quickly and conveniently. The Equation Editor does both. And even though it previously sold as a stand-alone application, Word includes the Equation Editor free.

Figure 1-18: The Equation Editor brings scientific equations into the desktop-publishing world.

A Philanthropic Consideration

It's difficult to calculate the value of these utilities. Collectively considered, Word and its utilities comprise a complete desktop-publishing library, with few compromises. Coupled with Windows Paintbrush (Windows's free raster-graphics utility), Word users possess a more complete system than that of most desktop publishers, and Word—including all its utilities—sells for $495. Dollar-for-dollar, nothing comes close.

ODDS 'N' ENDS

I conclude this chapter with a look at those features most desktop publishers consider compulsory: text wrap, color, zooming, file importing and the ability to produce pages of various sizes. I'll add to that list two more significant items: object linking and cross-platform compatibility.

Text Wrap

If there's one feature that epitomizes desktop publishing, it's text wrap. Where would we be without text neatly flowing around graphics, imprinting our documents as "desktop-published." Nothing clarifies desktop publishing quite so distinctly as text wrap.

Word makes few concessions here. Using frames, Word wraps text with the best of them, providing you with the ability to drag graphics anywhere on the page and watch text flow around them as a stream flows around an island (see Figure 1-19).

Irregular wraps unraveled

Word doesn't wrap text around an irregularly shaped graphic. Text wraps must be rectangular; there's no compromise. One strategy is to place a border around the graphic (Format menu, Borders and Shading) as I've done in Figure 1-19. Borders define graphics and are always rectangular. Picture frames are rectangular, after all, and no one seems to mind.

Figure 1-19: Word's frames and interactive page-layout zooms facilitate text wrapping.

Coupled with Word's document view and full-page zooms, Word's text wraps are without peer in the word-processing field, and nearly equal to anything desktop publishing has to offer.

Give Word two more points for superior text wrap.

Color

This feature is critical for some users and insignificant for others. If your budget supports it, there's nothing like color to add pizzazz to a design.

Word's character-formatting dialog box lets you apply color to any character or grouping of characters, and Windows's printer-options dialog boxes accommodate printing for color printers (see Figure 1-20). The Drawing toolbar,

Paintbrush and WordArt can apply color to graphics as well, and Word accepts colored graphics without so much as a sigh. Word displays color on color monitors and prints color on color printers.

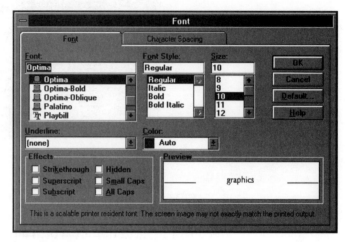

Figure 1-20: Colored text is accommodated with Word's Format-Font dialog box.

Making color masters

Though not directly, Word will print spot-color masters—if you know how. Use a basic style (discussed in Chapter 6, "Styles") for each color. As you edit, assign black to all styles. When it's time to print, print one color master at a time by assigning white to all styles except the one you want printed. Follow these steps for each color. You will get nicely registered masters, one for each color in the document.

This discussion applies only to those of you who have access to color printers, though Word has limited potential for making spot-color masters (see sidebar). Process color separations are not in Word's vocabulary, which is no particular hindrance to the casual desktop publisher: those who need to make process color separations require exacting and very expensive hardware and software that are out of Word's league.

Give Word a point for color.

Zoom Controls

Wow! What's a word processor doing with zoom controls? Zooms are common to dedicated desktop-publishing and graphics programs, but they're rare in word processing. Of those word processors that do offer zooms, only Word offers infinitely selectable enlargements or reductions (from 10 to 200 percent) *and* editing while in an enlarged or reduced view.

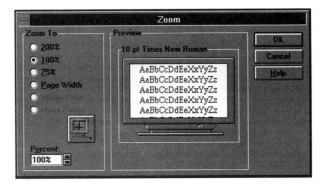

Figure 1-21: Word offers abundant zoom potential.

Word's zoom feature is not only *very* desktop-publishing, few dedicated desktop-publishing programs can equal it. This capability is definitely worth a point.

File Importing

In Chapter 7, I describe at least 12 graphic formats familiar to Word. Microsoft is always adding filters to Word's repertoire, so there may be more by the time you read this book.

This list may sound finite, but Word reads every standard raster, vector and metafile graphics format. Every graphics program of which I'm aware can save to one of these formats. Moreover, you can edit most of these files using either the Drawing toolbar or Paintbrush.

Word's chameleon-like adaptability extends to text as well. Word accepts text files from nearly every word processor, spreadsheet and database, including formatted Macintosh Word files (from the Tools menu, choose Options; then click the Compatibility folder's tab).

In other words, Word can probably read your stuff, no matter how peculiar its file format may be. Desktop publishers require this adaptability, and Word receives a point for recognizing that need.

Page Size

The largest paper Word's Page Setup dialog box (File menu, Page Setup) will accept is 22 by 22 inches. Although this limit accommodates tabloid-sized paper (17 by 22 inches), it doesn't accommodate signage.

"So what," you say. "Who has a printer that big anyway?" While that may be true, most dedicated desktop-publishing programs automatically tile the printing of large documents on smaller paper. The tiles are then taped together (or pasted up) and sent to a screen-printing shop for mastering and printing.

If you make large signs, T-shirts or billboards, perhaps you shouldn't be using Word. If you don't require anything larger than tabloids, Word receives another point.

Object Linking

In Chapter 7, we discuss object linking and embedding (OLE). No other category of user stands to benefit more from this software development than desktop publishers. Almost by definition, desktop publishing represents amalgamations of independent documents, pieced together into comprehensive publications. Some line art from Paintbrush, a chart from Excel, a graphic from FreeHand—they might all be included in a single desktop-published document.

Now imagine double-clicking on any one of these objects and immediately finding yourself within the program that created it. Double-click on a Paintbrush graphic and you're in Paintbrush, ready to edit the graphic as you please. When you're done, exit from Paintbrush and you're back in Word, where the graphic now reflects the results of your editing.

Printing envelopes
The Envelopes and Labels command under the Tools menu addresses (pun intended) one of the most tormenting nemeses of computer-based printing: envelopes and labels. Select the address, put an envelope (or page of labels) in your printer and press the button. It works so well that you will find yourself looking for opportunities to print envelopes and labels, heretofore unheard-of behavior on behalf of computer users.

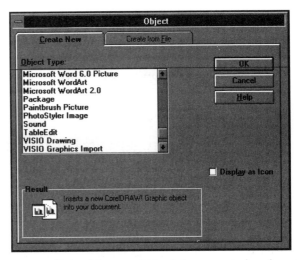

Figure 1-22: You link objects to Word documents by choosing Object from the Insert menu.

With OLE, a desktop-publishing session becomes document-oriented: your attention is devoted to the document, not to the individual programs that created it. To the user, documents are entities rather than aggregations. Word skillfully plays the role of narrator: telling the story, introducing the supporting acts and unifying the performance.

Though OLE is a Windows rather than a Word feature, Word's implementation of it is convenient and practical. Award another point.

Cross-Platform Compatibility

Let's face it: desktop publishing began on the Macintosh, and the Macintosh system remains its mainstay. Any Windows program that ignores its Macintosh heritage is in self-exile, and that gets pretty lonely.

Fortunately, Word for Windows 6 and Macintosh Word 6 were developed simultaneously, and the two programs share common command structures and file formats. Word can import and export Macintosh Word files with little change in content. And Word for Windows users feel right at home with the Macintosh version (and vice versa).

You may never need it, but it's nice to know it's there if you ever do.

Three-to-One in Favor

So is Word really desktop-publishing software? Look at Figure 1-23 and we will review the tally:

Feature	Benefit	Barrier
Free-form, object-oriented architecture		✔
Linear, lock-step architecture	✔	
Long-document support (sections, outlines)	✔	
All-in-one document management strategy	✔	✔
Unequal-width columns	✔	
Jumps		✔
Templates	✔	
Zoom controls	✔	
File importing	✔	
Color	✔	
Kerning	✔	
Letter spacing and justification		✔
Hyphenation	✔	
Text wrap	✔	
Mirrored layouts	✔	
Spelling, thesaurus, grammar	✔	
Tables	✔	
Macros	✔	
Footnotes	✔	
Utilities (WordArt, Drawing toolbar, Graph, and Equation Editor)	✔✔✔	

Figure 1-23: Although somewhat subjective, our final tally quantifies Word's exemplary desktop-publishing performance.

There really is little doubt about it: Word is desktop-publishing software. Indeed, with its included utilities, Word is a comprehensive desktop-publishing ensemble. Many users will require nothing else.

For those who fit the definition of the desktop publisher as a generalist, pauper and part-timer, you would be hard-pressed to identify a superior product.

MOVING ON

If Word is the desktop-publishing software for you, you're probably eager to get to the specifics. So am I. In the next chapter, we'll tackle what is probably the most significant yet least respected subject of desktop publishing: body type. Turn the page. Let's get to the specifics.

2

Body Type

Body type is blue-collar stuff. It's the Willy Loman of the printed word, toiling unceasingly at its pedestrian task, thanklessly obliging the relentless demands of workaday communication. There's no glory in body type. Even though it typically comprises over 90 percent of the page, it's perceived as being amorphous, arid and lackluster.

This dichotomy—ubiquity and triviality—poses a unique challenge to the desktop publisher. If no one is going to notice body type, why bother designing it?

Chocolate-chip cookies come to mind. Though we tend to notice the chips, the dough makes the cookie. Lackluster dough makes a lackluster cookie, no matter how many chips you use. Conversely, really great dough can disguise stale chips. If you want a tasty cookie, put your effort into the dough. If you want a tasteful design, put your effort into body type.

Despite its lack of respect, body type exercises an influence over the page that is both subtle and profound. It doesn't reach out and grab the reader's attention the way illustrations and display type do. But it determines the texture, the flavor, the *quality* of the document. Chocolate chips, after all, come from the store. Great cookie dough comes from the heart.

All this talk about cookies and Willy Loman may have clouded the issue. Body type is formally defined as type that measures 8 to 12 points in size, comprising the text of the document. All the rest is display text. You're reading body text right now; the following subhead, "Determining the Font," is display type.

Now let's put on our aprons and cook up some body type.

DETERMINING THE FONT

Think points

As the term is used, a *point* measures 1/72 of an inch. Because typographical specifications are so infinitesimal, coarser units of measurement—the inch in particular—are simply inadequate. Thinking in terms of points is learned behavior, but it's a habit you'll acquire quickly.

First, we had best define the term *font*. In the old days, before Nestlé put chips in cellophane bags, fonts were typesetters' domain. Typically, fonts were placed in shallow wooden drawers divided into 50 or so small compartments. Each compartment contained a number of *stamps*, or individual blocks of type. All *A* stamps were in one compartment, *B* stamps in another and so on. A font consisted of all letters of one typeface, one style and one size. Twelve-point Times Roman, in other words, was a font. Ten-point Times Roman was another. Ten-point Times Italic was a third.

With the advent of phototypesetting machines, changing a point size was accomplished not by selecting another font, but by changing the optics of the system—similar to the way you might zoom the optics of a camcorder. A font, then, became all the characters of one style in all sizes of a typeface.

Then the personal computer arrived. Programs for the Macintosh, in particular, often featured a font menu, which not only offered a choice of typeface and point size, but also a selection of font "styles." You could italicize a font or make it boldface.

Case in points

In the days when type was set by hand, typographers placed capital letters in compartments at the rear of the drawer, or *case*; they kept noncapital letters toward the front. When setting a page, the typographer placed the case on a rack that was elevated and angled, something like a music stand. The capital letters—now in the upper portion of the angled case—became known as "uppercase" letters, the others "lowercase."

Thus, the word *font* came to be known as all the characters, all the sizes and *all the styles* of a single typeface. This use is a gross simplification. Look, for instance, at the italics two sentences back. Compare the *a* in the word *all* with the *a* in the word *and* preceding it. The italic is not simply the roman (regular) leaned over. The characters are entirely different designs. In fact, most italics are uniquely separate designs, configured to complement their roman (regular) counterparts.

For the remainder of this book, I am going to use the word *font* as phototypesetters did: all the characters and sizes of one style of a typeface. I will use the term *font family* to refer to the complementary styles—roman (regular), italic, bold and bold italic—of a typeface.

Picky, picky. But as desktop publishers, we have a responsibility to clarify the vocabulary and perpetuate the language of design. And the word *font* begs clarification.

Font Races

Our first task is an onerous one: we must decide on a font appropriate to our reader and subject. Depending on your system, you may have scores of fonts from which to choose. Where to begin?

Old English

We'll begin by eliminating all but one type race. Gutenberg's Bibles were set in a type race variously referred to as text, blackletter or, more contemporarily, Old English.

As you might assume, Old English typefaces are hardly appropriate for body type. A page of Old English type is, well, black (see Figure 2-1).

Figure 2-1: The Old English typeface Lino Text is typical of blackletter type.

Serif (Roman)

We'll move forward chronologically. The next type race to come along was serif (or *roman*) type. All serif typefaces feature cross strokes at the end of the letterform, such as the small "feet" you see at the ends of the *T* in the word *Times* in Figure 2-2.

SansBoldItalic

We need a word for "regular" type—type that's not italic and not bold. The language of typography is full of synonyms: *roman*, *light*, *book* and *medium* are all proper, but none is universally appropriate. Intentional obfuscation such as this must have something to do with job security.

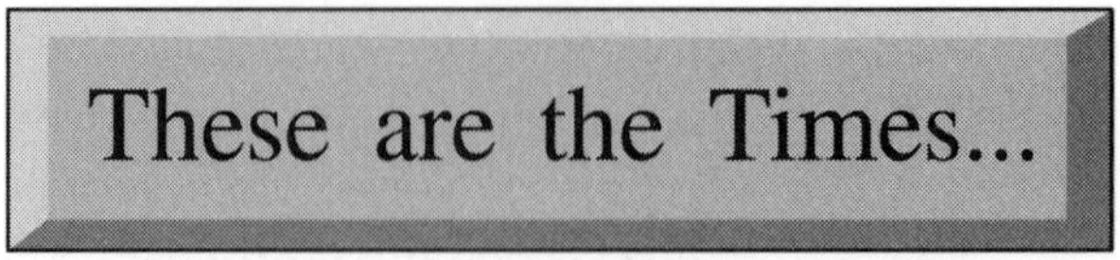

These are the Times...

Figure 2-2: The most popular roman typeface, Times, was designed for *The Times* of London in 1931.

Times's legacy
The typeface Times New Roman was designed by Stanley Morison for *The Times* of London in 1931. It's a marvel of efficiency: if you want to fit the maximum amount of text into a finite area, use Times.

Serifs also prescribe a strong horizontal baseline, which aids the eye as it reads from left to right and back again.

Serif typefaces are also characterized by variation in the thickness of strokes. Note how the strokes of the *m* in Times (Figure 2-2) differ in thickness.

The overall effect is readability. Of all the various type groups, serif is considered to be the most readable.

Sans-Serif

Keep readability in mind as we consider the next race, *sans-serif*. As you might expect, sans-serif quite literally means "without serif." Sans-serif typefaces are an outgrowth of the 1920s German Bauhaus school of design, in which the guiding factors were simplicity and functionality (see Figure 2-3).

gesundheit!!

Figure 2-3: Helvetica, the most popular of sans-serif typefaces, didn't arrive in the United States until 1962.

Unfortunately, its simplicity severely limits sans-serif's usefulness as a body type. Serifs serve a purpose—readability—which is lost in sans-serif designs.

I'm being a bit harsh. Sans-serif typefaces often work well in small doses when you must read and interpret words quickly, or when reproduction may be less than ideal. Traffic signs, for instance, are set in sans-serif. Tiny type—where nuances like serifs would be lost—is also well suited for sans-serif. Captions for forms are often best set in a sans-serif typeface. Nonetheless, for body type applications, the serif type is usually your best choice.

Typewriter Faces

Monospaced fonts
Because most type-writer typefaces are monospaced—their characters are all the same width—they are appropriate for tables and charts, where columns of numbers must align atop one another.

Good old Courier. Most of us lived with it far too long in the days of Selectrics and daisy-wheel printers. When we got our LaserJets, we figured we were home free—until the first unformatted pages rolled out. In Courier.

For this we paid $2,000?

Frankly, there *are* a few applications where typewriter faces have a purpose as body text (see Figure 2-4). Think of flash forms: Courier type printed on yellow paper, telegram-like, declaring last-minute, late-breaking news. *Newsweek* magazine uses this technique. Courier might also be appropriate for business correspondence where the pretension of "type-set" text may be too formal.

Figure 2-4: Typewriter typefaces still have their place, though body type isn't usually one of them.

Normally, however, typewriter typefaces aren't considered to be body text material. The world has probably seen enough Courier.

Script

Don't confuse *script* typefaces with italics. Italics are complementary fonts designed to accompany their regular type counterparts. Script typefaces, on the other hand, have no such counterparts (no italics either). They're intended to stand alone for specific applications, but never as body type.

Use script typefaces on wedding invitations, on circulars, in ads or as display type (see Figure 2-5). Taken in large quantities, however, they get tedious. Avoid them especially in correspondence. If you want your correspondence to look as if it's handwritten, write it by hand.

Figure 2-5: Script typefaces can be appropriate for advertising or wedding invitations.

Specialty Typefaces

One more race deserves mention, if for no other reason than to clarify its exclusion from any of the type races mentioned earlier: *specialty type.* Have you ever peeked through the files of rub-on type at art-supply stores? There you find thousands of typefaces that defy categorization; and it's for that reason that the specialty race exists: to serve as a catch-all for those fonts that don't fit anywhere else.

You may safely assume that these fonts are not body typefaces (see Figure 2-6). They're intended for display purposes only, something we'll talk about in Chapter 4. These are the chocolate chips—rich, dark, Belgian chocolate chips. Sprinkle them lightly on your documents: a little bit goes a long way.

Figure 2-6: This eclectic trio of display typefaces can be used for special projects, but never as body type.

Font Families

Within each race are literally thousands of *families* of type. Users of PostScript systems will recognize Bookman, School-book and Palatino—all serif typeface families within the roman race.

As you might expect, a number of individuals comprise a family: roman (also known as regular), italic, bold and bold italic. You may have a limited number of families installed on your system, but you can purchase additional families from font vendors.

Look carefully at Figure 2-7. Note again that each font within the family is unique. Caslon Bold is not Caslon Roman made fatter; only the thick strokes are thicker. As mentioned earlier, the italics are entirely separate "cuts," as they used to say when type was chiseled out of lead.

Figure 2-7: The Caslon typeface used to be the standard. A familiar adage 50 years ago was "When in doubt, use Caslon."

If you want to develop a more elaborate font library than that supplied with your printer, you'll no doubt become an unwilling academic of the Byzantine architecture of Windows fonts. Though a later chapter is devoted to that topic, a word of wisdom begs to be spoken here.

User-installed fonts—PostScript fonts in particular—are usually sold as font families consisting of multiple font files. Though this distribution policy aligns with our theory of discrete fonts within a family, it imposes some operational idiosyncrasies of which you should be aware.

Suppose you purchase and install the Garamond font family: Garamond Light, Garamond Light Italic, Garamond Bold and Garamond Bold Italic. After the installation process is complete, Word's Font menu will display all four fonts (see Figure 2-8), not just the generic family name. This strategy is typical of many fonts that you purchase independently.

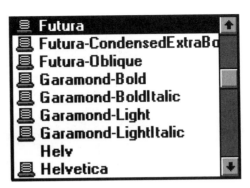

Figure 2-8: The user-installed Garamond and Futura font families appear under the Font menu with separate entries for each font within the family. For Garamond Italic, choose Garamond-LightItalic from this menu.

Pop quiz

Working productively on an article regarding the history of Western humor, you type the word *farceur* (French for one who writes farces). Because it is a foreign word, it should appear in italics.
Quick: How should you italicize the word?

A. Select the word; then click on the Formatting toolbar's Italic icon.
B. Select the word; then select "Italic" in the Format-Font dialog box.
C. Select the word; then press Ctrl-I.
D. None of the above.

When font families are displayed individually, declare typographical styles (italic, bold) by selecting the appropriate font, using either the Formatting toolbar's pull-down font list or the Format-Font dialog box. Don't click on the Italic or Bold button on the Standard toolbar, don't turn on the style in the Format-Font dialog box, and don't use keystroke shortcuts (such as Ctrl-I). This approach takes some getting used to, but it's the only method that works properly.

The answer to the quiz in the "Pop quiz" sidebar is D (None of the above). Refer to Figure 2-9. The word at the top is roman; the middle word is roman leaned over—the consequence of A, B or C in our multiple-choice quiz. The bottom word is Garamond Light Italic, created by changing the font to Garamond Italic. Changing fonts isn't as convenient as a button click or keystroke command, but it's necessary.

Figure 2-9: At top, Garamond Roman. Below that, Garamond Roman "leaned over," the result of applying the italic attribute. True Garamond Italic, a separate font, was used for the bottom word. Notice the differences, particularly the *f, a* and *r.*

Appropriate Body-Text Fonts

As you've no doubt gathered, roman typefaces are the preferred body type. They're plentiful and readable, especially when encountered *en masse* in most body-type applications. They're never showboats, always familiar and rarely inappropriate. They're also available in four primary categories, one of which is bound to be ideal for your purpose.

Old Style

Old-style fonts feature round circular characters—wide *m*'s and *w*'s—and bracketed serifs (see Figure 2-10). Collectively, these characteristics give old-style fonts elegance, affability and warmth. Their extreme width gives them a primary-school character, however, and a lack of efficiency. Use them where friendliness and elegance are appropriate, but you should avoid sizes larger than 11 points unless you want a Dick-and-Jane effect.

Figure 2-10: Bookman's heavily bracketed serifs (left) are typical of old-style typefaces.

Transitional

Look again at Figure 2-10. The typeface on the right, New Century Schoolbook, is commonly found in PostScript systems. A transitional typeface, it's characterized by sharp serifs and round finials (rounded ends of strokes such as the *f*). The rounded finials in transitional typefaces contrast starkly with their right-angled serifs. This look gives them a lively personality; and because their *o*'s are more ovoid and their *m*'s and *n*'s narrower, transitional typefaces have less of a primary-school character. Transitional typefaces are ideal for books, papers, newsletters and other applications that require more energy and maturity than old-style typefaces offer.

New Style

Naturally, if there's an old style and a transitional style, there must also be a new style. New-style typefaces feature small serifs and a distinct contrast between their thick and thin strokes.

Look at the *v*'s in Figure 2-11. The Times *v* on the right places less emphasis on its serifs and thin strokes than does the Schoolbook *v* on the left. The Times *v* is also a bit smaller, though both characters appear in the same point size. Collectively, these characteristics make for an extremely efficient typeface, though its more subtle serifs may cost the new-style typeface some of its personality.

Figure 2-11: Times's *v* (right) features more of a contrast between thick and thin strokes, and smaller serifs, characteristics typical of new-style typefaces.

Of all the new-style typefaces, Times New Roman is the most popular. It's a great choice when efficiency is your primary consideration. In body-type sizes, it's somewhat undistinguished (which may be an advantage); in display sizes, its thick/thin contrast gives it a "designer" quality, quite unlike its neutral, body-text personality.

The document pictured in Figure 2-12 illustrates Times's dual personality. The display type—headline, byline, subheads—is crisp and dynamic, whereas the body type is even-colored and efficient.

Figure 2-12: A text-only design, comprised entirely of Times: Times Roman, Times Italic and Times Bold. This style of single-family design is known as monotypographical harmony.

Personal

I mention this relatively narrow category because of the popularity of Palatino, a personal typeface designed by Hermann Zapf in 1950. Palatino was inspired by the hand-writing of Giambattista Palatino, a 16th-century Italian calligrapher. I mention its heritage because the heritage defines the intent: Palatino (and all other personal typefaces) was designed to satisfy the need for personal printed communication.

Look carefully at the ends of the strokes at the top of the *t*, the arm of the *r* and the tail of the *y* in Figure 2-13. Don't they resemble the stroke endings produced by a calligraphy pen? And look at that *Y*! This typography is affected, appropriate for uses that have an intimate familiarity: personal correspondence, fund-raisers—evocative documents, in which flamboyance and elocution aren't distracting.

Figure 2-13: Palatino, the archetypal personal typeface, exhibits its calligraphic heritage. Look at the chisel strokes on the *r, t* and *Y!*

Follow the Recipe

We've been merciless in our elimination of typefaces for use as body type, but it's warranted. Body type is no place for the inappropriate, the distracting or the affected. Its duty is communication—communication that's readable, dependable and appropriate. The very first design decision for nearly every document you produce will be that of selecting body type. Choose a typographical family from the fonts that are available, and appropriate to your reader, subject and system. You won't have many options; the decision should be easy and forthright. All you need to do is follow the recipe.

CHOOSING A FONT IN WORD

The Windows font environment is perplexing. Your system probably includes fonts that are available for onscreen display but aren't available on the printer. Other fonts may be available at the printer but not onscreen.

Variety is the spice of Windows

Every Windows configuration is different. Your collection of fonts won't match that mentioned in the text, and your Font menu won't match that pictured in Figure 2-14. Few Windows installations match one another. Wouldn't you prefer it that way?

TrueType fonts

With Windows 3.1, Microsoft incorporated TrueType font-imaging technology into the Windows system. True-Type fonts look good onscreen, regardless of the size in which they appear, and print beautifully on dot-matrix or ink-jet printers. You can always tell TrueType fonts: little TTs appear beside their names. Look again at Figure 2-14 and you'll see what I mean.

Thankfully, Word clarifies the situation by placing small printer icons next to the fonts appropriate for your printer. These icons are visible whenever you pull down the font list from the Formatting toolbar or from the Format-Font dialog box. Figure 2-14 represents a selection of fonts available for a PostScript printer; thus only PostScript fonts appear with printer icons. Because system and screen fonts (like System and Terminal) aren't intended for use with a PostScript printer, they aren't attributed with icons.

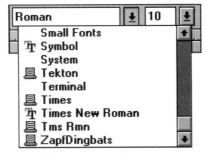

Figure 2-14: Fonts available for installed printers are marked with small printer icons. Use only these fonts when preparing a document.

How does Word know which fonts are appropriate to the printer? It confers with the printer driver you specified in the Print Setup dialog box (File menu, Print; then click on the Printer button).

This information becomes significant if you prepare or edit a document on one machine and print the document on another. Be sure both machines have the appropriate printer driver (Chapter 8 describes font installation methods) and that driver is declared (using Print Setup) even if the machine isn't the one connected to the printer.

Thanks to the printer-icon feature, you can clarify a muddy situation: choose the destination printer using Print Setup and then select only those fonts that appear with printer icons.

DETERMINING POINT SIZE

Now that you've determined the appropriate font family for your body text, it's time to select a size. A number of factors will affect your decision: the reader, the font family and, of course, availability.

The Reader

Forty is a devious age. We all experience a certain degree of trepidation with the arrival of a new decade in our lives. And though turning 30 isn't much of a crisis, turning 40 can be. The word *mortality* comes into focus. The grand-parenting potential must be confronted. A peculiar fascination with actuarial tables develops.

One physical change in particular dominates our anxieties: our arms start to shorten. Text we could read at arm's length a year ago now can't be read no matter how much we stretch our arms.

Of course, it's not the arms, it's the eyes. The medical profession obfuscates aging—aging provides its primary source of income, after all—with polysyllables. *Presbyopia* is one of its favorites. Presbyopia is a condition that produces a positive correlation between age and diopter: subtract 40 from your current age and divide by 3; then run down to the nearest drug store and buy a pair of reading glasses with a strength equal to that number.

In other words, the age of your reader has a lot to do with point size. Ten-point Times may do for the under-40 set, but 12 becomes the magic number thereafter. Young people simply can't understand this point. Take my word for it.

The Font

Old-style fonts, with their fat, round characters, are slightly easier to read in small sizes. Their large serifs hold up well in small point sizes, and their thin strokes don't disappear the way new-style fonts do.

Compare 8-point Times (new style) in Figure 2-15 with 8-point Bookman in the same illustration. Eight points is flirting with illegibility, but proper font selection helps.

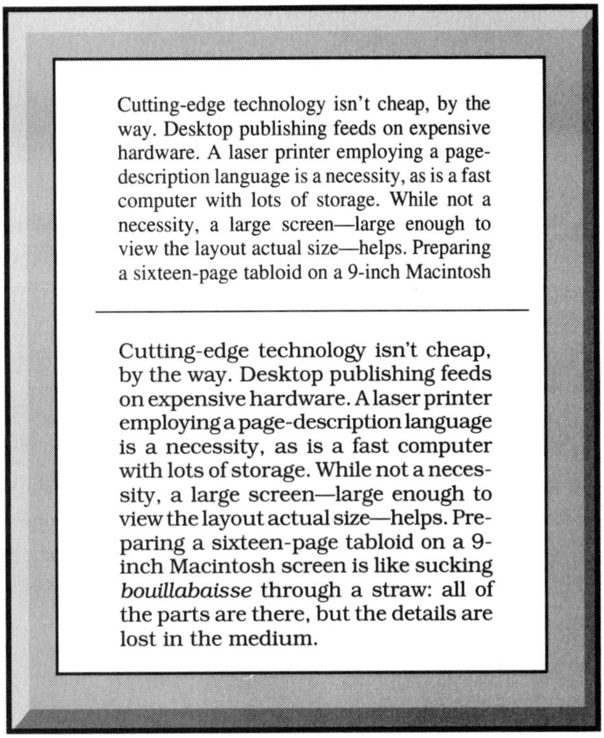

Cutting-edge technology isn't cheap, by the way. Desktop publishing feeds on expensive hardware. A laser printer employing a page-description language is a necessity, as is a fast computer with lots of storage. While not a necessity, a large screen—large enough to view the layout actual size—helps. Preparing a sixteen-page tabloid on a 9-inch Macintosh

Cutting-edge technology isn't cheap, by the way. Desktop publishing feeds on expensive hardware. A laser printer employing a page-description language is a necessity, as is a fast computer with lots of storage. While not a necessity, a large screen—large enough to view the layout actual size—helps. Preparing a sixteen-page tabloid on a 9-inch Macintosh screen is like sucking *bouillabaisse* through a straw: all of the parts are there, but the details are lost in the medium.

Figure 2-15: Eight-point Times (top) is slightly more difficult to read than 8-point Bookman.

Point size also affects personality. As mentioned earlier, 12-point Bookman bears a distinct resemblance to Dick and Jane. Ten-point Bookman, on the other hand, assumes an air of elegance that isn't apparent at 12 points.

In other words, know your typeface. Print a page of it at 10 points, another at 11 and a third at 12. Get to know its personality; then let that familiarity determine your point-size decision. Do that with each new typeface you acquire.

System Factors

Of course, none of this discussion amounts to a hill of Geritol if you don't have 12-point Bookman. Between the lines, we've been cultivating a good argument in favor of the infinite point-size selection offered by outline-technology fonts. Even though a point is only 1/72 inch, even half-point increments can affect personality and legibility.

Though Word's Point menu (whether you pull it down from the Formatting toolbar or from a dialog box) may offer limited choices, the Format-Font dialog box will accept any point size between 1 and 1638 in half-point increments, *if* your system can size fonts on the fly (see Figure 2-16).

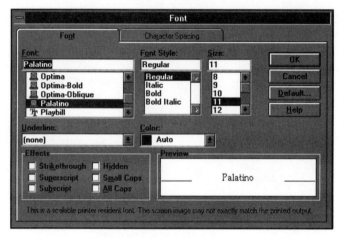

Figure 2-16: You can enter any point size between 1 and 1638 points—in half-point increments—in the Format-Font dialog box.

Realizing that the world is not a perfect place, we acknowledge those systems with only 10, 12 and 14 points from which to choose. If that's your situation, you're limited to those sizes, pure and simple. Nonetheless, print a page of everything you have to get to know it.

THE INGREDIENTS & THE PROCESS

All recipes, it seems, appear in two discrete sections. At the top, most recipes list the ingredients, and below that, instructions for the process. So far, we have listed the ingredients. The process—formatting type you have selected—follows in Chapter 3, "Setting Up Your Text."

3 Setting Up Your Text

Where cookbooks discuss mixing instructions, oven temperatures and baking time, we now discuss column width, leading and alignment. Whether recipe book or Word book, there comes a time for instructions rather than ingredients. Indeed, that's what this chapter is all about. Now that you've decided on the font and point size, it's time to put your text on paper.

With any recipe, even the most carefully chosen ingredients can be tasteless if you prepare them improperly. The same goes for body text: set in a column that's too wide or too narrow, or has improper leading, even the most carefully chosen body text has no more appeal than burned chocolate-chip cookies.

Go ahead and set the oven to 350, but while it's warming up, read this chapter.

DETERMINING COLUMN WIDTH

One of the primary differences between desktop publishing and word processing is multiple columns. Though Word can handle multiple columns, even columns of different widths, most word-processor users don't think in terms of multiple columns. Thus, 90 percent of their documents appear in one wide column.

That's a mistake.

Hidden benefits

Columns of proper width offer hidden benefits as well: because less leading is required, more text will fit on the page; more design flexibility is available; and the page offers more visual interest. Text in a single, page-wide column is about as appealing as an entire chocolate-chip recipe prepared as a single cookie.

Here's why: overly wide columns of body text confuse the eye. The "retrace" movement—the reverse scan that the eye has to make from the end of one line to the beginning of the next—can only be so long (see Figure 3-1). Any longer and the eye loses its place. This situation only has to occur two or three times before you've lost your reader.

Cutting-edge technology isn't cheap, by the way. Desktop publishing feeds on expensive hardware. A laser printer employing a page-description language is a necessity, as is a fast computer with lots of storage. While not a necessity, a large screen—large enough to view the layout actual size—helps. Preparing a sixteen-page tabloid on a 9-inch Macintosh screen is like sucking *bouillabaisse* through a straw: all of the parts are there, but the details are lost in the medium. Typically, a monochrome (no color) desktop-publishing system—computer, monitor, and printer—costs around $10,000.

Cutting-edge technology isn't cheap, by the way. Desktop publishing feeds on expensive hardware. A laser printer employing a page-description language is a necessity, as is a fast computer with lots of storage. While not a necessity, a large screen—large enough to view the layout actual size—helps. Preparing a sixteen-page tabloid on a 9-inch Macintosh screen is like sucking *bouillabaisse* through a straw: all of the parts are there, but the details are lost in the medium. Typically, a monochrome (no color) desktop-publishing system—computer, monitor, and printer—costs around $10,000.

Figure 3-1: An overly wide column of 8-point text (top) confuses the eye, causing it to struggle to keep its place as it retraces from right to left. The proper column width (below) is much easier to read.

Moreover, a column width designed for readability won't fill an 8 1/2-inch-wide page. The solution is either a lot of wasted space or multiple columns.

The Ideal Column Width

But how wide should a column be? The proper column width in Figure 3-1 is about 2 inches wide. Is that the perfect width?

It is if you're setting type in 8-point Times Roman. Eight-point Times Roman, however, is pretty rare stuff, reserved for warranty disclaimers and the fine print in lottery and direct-mail promotions.

Proper column width is a function of a number of factors. Point size is one: the proper column width for 12-point Times Roman is about 3 inches. Typeface is another: the proper column width for 12-point Bookman Roman is about 3 1/2 inches.

How can you be sure? Here's a trick: the proper column width is one and a half lowercase alphabets of the typeface and type size you've chosen for your document. It's that simple. Type

abcdefghijklmnopqrstuvwxyzabcdefghijklm

and measure its length. *Bingo!* There's the ideal column width.

The astute reader will perhaps note that this book doesn't follow its own advice. The text column you're now reading is actually about two body-text alphabets wide. Compromises aren't uncommon: a 1 1/2-alphabet column would be too narrow for our design. The page would be too vacant. Because the book designer knew she was going to stretch the ideal a bit, she compensated by increasing the leading (space between lines of text) of the body type, Palatino.

But leading is another topic. We'll discuss it in "Measuring Leading" later in this chapter.

Setting Column Widths in Word

You can set column widths at least four ways in Word.

> ✔ *Margins* are the brute-force method. Let's say you want a 2 1/2-inch column and you intend to print on 8 1/2-inch paper. You could declare 3-inch left and right margins, leaving a 2 1/2-inch text width.

Put it where you want it

You can frame and then move graphics, paragraphs, words, even single characters at will. Simply select the material you want framed; then from the Insert menu, choose Frame. Word will give you the option to switch to Page Layout View (if necessary), in which you can move framed objects by dragging them with the mouse.

Setting margins isn't as restrictive as it sounds. Word lets you declare both left and right indents (*outdents*, actually) outside the margins—even off the page, if you want. This capability gives you a lot of flexibility: you can place sections of your document entirely within the margins, partially within them and partially within the text area, or partially off the page and partially on it. You can make these settings for headers and footers as well.

You also can move (position) framed objects anywhere on the page (though not beyond the edge), regardless of margin placement. Frames are discussed in detail in Chapter 7, "Graphics."

In spite of this flexibility, using margin settings to declare column width is not the best of the four methods. Headers, footers and footnotes will all appear within the margins unless told otherwise. Footnote separators cannot be located outside the margin. Margins are section-level settings, which restrict format changes from one portion of the document to the next. And setting negative indent and position values is just too peculiar for productive work.

Though I'm not a stern advocate of dogged conventional behavior, I see no reason to toy with this kind of rascality unless there are *no* alternatives. There *are*; read on.

> ✔ *Indents* offer all the opportunities of margins, without the mischief. You can change indents in the midst of a document without a section change; indents don't affect headers, footers or footnotes (unless you want them to), and they're typically expressed as positive values. Indents are thus easier to conceptualize and manipulate than margins.

Let's say you're working with an 8 1/2-inch document, set up with Word's default 1 1/4-inch margins, left and right. The remaining text area measures 6 inches. If you want a 4-inch column, simply set the left indent to 2 inches. You then have 2 inches to the left of your text for subheads, graphics, captions, sidebars and the like. (See Figure 3-2.)

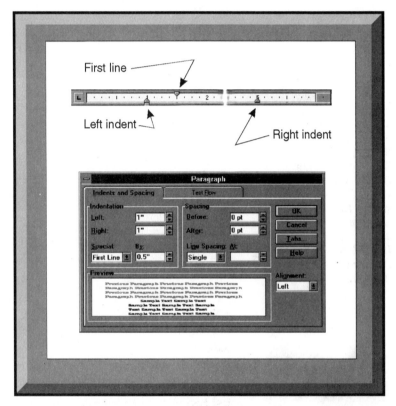

Figure 3-2: Indents can be set either on the Ruler or in the Format-Paragraph dialog box.

You can quickly describe a format similar to the one illustrated in Figure 3-3 by setting left and right margins to 1 1/4 inches (Word's default) and placing the left indent at 2 inches. This way, you create a body-text column of 4 inches. Subhead paragraphs for the text paragraphs are right-aligned with a 4 1/4-inch right indent. These three settings alone are all it takes to match the illustration.

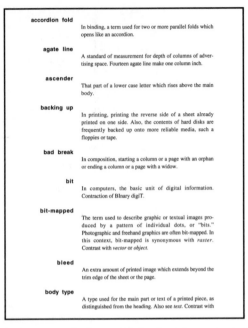

Figure 3-3: Body text is indented 2 inches from the left margin, the subheads are indented 4 1/4 inches from the right margin and right-aligned. Thus, you create a "multiple-column" layout with nothing more than indent commands.

✔ Consider an alternative to the format pictured in Figure 3-3 by using *tables*. By building a two-column table, we could not only match Figure 3-3's format, but also align the subheads with the paragraphs to their right. See the result in Figure 3-4.

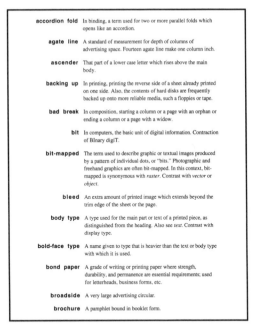

Figure 3-4: A variation on Figure 3-3, the subheads are aligned with the text by using Word's table feature.

The techniques illustrated in Figures 3-3 and 3-4 have advantages and disadvantages. The indent method lends itself well to styles (covered in Chapter 6, "Styles"), and it's slightly faster—faster to scroll and to edit (on slow machines in particular).

The table method aligns the subheads without mumbo-jumbo and may offer a formatting advantage when you don't use styles. Neither is really better than the other.

✔ Naturally, Word's Column command offers a fourth alternative. This option has its advantages and disadvantages as well. It's simply not appropriate for the extended-subhead format shown in the two previous illustrations. But for multiple-column layouts in which text "snakes" from one column to the next, it is the only choice (see Figure 3-5).

accordion fold
In binding, a term used for two or more parallel folds which opens like an accordion.

agate line
A standard of measurement for depth of columns of advertising space. Fourteen agate line make one column inch.

ascender
That part of a lower case letter which rises above the main body.

backing up
In printing, printing the reverse side of a sheet already printed on one side. Also, the contents of hard disks are frequently backed up onto more reliable media, such a floppies or tape.

bad break
In composition, starting a column or a page with an orphan or ending a column or a page with a widow.

bit
In computers, the basic unit of digital information. Contraction of BInary digiT.

bit-mapped
The term used to describe graphic or textual images produced by a pattern of individual dots, or "bits." Photographic and freehand graphics are often bit-mapped. In this context, bit-mapped is synonymous with *raster*. Contrast with *vector* or *object*.

bleed
An extra amount of printed image which extends beyond the trim edge of the sheet or the page.

body type
A type used for the main part or text of a printed piece, as distinguished from the heading. Also see *text*. Contrast with display type.

bold-face type
A name given to type that is heavier than the text or body type with which it is used.

bond paper
A grade of writing or printing paper where strength, durability, and permanence are essential requirements; used for letterheads, business forms, etc.

broadside
A very large advertising circular.

brochure
A pamphlet bound in booklet form.

byte
In computers, a unit of digital information, equivalent to one character of eight bits.

camera-ready
Copy which is ready for photography.

caps and small caps
Two sizes of capital letters made in one size of type. Commonly used in most roman type faces. See *small caps*.

Figure 3-5: Word's Column command provides another alternative, better suited to "snaked" text that flows from one column to the next.

Word is certainly generous when it comes to supplying methods to set column width, and that generosity underlines my point: don't blithely accept Word's 6-inch column width every time you begin a new document. Few projects are appropriate for a column that wide. Become familiar with Word's column-width tools; then set your column width to complement your typeface and type size. Your readers will thank you for it.

ANATOMY OF A FONT

Originally, all type was made out of lead. Lead could be cast without much effort, yet it was relatively hard and smooth.

All typographical terminology is based on the original *stamp* of lead, illustrated in Figure 3-6. These little stamps were plucked from the font case with what amounted to tweezers and slid into a composing stick. After an entire line of type was set on the composing stick, it was locked into place on the printing plate, which was then inked with a roller and pressed onto the paper, a kind of printing known as letterpress.

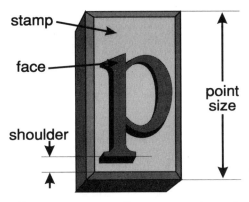

Figure 3-6: All type was originally set using these tiny stamps.

Mind your p's & q's

In fact, the illustration shown in Figure 3-6 is backward. Because it was pressed onto the paper, the stamp produced an image that mirrored the original. Because all stamps were mirror images of the characters they represented, beginning typesetters had difficulty distinguishing between *p*'s and *q*'s. Thus, the age-old adage, "Mind your p's and q's."

Referring again to Figure 3-6, note that the point size of a specimen of type is measured from the top to the bottom of the stamp. This measurement confuses the issue because there are no stamps in this electronic age of desktop publishing.

The issue is further muddled when you consider the *shoulder*, the small distance from the bottom of the face to the bottom of the stamp (or from the top of the face to the top of the stamp). The shoulder differs from typeface to typeface. Times, for instance, has a considerable shoulder. Bookman does not. Because the stamp doesn't really exist any more, the shoulder is something of a nebulous concept, but it's significant nonetheless.

This matter of measuring type becomes even more mystical when you consider *ascenders* and *descenders*. Refer to Figure 3-7. The portion of lowercase *b*'s, *d*'s, *f*'s, *h*'s, *k*'s, *l*'s and *t*'s that extends above the mean line is known as an ascender. Lower-case *g*'s, *j*'s, *p*'s and *q*'s all feature descenders, or portions of the character that extend below the mean line.

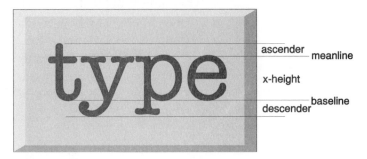

Figure 3-7: Ascenders and descenders provide a unique silhouette for familiar words and phrases. The eye recognizes the resulting shapes and patterns as it reads, rather than individual letters.

The problem is, no character contains both an ascender and a descender. Thus, even if the shoulder weren't an issue, you still couldn't measure a single character of type to determine its size. And because the shoulder *is* an issue, you can't measure a line of type (containing both ascenders and descenders) either.

Measuring type, in other words, isn't done with a ruler. If the document is a Word document, simply select the type to be measured and look at the number on the Formatting toolbar or call up the Format-Font dialog box. If the document appears on paper only, you will have to use a template containing specimens of the typeface you're measuring in stated point sizes.

MEASURING LEADING

As mentioned earlier, as the eye reads, it has to "retrace" from the end of one line of type to the beginning of the next. To facilitate retracing, space between lines that isn't cluttered with ascenders or descenders should exist. Typefaces with extensive shoulders offer uncluttered space without assistance, but typefaces without much of a shoulder require some help.

Pop quiz
Quick: Name a heavy, soft, gray metal that's commonly used to sink fishing lines. "Lead," you say. Good. Now pronounce the word *leading*. If you rhymed the word with "bedding," it's now your responsibility to correct those who rhyme the word with "weeding."

In the days of lead type, this assistance was provided by inserting a shim made of lead between each line of type. Thus, the process became known as leading.

Leading is measured from the top of the stamp to the top of the next stamp (see Figure 3-8). Thus, if 12-point type is shimmed with 2 points of leading between each line, the leading specification is said to be 14 points, not 2. Traditionally, type is specified by point size, then leading, then typeface. Twelve-point Times with 14 points of leading is written "12/14 Times," and said aloud as "12 on 14 Times."

Figure 3-8: Leading is measured from the top of the stamp to the top of the next stamp, inclusive of point size.

Leading & Typeface

Your typeface will determine your leading specification. It depends upon the size of the typeface's shoulder. Times, for instance, was destined for newspaper use and was thus designed with an extensive shoulder. In many situations it can then be set "solid"—with no leading—and still accommodate eye retracing.

Print out some examples of the font families available in your system. Print them at the same size, with the same leading and column width. You'll have no trouble identifying those with significant shoulders and those without.

Look at Figure 3-9. Here, differences in shoulder design become apparent. At the bottom of the illustration, 10-point Helvetica set "solid"—without leading—exhibits near-collisions between its descenders and ascenders (look at the *y* in the word *way* in the top line). At the top of the illustration, 10-point Times set solid avoids collisions.

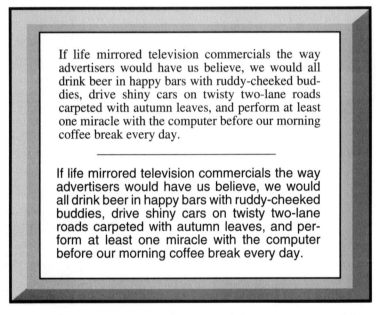

Figure 3-9: Times (top), even when set solid, is easier to read than Helvetica. The difference is the shoulder.

Leading & Column Width

Column width should also influence your choice of leading. Remember that the ideal column width is 1 1/2 alphabets of the typeface and size you intend to use. If that's possible, then use another rule of thumb as a starting point: set leading to 120 percent of point size. If you're using 10-point Caslon (and your column width is the 1 1/2-alphabet ideal), try 12-point leading (120 percent of 10). Print a few paragraphs and adjust leading according to what you see.

If the column has to be wider (as it is in this book), add more leading to help the eye travel a greater distance when it retraces. You may want to set it at something greater than 120 percent, print a page, and let your eye be your guide.

If your column has to be narrower than the ideal, don't reduce leading below 120 percent unless the typeface has a considerable shoulder. With most typefaces, anything less than 120 percent of point size seems crowded.

Leading & Word

True to its word-processing heritage, Word downplays leading. Indeed, Word even ignores the term: leading is "line spacing" as far as Word is concerned. With Version 2, Word became a little more accommodating, but it muddled the issue somewhat in the process. Figure 3-10 shows the six leading options offered by the program, but only one is relative to our discussion.

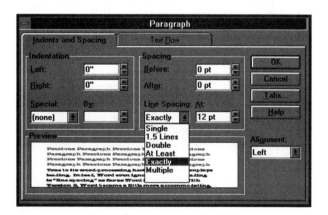

Figure 3-10: Word's line-spacing options reveal its word-processing heritage. Only the Exactly option is appropriate for desktop publishing.

Use points

Always enter leading specifications in points, not inches or lines. Follow your specification with "pt" and Word will understand. Using this system of measurement, you may specify leading by half-point increments, a dimension much finer and easier to comprehend than something as coarse as an inch.

Let's examine these options:

✔ *Single* sets leading equal to the "tallest character." This setting is ambiguous. Twelve-point Helvetica with single line spacing, for instance, is set 12/14. Schoolbook, however, is set 12/19.

The word *single* refers to text with mixed point sizes or in-line graphics that are taller than the point size. In this case, Word increases leading for the affected line to equal the largest text or graphic on the line, which can produce some really awful typography.

Figure 3-11 shows what happens when single line spacing is used and the paragraph's initial character is enlarged. Because the initial character measures 24 points, Word has based leading for the first line on the 24-point initial character. Leading for the remainder of the paragraph is considerably smaller.

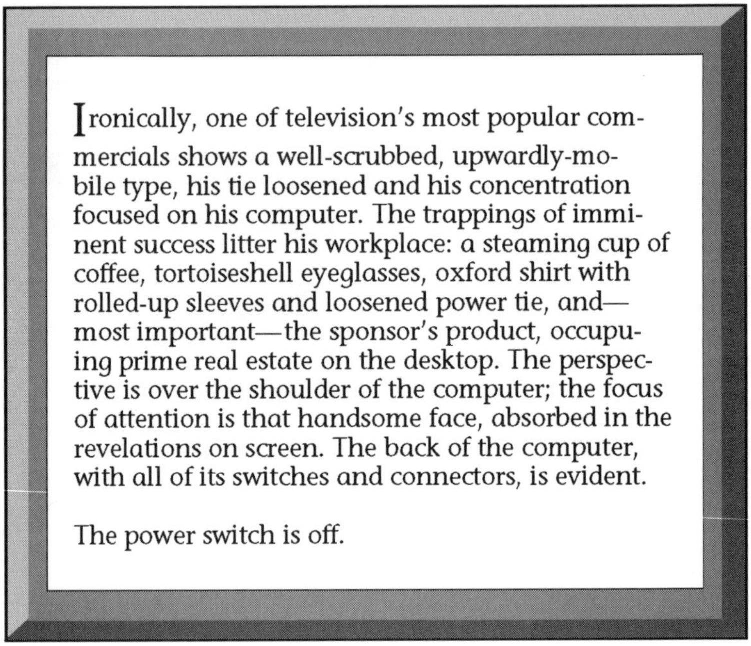

Ironically, one of television's most popular commercials shows a well-scrubbed, upwardly-mobile type, his tie loosened and his concentration focused on his computer. The trappings of imminent success litter his workplace: a steaming cup of coffee, tortoiseshell eyeglasses, oxford shirt with rolled-up sleeves and loosened power tie, and—most important—the sponsor's product, occupying prime real estate on the desktop. The perspective is over the shoulder of the computer; the focus of attention is that handsome face, absorbed in the revelations on screen. The back of the computer, with all of its switches and connectors, is evident.

The power switch is off.

Figure 3-11: Because single line spacing sets leading equal to the largest character on a line, the first line of this paragraph is spaced apart from the rest.

Even if you don't mix sizes or graphics within a paragraph, remember that single line spacing varies with the point size of the paragraph's dominant typeface. You never know if your foot is on the brake or the throttle. Unfortunately, this kind of anarchy is Word's default. You'll have to override it.

✔ *Double* and *1.5* are the same as Single, just bigger.

✔ *At Least* is the same as Single, Double or 1.5—except you (not Word) determine the minimum leading. Though you may rest assured that leading won't drop below your stated minimum, you'll never be sure of what Word is doing over and above the minimum. Though your foot is on the brake, Word still has the throttle.

✔ *Exactly* is your best choice. All you need do is type in an absolute leading specification, and Word will keep its feet off the pedals. Not only is this method predictable, it's the only way you'll develop a feel for leading. After a while, you'll come to recognize, say, 11/14 Garamond, but only if you've been observing 11-point Garamond reliably set on 14-point leading. Leading should never be a moving target. (See Figure 3-12.)

✔ *Multiple* is similar to Double and 1.5 in that line spacing is expressed in multiples of Word's "Single" line spacing. Anything between 0 and 132 lines is acceptable. This setting also is too ambiguous for desktop-publishing work. Always use Exactly.

Of all the formatting controls Word offers, leading may be the most critical. Improperly leaded documents will return to haunt you. Appearing in silhouette on "60 Minutes," you'll be forced to confess your naiveté in humiliation and shame as Mike Wallace ruthlessly hammers at the trail of insensitivity and ineptitude you left behind. Don't provide him with the opportunity. Be uncompromising. Lead body text scrupulously.

— ❦ —

Of all the formatting controls Word offers, leading may be the most critical. Improperly leaded documents will return to haunt you. Appearing in silhouette on "60 Minutes," you'll be forced to confess your naiveté in humiliation and shame as Mike Wallace ruthlessly hammers at the trail of insensitivity and ineptitude you left behind. Don't provide him with the opportunity. Be uncompromising. Lead body text scrupulously.

Figure 3-12: You can specify leading in half-point increments using the Exactly line-spacing option.

Of all the formatting controls Word offers, leading may be the most critical. Improperly leaded documents will return to haunt you. Appearing in silhouette on "60 Minutes," you'll be forced to confess your naiveté in humiliation and shame as Mike Wallace ruthlessly hammers at the trail of insensitivity and ineptitude you left behind. Don't give him the opportunity. Be uncompromising. Lead body text scrupulously.

SETTING PARAGRAPH ALIGNMENT

Now that you've determined font, size, width and leading, the only body-text decision remaining is that of alignment. Fortunately, only two choices are appropriate in most cases: left-align or full justification. Right and center alignment are reserved for non-body text applications.

Full Justification

Justification is formal, predictable and traditional. For example, Gutenberg's Bible was justified. Legal documents, textbooks and novels are justified.

Gutenberg probably was the first to justify type: by inserting tiny spaces between characters and words, he dramatized the versatility of movable type. Other typesetters followed suit, demonstrating their expertise similarly. Justification became an emblem of typographical mastery. Later, when typewriters became commonplace, justification served to distinguish typesetting from typewriting. Justification, in other words, was and is perceived as fancy stuff.

Like many word processors, Word justifies only by adding spaces between words. The distance between the characters within each word remains constant.

**Say it right
(or left...)**
The terms *left justify* and *right justify* are misnomers. Only fully justified text is deserving of the term *justify*. If text isn't justified, it's aligned left, right or center. This proper lexicology is not a description of political affiliation.

Rivers of White

Justification achieved by adding space between words, instead of words and characters, can open up large, irregular spaces within the text. Invariably, some of these spaces align atop or near one another. The result is a series of worm-like white patterns squirming over the text, compromising its "color," as typesetters used to say.

Hold Figure 3-13 far enough away so that you can't read the words. Note the lower section's uniform gray color. The upper section, however, is riddled with "rivers of white." Do you see one that runs the full height of the paragraph? It starts between the words *especially* and *advertising* on the first line, and continues all the way down to the double-quotation mark after the word *error* on the last line.

Popular media—especially advertising media—glorify computerdom, making alluring promises computers can't keep. In response, we buy computers with cold-remedy expectation—and cold-remedy prospects for success. That handsome fellow wearing the power tie is no more using his computer than swimsuit models are swimming. If he was, he would probably be staring blankly at the screen wondering what "Non-system disk or disk error" means.

Popular media—especially advertising media—glorify computerdom, making alluring promises computers can't keep. In response, we buy computers with cold-remedy expectations—and cold-remedy prospects for success. That handsome fellow wearing the power tie is no more using his computer than swimsuit models are swimming. If he was, he would probably be staring blankly at the screen wondering what "Non-system disk or disk error" means.

Figure 3-13: "Rivers of white" run rampant throughout the upper sample of type, caused by Word's ability to only add space between words as it justifies.

No double spacing!
Word interprets two spaces—one beside the other—as two words. If it needs to stretch a line and the line contains adjacent spaces, Word may add as much as two more spaces on either side of those already there. Therefore, you should never double-space between sentences: huge holes can develop if you're using justified alignment. You're no longer behind the keyboard of a 1938 Underwood; place a single space between sentences.

You may not consciously notice rivers of white at a normal reading distance, but you notice them subconsciously. Rivers of white are like static on the radio: no matter how compelling the message, eventually the audience tunes out.

Figure 3-13 is an exaggeration. Word can do better, but only if you intervene. By hyphenating the paragraph, you can eliminate some of the rivers. Word, however, will not hyphenate unless you turn on automatic hyphenation or hyphenate the document yourself. It won't even give fair warning, contrary to the counsel pictured in Figure 3-14. Hyphenation is your responsibility.

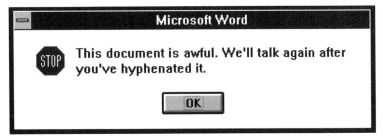

Figure 3-14: Don't count on it. Word never tells you when hyphenation is required.

When Is Justification Justified?

Am I saying you should never use Word's justification? No. I'm saying you should challenge the motive behind every justified paragraph. Is justification really necessary? If you answer yes, be aware of the space-between-words method Word uses to justify; then search ruthlessly for rivers of white.

Ideally, only wide-column text should be justified—and leaded accordingly, of course.

Left Alignment

The color of left-aligned, ragged-right text is never compromised. Because Word has no need to add spaces, all words are spaced uniformly. The typographical texture of left-aligned text is consistent. Some say its ragged-right margin adds interest to the page as well.

One thing is certain: left alignment is the only alternative when columns are narrow. The text column in Figure 3-15 measures about 40 characters, just about optimum. Nonetheless, not enough words appear on each line to let Word justify without excessive word spacing.

Without their allure, computers are simply appliances—new-technology appliances not unlike microwave ovens, but appliances just the same, in the most mundane sense of the word. Microwave ovens heat leftovers and warm soup very well. They don't cook gourmet meals or bake pastries very well, in spite of cute cookbooks and pricey entrees to the contrary. Computers are just the same: high-technology appliances best applied to robotic but essential tasks.

Without their allure, computers are simply appliances—new-technology appliances not unlike microwave ovens, but appliances just the same, in the most mundane sense of the word. Microwave ovens heat leftovers and warm soup very well. They don't cook gourmet meals or bake pastries very well, in spite of cute cookbooks and pricey entrees to the contrary. Computers are just the same: high-technology appliances best applied to robotic but essential tasks.

Figure 3-15: The text at top illustrates an excessive ragged-right margin. Below it, Word's hyphenation tool smooths the margin, providing a more pleasing silhouette.

Hyphenation

With Version 6.0, Microsoft added automatic hyphenation to Word (see Figure 3-15). Automatic hyphenation hyphenates as you type, automatically looking up words in its dictionary, noting their syllable breaks, and hyphenating when necessary. This process slows the program somewhat, but with today's fast machines it's hardly noticeable.

Selective hyphenation

Unless you tell it otherwise, Word hyphenates everything when automatic hyphenation is turned on. Every so often, you'll encounter a paragraph or two in the midst of a document that you don't want Word to hyphenate. When that's the case, select the text that's to remain unhyphenated and, from the Format menu, choose Paragraph. Click the Text Flow tab and turn on Don't Hyphenate. Word will do as it's told.

Unfortunately, automatic hyphenation isn't the default. You'll have to turn it on (Tools menu, Hyphenation) for each document you write (or you'll have to use a template that includes automatic hyphenation—more about templates in Chapter 9, "AutoFormat, Wizards & Templates"). Don't forget to do that.

Typically, left-aligned text set in a narrow column will produce an exaggerated ragged-right margin. Although this "silhouette" may provide interest, it can become noisy if excessive. The solution is hyphenation.

Referring to Figure 3-16, note the "hyphenation zone" control. This control indirectly affects Word's enthusiasm for hyphenating: if the width of the hot zone is increased, fewer hyphens are inserted; if it's reduced, more hyphens appear. You can use the hyphenation zone control, in other words, to shape the silhouette of left-aligned text.

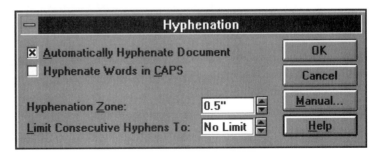

Figure 3-16: Word's hyphenation tool smooths the silhouette of left-aligned text and reduces the rivers of white in justified type.

Caution: Setting the hyphenation zone too narrow results in an overabundance of hyphens. Setting it too wide results in no hyphens at all. Most important, understand that this setting is an absolute measurement: it doesn't get wider as point size increases, for instance. A 1/4-inch hyphenation zone will produce more hyphenation in a 13-point deposition than in a 14-point *McGuffy Reader*. Don't assume the default is appropriate for any document.

When to Use Left Alignment

This one is easy: always use left alignment for body text, unless you have a profound argument in favor of justification. Don't misinterpret the abundance of justified text today. Most of it has been prepared with systems that control inter-word and inter-character spacing, both positive and negative.

You may hear many arguments in favor of justification: it's familiar; it's best for long works; it conveys a sense of orderliness. Avoid the dispute: it doesn't apply to us. Until Word offers complete word- and letter-spacing controls, justification will always involve compromise.

Declaring Alignment

Word offers a number of methods by which you can declare alignment. It probably won't be necessary, however, because left alignment is Word's default and should be yours as well.

To declare alignment, begin by selecting the paragraph (or paragraphs) to be aligned. After you've made the selection, click on the appropriate button on the Formatting toolbar, call up the Format-Paragraph dialog box and select alignment there, or type one of the following commands (see Figure 3-17):

Ctrl-J .... Justify

Ctrl-L .... Left align

Ctrl-R .... Right align

Ctrl-E .... Center

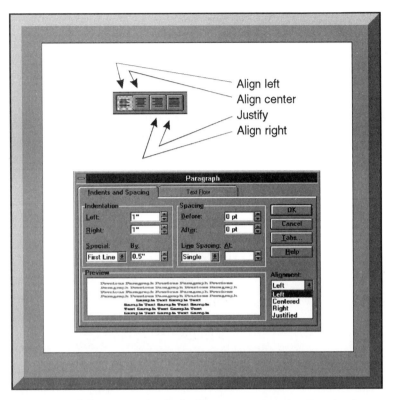

Figure 3-17: Select a method of alignment using the Standard toolbar (top), the Format-Paragraph dialog box (bottom) or Ctrl-key combinations.

FLATTER THE COOK

Let's review our recipe for setting body type:

✔ With an eye toward the reader and the subject, determine the font family that will comprise your body text. Choose from the serif typefaces available in your system.

✔ Next, choose a point size. Print a number of pages in various point sizes of the typeface you've chosen. Eye them for readability and personality to choose the size.

✔ Type 1 1/2 lowercase alphabets of your typeface in the size you've chosen. That's the ideal column width for your document. You may make compromises to accommodate the overall design. But, if possible, try not to deviate from the optimum unless it's necessary.

✔ Declare line spacing (leading) using Word's Exactly method. Start with leading equal to 120 percent of your point size. If your column is wider than the ideal, increase leading a bit. Print samples using two or three leading specifications and eye them for readability and suitability.

✔ Finally, choose an alignment option: left-aligned or justified. Left-aligned should be your default. Justify type only when you have a good reason to do so. In either case, don't forget to hyphenate.

The recipe for setting up your text may be more complex than you originally assumed, but it's worth the trouble. When the proper ingredients are mixed in the proper order, the result is an unobtrusive but exceptionally palatable page, guaranteed to flatter the cook and whet the appetite of any reader.

THE MASTER CHEF

Admittedly, body type isn't the most exciting stuff, either to discuss or to format. It *is*, however, the heart of most documents. Its appearance establishes the document's texture, tone and readability. Failure to attend to body type properly is probably desktop publishing's most common omission, and it often shows.

You're wiser now. You have mastered the ingredients and the preparation of body text. You're becoming a sage (excuse the pun) chef and you deserve a reward. That reward is display type, which we discuss in the next chapter.

Display Type 4

There sits the cookie dough in the stainless-steel mixing bowl: elegant, cultivated, delectable and...well, monotonous. Oh sure, cookie dough is great stuff for licking off the beater, but it's not very appetizing to look at, no matter how much effort went into preparing it.

Which, probably, is why somebody thought up the chips. With the simple addition of a few gobbets of chocolate, lifeless cookie dough comes alive with texture and intrigue. And, as I mentioned in Chapter 2, "Body Type," chips come from the store. Adding them to a recipe requires little talent: just open the bag and pour.

Which leads us to display type. Display type is to desktop publishing what chocolate chips are to cookies. Without display type, most documents are about as provocative as cookie dough: worth sampling perhaps, but no one wants the whole bowl.

Display type adds interest and texture, doesn't cost much, demands little talent and never requires a trip to the store—at least not for those of us who use Word.

The Toll House

The "somebody" who thought up the chips in chocolate-chip cookies is Ruth Wakefield, proprietor of the 300-year-old Toll House Restaurant (which really was a toll house at one time) on Highway 18 in Whitman, Massachusetts. Ruth's cookies were so celebrated that the Nestlé company saw cause to buy the name. The term *Toll House* has been a part of the American lexicon ever since.

WHAT IS DISPLAY TYPE?

Before we go any further, let's define the term *display type*. In Chapter 2, we defined body type as that which measures 8 to 12 points in size. Display type, therefore, is the big stuff: everything over 12 points—headlines, subheads, drop caps, pull-quotes, etc. The subhead directly above, "WHAT IS DISPLAY TYPE," is display type. The text you're now reading is body type.

Unlike body type, display type rarely appears in quantity. A paragraph of display type is an abundance. You won't be spending your time *writing* display type; you'll be spending your time *formatting* it. And well you should: more often than not, neglected display type has given "desktop publishing" its bad name. Design scholars shout epithets at desktop publishers. The indignities experts point to, however, are usually simple transgressions that could be avoided with a few moments spent formatting display type. This challenge isn't monumental: all you need is a basic awareness and a few tools. Word provides the tools; this book provides the awareness. Read on.

Sources of Display Type

For those with unlimited budgets, the sky's the limit for access to display fonts. CorelDRAW software ($695), for instance, ships with over 500 custom typefaces, many of which include multiple fonts. Micrografx Designer software ($695) includes 40 fonts. Adobe and Bitstream each offer thousands of system fonts. In fact, Adobe will sell you its entire font library on a single CD-ROM disk for about $12,000.

On the other hand, those of us with no budget have to make do with what we have, which isn't really all that bad. Word provides two sources which together should address nearly all your needs.

System fonts

The term *system font* refers to a font installed for use by the Windows system. In Word, system fonts appear on the Formatting toolbar and in the Format-Font dialog box. System fonts are *machine-specific:* not all machines offer the same fonts. Be careful: documents prepared on machine A may not look the same on machine B, unless both machines offer identical system fonts.

System Fonts

Naturally, any large system font qualifies as display type. Depending on the printer, Word allows any size from 1 to 1638 points in half-point increments. Remember that a point equals 1/72 inch. Thus, Word can produce text over 22 inches high (see Figure 4-1).

Big Stuff!

Figure 4-1: Word can provide system text up to 1638 points in size. This text, appearing at 127 points, is less than one-tenth the size of Word's maximum.

Though you rarely need text this large, it's nice to know that Word offers the potential. Furthermore, you can apply any of 16 colors to text, which can be superscripted or subscripted, expanded or condensed, underlined, italicized, boldfaced, or presented in small or all caps. Indeed, system text offers such a diversity of combinations that you really don't need anything else—if money is no object.

But money *is* usually a limiting factor. Outline-font technology printers, which can print fonts in all the sizes Word offers, are expensive, as are system fonts. Because display type is a supporting player, purchasing fonts exclusively for display purposes can be hard to justify.

Sagacious desktop publishers that we are, we know that display type is *not* a supporting player. Display type has a powerful presence: it whispers; it shouts; its personality dominates, no matter how many characters make up the cast. Anything but a bit player, it deserves equal billing—right up there with body type and graphics.

WordArt

Thankfully, Word complements our cast with Microsoft WordArt, a display-text utility joining the troupe in full costume, including 15 free display fonts (see Figure 4-2).

Figure 4-2: A sample of five WordArt fonts: a versatile cast of players, each ready for top billing in your documents.

Double-click to edit

To edit existing WordArt text, double-click on it. Word will launch and load your text into WordArt, where you'll work until you're ready to return to Word. This feature is known as *object embedding*, discussed in Chapter 7, "Graphics."

To access WordArt, choose Object from the Insert menu and then choose "Microsoft WordArt." (If you have upgraded from a previous version of Word, or if you use certain other Microsoft applications, you should choose "Microsoft WordArt 2.0," the latest version.) You may then select the font, size, style and color you want. Type in your text; select the style, font, size, color and other features you like from WordArt's toolbar; click on OK, and your display type plays its scene right where you placed the cursor.

The beauty of WordArt text is that it can be printed on any printer in any size, from 1 to 1638 points. Here's the trick: after you return to Word, WordArt text appears *as a graphic*—eight graphics handles surround it (see Figure 4-3). Thus, any printer that can print graphics can print WordArt text—a godsend for those of us with an unadorned LaserJet.

Figure 4-3: Eight graphics handles surround WordArt text.

The fact that WordArt text appears as a graphic is something of a mixed blessing (see Figure 4-4). For instance, you can use all of Word's graphic controls to manipulate WordArt text: you can size, crop, border, color and distort it. On the other hand, you cannot use any of Word's textual controls—word, letter or line spacing (though WordArt offers letter-spacing controls of its own)—with WordArt. Nonetheless, WordArt offers an abundant source of material for display type. Purchased on the retail market, WordArt's 15 typefaces would cost more than Word does in the first place.

Pluses	Minuses
✦ Fonts free of charge.	— Limited number of fonts available.
✦ Lots of effects available.	— Can become hackneyed.
✦ WordArt text may be enlarged, reduced, bordered and distorted within Word.	— Must use WordArt to edit text.
✦ Any machine can display and print WordArt text—neither WordArt nor WordArt fonts are required at the destination machine.	— WordArt text may not be edited in the destination machine unless WordArt is installed on that machine.
✦ WordArt text may be copied to the clipboard and pasted into any graphics program.	— Many graphics programs offer a larger selection of fonts and styles.
✦ Text may occupy multiple lines.	— No control over leading.
✦ Sizes up to 1638 points are available, regardless of printer type.	

Figure 4-4: WordArt is something of a mixed blessing.

Perhaps WordArt's best feature is that it's easy to learn and use. Spend an hour fooling around with it, and you'll know it all. You'll probably never even have to open the manual (which is just as well: the manual barely mentions WordArt). One suggestion is worth mentioning, however. Prepare a page of WordArt text displaying all 15 typefaces and their names and print it out (see Figure 4-5). Refer to it whenever you need display type.

ALGERIAN
Arial Rounded
Bookman Old Style
Braggadocio
Brittanic Bold
Brush Script
Century Gothic
Colonna
DESDEMONA
Footlight
Impact
Kino
Playbill
Matura
Wide Latin

Figure 4-5: WordArt's 15 beautiful fonts are added to your system when you install Word, and become available to all of your applications.

We're far from done with WordArt. We discuss it now and again in this chapter and the next. It's a powerful tool somewhat ignored by the Word *User's Guide*. This book will correct the oversight.

FORMATTING DISPLAY TYPE

Because display type plays such a different role than body type, its formatting requirements are considerably different. Here's an example: the eye doesn't really read body type; it recognizes patterns. Combinations of ascenders and descenders provide each word or phrase with an easily recognizable silhouette. That's why we can read body type so quickly and why we fail to note typos appearing within common phrases.

Display type, however, is different. Because of its size, individual characters dominate, reducing pattern recognition. Each character's appearance and the way it fits together with other characters are of utmost significance.

Leading

In the previous chapter's section on leading, you learned that Word's Exactly leading specification is usually your best bet. This advice applies doubly to display type. Of all the linespacing (leading) options offered in the Format-Paragraph dialog box, only Exactly and Multiple let you use negative leading: leading that's smaller than the type's point size. (Notice that negative leading isn't really negative; it's just smaller than point size. Word won't accept negative values in the Format-Paragraph dialog box.)

In display-type sizes, even text set solid (no leading) seems too loose (see Figure 4-6). Typically, about half of any font's point size is reserved for ascenders and descenders. A headline set in 36-point Times, for instance, devotes 22 points to ascenders, descenders and the shoulder. The remaining 14 points is the x-height. (Review Figure 3-7 for an illustration of ascenders, descenders, shoulders and x-height.) In other words, more space is devoted to the area between lines than the lines themselves, even when Times is set without leading.

Figure 4-6: At top, Word's default Single line spacing (leading). In the center, type set without leading. At bottom, 36-point type on 30-point negative leading.

This amount of line spacing makes sense for body type, where broad horizontal "stripes" help the eye scan the page. For display type, however, broad areas of white between lines only serve to confuse. Indeed, if the amount of space between lines approaches the amount of space between words, the eye doesn't know whether to read left-to-right or top-to-bottom.

The solution is negative leading. The lower example in Figure 4-6 is set with negative leading; notice how the ascenders and descenders tuck around each other. Extreme negative leading such as this is only successful when ascenders and descenders don't collide.

Leading System Fonts

You may want to use negative leading when preparing display type using system fonts. Fortunately, Word makes it easy: simply select the text that's to be leaded, choose Paragraph from the Format menu, change Line Spacing to Exactly and type in the leading specification (see Figure 4-7).

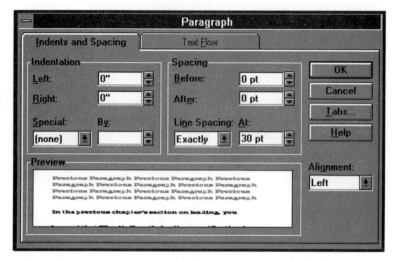

Figure 4-7: The 36-point Times in Figure 4-6 was leaded by declaring line spacing of Exactly 30 points.

The multilingual Word

Word's Format-Paragraph dialog box accepts dimensions in points (pt), picas (pi), inches (in or "), centimeters (cm) or lines (li). Just include the appropriate abbreviation.

Note that this command appears within the Format-Paragraph dialog box, thus leading is a paragraph-level attribute, which has a number of implications:

✔ Only a partial selection (an insertion point will do) is required to identify a paragraph for which a leading command is to be issued. The command will affect the entire paragraph, regardless of the extent of the selection.

✔ Negatively leaded system fonts appear cut off on the screen, but they print in their entirety (see sidebar).

Headless characters

Often, Word seems to cut off the tops of characters when you declare negative leading. Don't let it worry you: though the characters are cut off onscreen, they'll print without a problem.

✔ All paragraph attributes are carried forward to subsequent paragraphs. Be careful: exact leading continues from one paragraph to the next. In the left illustration in Figure 4-8, the title's 30-point leading was inadvertently carried forward and applied to the quote beneath, even though the quote's point size was reduced to 14.

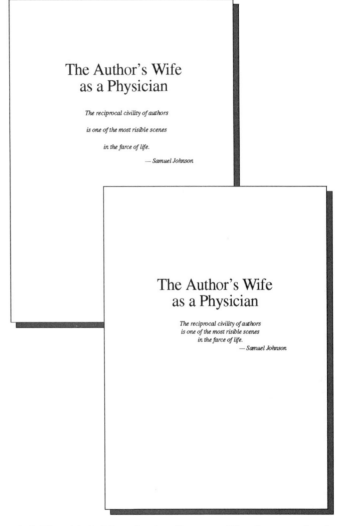

Figure 4-8: The title's 30-point leading specification was inadvertently applied to the top quote. On the bottom, the quote's leading was manually reduced to 18 points.

Leading WordArt Text

Though system fonts should be your first choice for display type, you may want a font or size not offered by your system. No problem: use WordArt.

Even though WordArt can accommodate multiple lines of text, even though it gives us 15 fonts, and even though it provides a nearly unlimited choice of font sizes, it gives us absolutely no control over leading (see Figure 4-9).

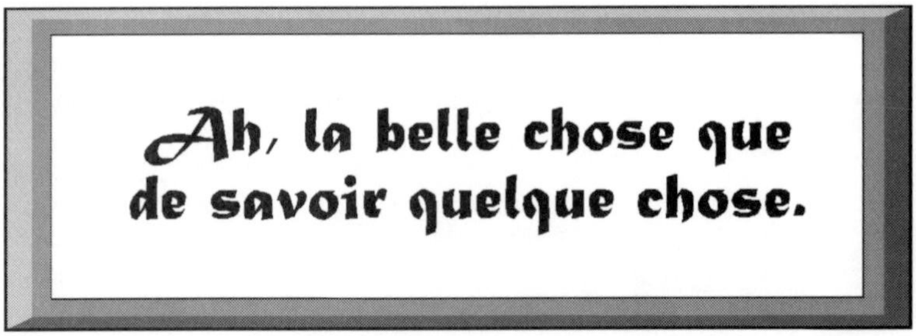

Figure 4-9: WordArt's default leading is its only leading option. If you want to override it, you will have to do so using Word's line-spacing control, described in the text.

To assert any control over WordArt's leading, you have to prepare each line of type in WordArt separately and then use Word's line-spacing control to manipulate the text. It's a work-around—WordArt should offer leading controls—but it's no trouble.

Interestingly, WordArt text that has been negatively leaded using Word's line-spacing control appears cut off when you view it on the screen (see Figure 4-10), but it prints satisfactorily just the same.

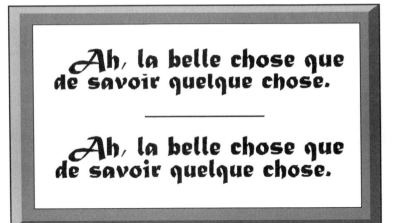

Figure 4-10: At the top, 24-point WordArt Matura text on 22-point leading. Note how some of the characters have been cut off (look at the dot over the *i*). Below that, the printout of the same text. (Ah, it's a lovely thing, to know a thing or two. —Molière)

Here's how I did it:

✔ I used WordArt to create each line of text separately, giving each its own paragraph in Word.

✔ Using Word, I selected the second line; then I chose Paragraph from the Format menu.

✔ I changed the Line Spacing setting to Exactly and specified 22 points.

This procedure is not casual. It takes a bit of work. The results, however, justify the effort, and these little courtesies provide the sparkle that makes everyday documents glisten in publishing's surfeit of mediocrity.

There's no formula for setting display-type leading, nor is it a black art. It's more a matter of developing an eye. Anyone can do it; it doesn't take long. Begin by *observing* rather than reading type. Open any magazine and spend five minutes analyzing its display type. Note how often negative leading is used (look for descenders extending below the tops of ascenders). Try to guess its point size and leading; then duplicate the effect using Word. After about two weeks, you'll become a leading expert, able to recognize the need and issue the commands without conscious thought.

Kerning

Mirror images
In fact, all my "stamp" illustrations are mirror images of reality. True typographical stamps were reversed left-to-right to provide the proper image when the stamp was pressed against the page. Hold Figure 4-11 up to a mirror if you're a purist about this kind of thing.

It's time to stop thinking vertically. You have just as much need to control the space between characters horizontally as vertically. Look at Figure 4-11. We're back to the stamps from the previous chapter, in this case four of them lined up neatly to form the word *Type*.

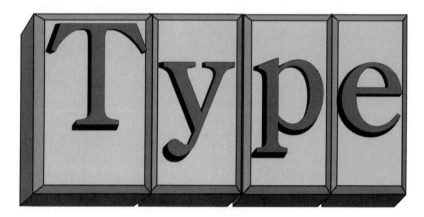

Figure 4-11: The unkerned *Type* seems to burp between the *T* and the *y*. You can narrow the gap by kerning the first two characters of the word.

Do you see the large gap between the *T* and the *y*? The *T*'s stamp has to accommodate its wide arms, creating an unnatural distance to the right of the *T*. When printed in display-type sizes, the word looks more like two words: *T* and *ype*. The word burps. The eye will most likely assemble the pieces, just as the ear would if the speaker burped in the middle of the word; but the interruption is distracting and anything but elegant.

The solution is kerning. The term refers to the horizontal positioning of pairs of characters. You should, in effect, file off the right side of the *T*'s stamp, leaving the right arm of the *T* hanging beyond the edge (see Figure 4-12).

Figure 4-12: The right side of the *T*'s stamp has been kerned, allowing the adjacent *y* to fit under the arm of the *T* to create a more pleasing fit.

The Kern Type Shop

I heard this story from a student at the University of Oregon—hardly an unimpeachable source. The Kern Type Shop in Portland was where stamps were first filed to "kern" pairs of characters. Other Oregonians claim the Intel Pentium was designed in Hillsboro over a pint of Terminator Stout and that the sarcophagus of Tutankhamen is buried at the base of Mount Hood. All these stories are suspect. Indeed, the very existence of the state has been disputed by scholars and politicians for decades.

Which is exactly what the old-timers used to do: they would get out the file and "kern the T." Typesetters prized their kerned characters, which were delicate, used rarely and served to identify the attentive professional.

Fortunately, the days of lead type are over. Files are no longer required to kern pairs of characters. But you still have good reason to take pride in your work, and kerning is another way to demonstrate that attitude.

Kerning System Type

Kerning is another typographical term Word ignores. Instead, the Format-Font dialog box offers an entire Character Spacing tab section (see Figure 4-13). In fact, because of the difference between kerning and letter spacing, Word uses the term properly in some situations: *kerning* refers to the relationship between pairs of characters; *spacing* refers to letter spacing over a group of characters—always more than two. If you select a group of characters before you invoke this dialog box, all those characters within the selection will be affected. If you kern more than two characters at once, that's spacing.

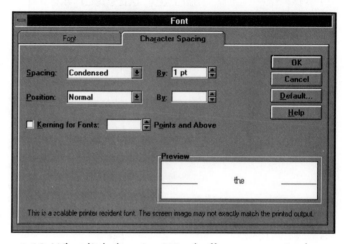

Figure 4-13: What little kerning Word offers appears in the Format-Font dialog box as Condensed Spacing. The maximum is 1584 points.

With Version 6.0, Word now offers truly effective kerning controls for system text, in tenth-of-a-point increments. All you have to do is select the leftmost character of the two characters you want to kern, choose Font from the Format menu, click on the Character Spacing tab, choose Condensed from the Spacing pop-up menu and specify the amount of kerning you prefer in the By text box (refer again to Figure 4-13). Word will even preview the effect for you before you apply it to your text.

Select one, not two

Select only a single character to kern a pair. Selecting both characters of a pair "kerns" not only the pair, but the character following the pair as well. Officially, Word's letter-spacing control "removes space from the right side of the selected characters," to quote the Help file.

Automatic kerning

Most printer-font technology embraces some form of automatic kerning, as does WordArt. To see whether your computer and printer accommodate automatic kerning, print the word *WAVE* in all uppercase in a large point size. Now look at the results carefully. Are the *W*, the *A* and the *V* kerned? Don't be surprised if they are: it's pretty common.

In the old days, typographers had a saying: "TNT," meaning "tight not touching." This saying described their preferred method of setting display type. Indeed, the eye expects to see display type set very tight, both in terms of leading and letter spacing. Kerning isn't something Word accommodates automatically, but specifying it manually isn't too much trouble, and the results are well worth the effort (see Figure 4-14).

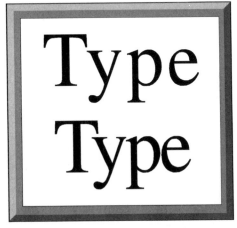

Figure 4-14: Above, the word *Type* without kerning. Below, manual kerning has been applied to better marry the individual characters in the word.

Kerning WordArt Text

Word offers a second solution to the kerning problem, and that's WordArt. It's something of a mixed blessing: though WordArt can kern automatically, "kerning," as far as WordArt is concerned, applies to a WordArt object in its entirety, not specific pairs of characters.

Let's begin with the good news: WordArt, interestingly enough, kerns quite well without having to be told. If you stop to think about it, a finite number of pairs of characters need to be kerned. You should always kern an uppercase *T* and a lowercase *y*, for instance; but you should never kern an uppercase *T* and a lowercase *h*. When you consider all the possible combinations, you will discover a need for about 100 "kerned pairs." WordArt is aware of these pairs and can be instructed to kern them automatically.

The top example in Figure 4-15 illustrates WordArt text, set without kerning. The example directly below it illustrates WordArt's automatic kerning. It's a subtle change, but significant.

Figure 4-15: At top, WordArt text without kerning. WordArt's automatic kerning is subtle but evident in the middle example; the lower example adds additional, "custom" kerning.

As you can see from Figure 4-15's second example, WordArt's automatic kerning feature is subtle at best. Typically, you will need to assist it with some additional kerning of your own. WordArt anticipates the need, allowing you to specify custom kerning values ranging from 0% (which piles all of WordArt's characters on top of one another) to 300% (which is great if you're after a "missing teeth" effect, but not for much else).

Figure 4-15's lower example illustrates WordArt text with automatic kerning turned on and custom kerning set to 90%, as shown in the dialog box pictured in Figure 4-16. To specify automatic and custom kerning, choose Spacing Between Characters from WordArt's Format menu (or click the corresponding button on WordArt's toolbar).

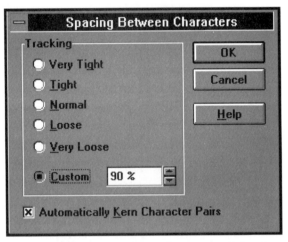

Figure 4-16: The Spacing Between Characters dialog box provides the opportunity to kern WordArt's text.

TAKING OFF THE GLOVES

Our discussion of display-text formatting has ended. Aside from WordArt leading, Word has missed few tricks when it comes to formatting of this nature. This version is a significant improvement over the previous version of the program—one that's perfectly suited to the world of the desktop publisher. It is a world where fun abounds, pages glisten and your finances remain unchallenged. It is the world of cheap tricks, and it's coming up next.

5 Cheap Tricks With Display Type

Though the term *cheap tricks* has derogatory connotations, none should be read into the above title. I'm using the term literally, not figuratively. Everybody is looking for cheap tricks, bakers and desktop publishers alike. Commercial bakeries, for instance, learned a long time ago that fresh milk is expensive, bulky, and doesn't keep well. Milk *fats*, on the other hand, are cheap, take forever to spoil and store in a fraction of the space required by whole milk. Moreover, milk fats reconstitute into a product that may frequently be substituted for whole milk. Most chocolate chips are produced from milk fats and no one is the wiser.

Desktop publishers aren't exempt from frugality, either. The desktop publisher's constant nemesis is money—or the lack of it. Were it not for the scarcity of funds, there probably would *be* no desktop publishing. Why would anyone bother?

Plenty of experts are willing to prepare documents: exquisite, trouble-free, professional documents. Of course, experts expect to be paid, and therein lies the rub. Many of us got into this business because we couldn't afford the experts. Desktop publishers are eternally juggling limited resources: fonts, graphics and time. Anything that helps is welcome—as long as it's free.

Which brings us to our discussion of cheap tricks: bountiful, malleable, cost-free ornaments with which we can embroider the fabric of monotony that challenges us each day.

The first resource that comes to mind is graphics. A graphic gobbet here and a graphic gobbet there can do wonders for the tedium of the textual page. Although this observation may be true, the fact of the matter is that most graphics fail to meet our criteria: they're bountiful and malleable, but few are free. What's left? Display text. Sidebars, pull-quotes, drop caps, blurbs: these are the resources of the inventive desktop publisher. They're bountiful, malleable and—best of all— absolutely free. (See Figure 5-1.)

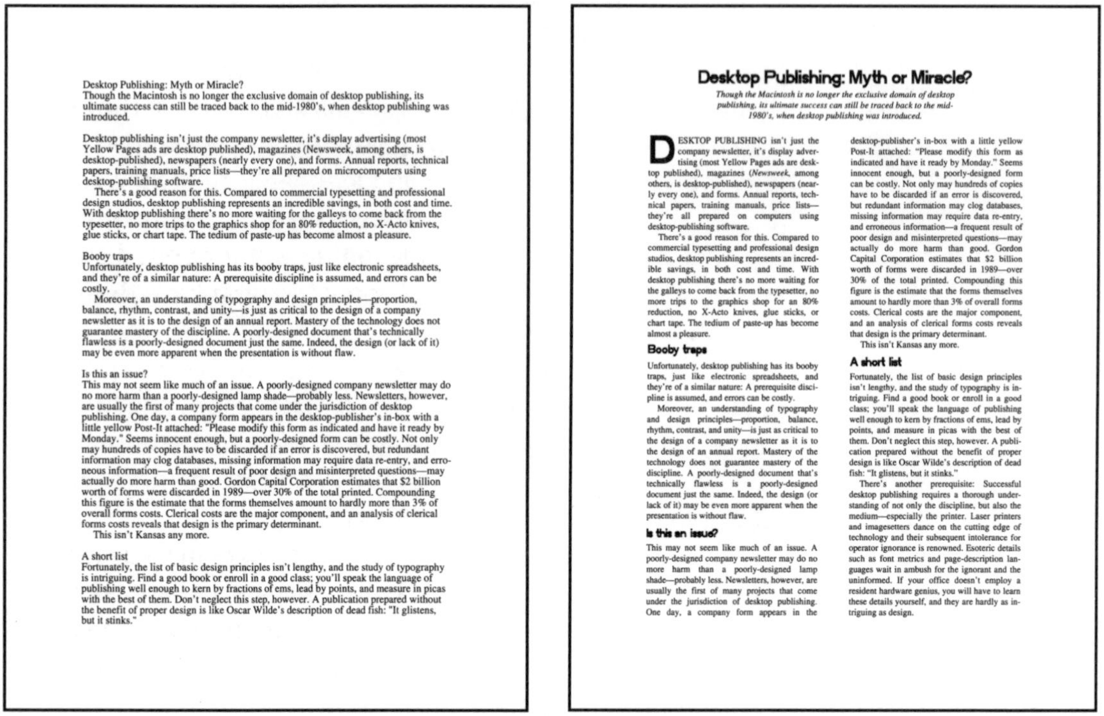

Figure 5-1: Though the story may be captivating, the design at left is listless. The simple addition of display type—cheap tricks— provides more allure to the page on the right.

HEADLINES

More of an obligation than an ornament, headlines hardly qualify as a cheap trick; but they *do* preclude monotony and they're free. Headlines, in other words, satisfy the spirit of this discussion, if not its implication.

Monotypographical Harmony

A review

For a good example of monotypographical harmony, turn back to Figure 2-12 in Chapter 2. The entire design is Times—Times Roman for the body, Times Italic and Times Bold for display—and the page sparkles. Don't equate monotypographical harmony with monotony. They may be spelled similarly, but there the similarity ends.

Your first display-type decision will be academic: which typeface should you use? Before laboring unnecessarily over academics, try using the typeface you've selected for your body text. Using the same face for both body and display is known as *monotypographical harmony*, and it's often the best place to begin. Prepare a few pages this way, print them out, and look them over. Is there an identifiable need for a contrasting display face? Chances are there isn't. Many designs are lively enough with just one font family for both display and body type. If nothing else, monotypographical designs are reliably unified.

On the other hand, your design may need typographical contrast. The use of a contrasting typeface for display purposes may enliven the design and provide a counterpoint for the monotony of body type. If this is the case, all you need do is decide upon the contrasting face.

You may recall our discussion of type *races* in Chapter 2, "Body Type." Old English is a race. Roman is a race, as are sans-serif and specialty typefaces. Though roman is the most appropriate race for body text, when it comes to display text, anything goes.

There you have it: if your design needs typographical contrast, fill it with any font family you like. But if you aren't going to employ monotypographical harmony, fill the need with a font family from a race other than that of your body text. Assuming your body text is roman, use a script, a sans-serif or a specialty face for display. On a PostScript system, Avant Garde, Helvetica and even Zapf Chancery would provide appropriate contrast to roman body text—but not Bookman, Schoolbook or Palatino.

Line Breaks & Hyphenation

Headlines, like many display applications, require particular attention to line breaks and hyphenation. Readers comprehend headlines in small chunks, and these chunks should be as readable as possible. The implication is especially significant when it comes to line breaks: multiple-line headlines should always break the same way your voice would break them were you to read them aloud (see Figure 5-2).

Multiple-line subheads

Line breaks are commands that start a new line but not a new paragraph. They are perfect to use to break the lines for headlines and other multiple-line subheads. To declare a line break, position the insertion point where the break is required and then press Shift-Enter.

> # Bugs and frogs, even clods, kids eat 'em up
>
> ---
>
> # Bugs and frogs, even clods, kids eat 'em up

Figure 5-2: Allowed to determine line breaks on its own, Word bungles the job (top). At bottom, manually inserted line breaks make the text more readable and improve its silhouette.

Capitalization

If you've ever pondered the purpose of ascenders and descenders, think of shapes and silhouettes. In fact, most of us read by *recognizing patterns*, rather than by observing characters and words. That's why we have ascenders and descenders: they give words and phrases familiar shapes that we use for pattern recognition.

Practice what I preach

In spite of my advice to the contrary, capitalized subheads appear throughout this book. In Chapter 2, "Body Type," I say that Palatino is a poor choice for body text, yet this book's body text is set in Palatino. Why the hypocrisy? Because the people at Ventana offer a family of products, and they prefer a family resemblance among them. Capitalization and Palatino run in the Ventana family. They really are quite nice people otherwise.

The Outline View

If headlines and multiple-level subheads are attributed with "heading" styles—Heading 1, Heading 2 and so forth—you can switch from Document View (the trees) to Outline View (the forest) by simply choosing Outline from the View menu. Using the Outline View to display only heads and subheads helps organize thoughts, arrange material more effectively and navigate long documents. And it's only a mouse move away.

In Other Words, You Should Never Capitalize Every Word Of Any Body Of Text. It burps. It stumbles. It destroys pattern recognition. My preference is to capitalize display text just as you would body text: initial words and proper nouns only.

Newly enhanced in Version 6.0 is the Format-Change Case command. This dialog box controls—for the selected text—Sentence case, lowercase, UPPERCASE, Title Case, or tOGGLE cASE.

Grazing

You will frequently encounter the word *grazing* during the next few pages. Grazing is what display type is all about: readers graze in fields fertile with information—more information than they need or have time for. With such a glut of potential, readers graze languidly, tasting only material that appeals to their senses and stopping to consume only that which seems particularly alluring. Display text provides the allure.

Headlines are primary grazing material. They're the bait; other display text is the hook. If the reader isn't attracted to the bait, everything else is immaterial. Put extra effort into your headlines. Word them compellingly and format them appropriately.

SUBHEADS

After the reader has taken the headline's bait, subheads provide the secondary source of grazing material. Readers judge the extent and suitability of your material by grazing on subheads. They use subheads as signposts, for indexing and navigation. Subheads provide the primary rhythm of your document, allowing it to flow smoothly from one subject to another. Subheads also let the writer concentrate on the overall arrangement of the document: to see the forest when the trees get in the way (see sidebar).

Accordingly, use subheads and make them stand out. Give them a paragraph or column of their own. Set them in a contrasting font. Keep their rhythmical function in mind and avoid spacing them irregularly.

Sideheads

A familiar design for desktop-published documents is the *sidehead* format. You've seen this design before: subheads placed in a large margin outside the body text column. The resulting unified white space gives the eye a rest area and provides the reader with an unobstructed view of the document's subheads, an especially effective way to facilitate grazing (see Figure 5-3).

Figure 5-3: Sideheads receive a "column" of their own, providing ample white space to set them apart from the text and facilitate grazing.

An additional benefit is the reduced column width imposed upon the body text. As we mentioned in Chapter 3, "Setting Up Your Text," a column width of 1 1/2 alphabets is ideal. Paper that's 8 1/2 inches wide hardly promotes such a narrow column. Sideheads are one way of accommodating the need.

Sideheads are best formatted using frames. Though frames will be discussed later in Chapter 7, "Graphics," a description of the sidebar technique I used to create Figure 5-3 seems appropriate here. Refer to Figure 5-4 as you follow these steps:

Frame borders

Word places a border around text you frame. This border is rarely appropriate for sideheads. To correct this problem, leave your sidehead selected, choose Borders and Shading from the Format menu and click on None in the Presets area.

✔ Enter all your text normally. Each subhead should reside in a paragraph of its own; but don't worry about formatting until text entry is complete.

✔ Choose Page Setup from the File menu and declare an exaggerated left margin. I used a left margin of 16.5 picas (2 1/2 inches) for the document illustrated in Figure 5-3. If you're not in Page Layout View, your text will still appear on the left. It isn't. Word always positions the left margin against the left edge of the screen, unless you're in Page Layout View.

✔ Select a subhead; then choose Frame from the Insert menu. Word will ask if you want to switch to Page Layout View (if you're not already there); answer Yes. Your body text will probably now be wrapped around the subhead.

✔ Leaving the subhead selected, choose Frame from the Format menu. Set the frame's Horizontal Position: Left, Relative To: Page; set its Vertical Position: 0, Relative To: Paragraph. Set its width Exactly to the width of your left margin, less the distance you want between your subheads and body text and less the amount of white space you want from the edge of the paper. Because I wanted a pica between the subheads and body text, I set my subhead's width to 11 picas. Choose OK to close the Frame dialog box.

✔ Back at the layout, right-align the subhead (use the Formatting toolbar or press Ctrl-R), and apply any other formatting attributes (font, style, size) you want.

Mirror margins

The sidehead format is available for two-sided, facing-page documents as well. Turn on Mirror Margins in the File-Page Setup dialog box and declare an exaggerated outside margin. In the Format-Frame dialog box, set the Vertical Position to the Outside of the Page. That's all: Word takes care of the rest, even if you edit the document after you format the sideheads.

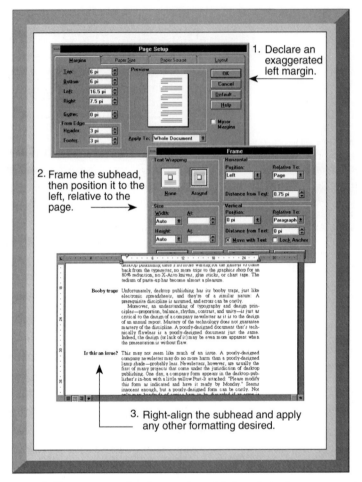

Figure 5-4: The process for formatting sideheads isn't too complex. Frames make it all possible.

Look again at the Format-Frame dialog box pictured in Figure 5-4. Note that I have selected Move with Text in the Vertical section. This selection infers that the subhead will move with the paragraph to its right as you edit the document, a valuable (and necessary) feature.

If your document contains a number of subheads, you'll have to repeat this process for each one. This process would be laborious were it not for styles (see Chapter 6).

SIDEBARS

Don't confuse side*heads* with side*bars*. Sidebars are parenthetical notes often placed at the side of body text. They're used extensively in this book, where they appear in the left margins. If you purchased *Desktop Publishing With Word for Windows* in a store, did its sidebars influence your decision? I put extra effort into their content and format to attract bookstore browsers.

Sidebars illuminate or elucidate the subject material of the body text. From a design standpoint, sidebars are another cheap trick: they provide graphical interest, add some "color" to the page, attract grazers and don't cost a dime.

It's important that you format sidebars in such a way as to distinguish them from the body text. Typically, you use a contrasting type race, use different leading, include borders or add a shade behind the sidebar text. It's just as important that sidebars contain information that's compelling to read (sidebars are primary grazing material) and corollary to the body. Oftentimes, sidebar material fails to warrant sidebar emphasis and is really nothing more than rehashed body text. Repeating the same old information defeats the purpose. Save your best stuff for sidebars.

Sidebars need not always appear at the side. Figure 5-5 offers three sidebar formats, of which only one is traditional. Sidebars may appear within the text column itself, isolated on a page or even as footnotes. Indeed, footnotes are often read before anything else. We're not talking about academic documents where footnotes typically provide reference information; we're talking about everyday documents where footnotes present corollary information, often with a glint of humor or an effective turn of phrase. Sound familiar? They aren't really footnotes at all; they're sidebars masquerading as footnotes, where they capitalize on the footnotes' readership.

Be consistent
No matter what format you choose for your sidebars, be consistent. If you box one, you should box all of them. Consistency establishes convention, convention comforts readers, and comfortable readers abide the objectives of persuasion.

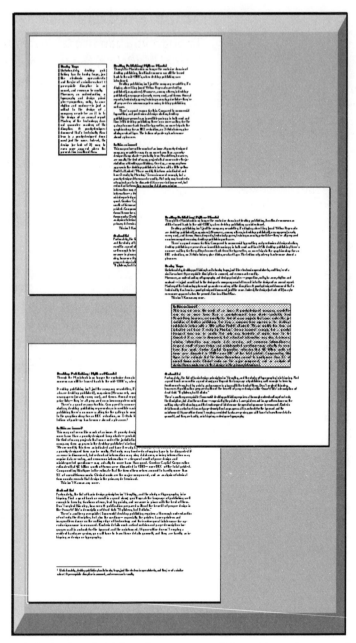

Figure 5-5: A trio of sidebar formats—traditional (top, formatted with a frame), boxed and shaded (middle, formatted with borders), and as a footnote (bottom).

Framed Sidebars

Though you can use tables, multiple columns and Draw to format a sidebar, the two most common (and easiest) methods are frames and paragraph borders.

Whole Page View

After a frame is established, you may find it easier to position a sidebar by zooming out to Whole Page View. Choose Zoom from the View menu; then click on Whole Page. This view is not only WYSIWYG, it's also interactive.

If you frame a sidebar, you can position it on the page by simply dragging it with the mouse. And there's not much to it:

✔ Switch to Page Layout View (View menu), if necessary.

✔ Select all the sidebar text, including the title (if any).

✔ Choose Frame from the Insert menu.

That's it. Word returns with eight black handles surrounding the sidebar. Dragging on any of the four side handles resizes the sidebar in the direction corresponding to the handle; dragging on a corner handle resizes the sidebar in two directions at once. Dragging on the perimeter of the frame (not on a handle) when a four-headed arrow appears moves it around on the page. (See Figure 5-6.) No matter what, Word automatically wraps the remaining text around the frame. Nothing could be easier.

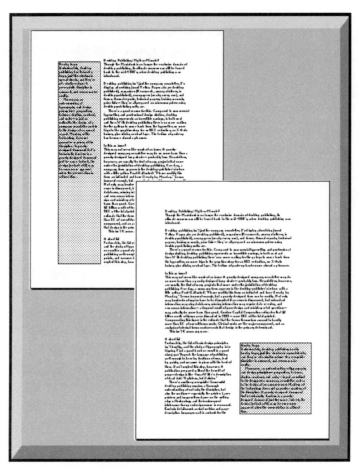

Figure 5-6: Instant redesign: by simply dragging frame handles in Page Layout View, you can go from the design at top to the design at bottom in a matter of seconds.

Frames and zooms are Word's primary tools for the desktop publisher. We'll discuss both of them in Chapter 7, "Graphics."

Bordered Sidebars

The complexity and flexibility of frames are often unwarranted. Many sidebars are simply indented paragraphs, similar to the middle example in Figure 5-5. In these situations, some kind of border often helps. It can be as simple as a single rule at the side, or as elaborate as a shadowed outline, filled with a shade or pattern.

You accomplish these changes via Word's Format-Borders and Shading command. Here's the process:

✔ Select the sidebar paragraph(s).

✔ Choose Borders and Shading from the Format menu.

✔ Choose the appropriate border location, style and shade (see Figure 5-7).

✔ Back at the layout (with the sidebar paragraph(s) still selected), set the left and right indents (if appropriate) using either the Ruler or the Format-Paragraph dialog box.

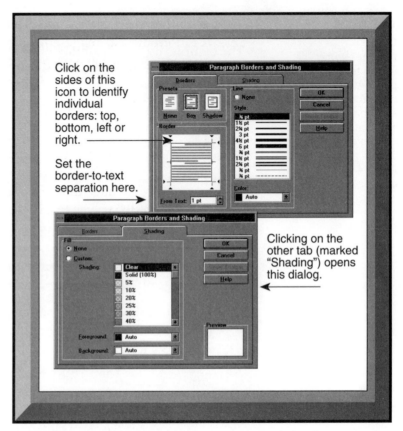

Figure 5-7: The Format-Borders and Shading dialog box provides ample control over border appearance and position.

Be careful with shades. Most 300 dpi laser printers produce a screen frequency of 60 to 75 lines per inch. That's print-shop talk, but it means that the individual dots of a shade (screen) produced on a laser printer may measure more than a point across. This *very* coarse dot pattern can obliterate details such as serifs and the dots over *i*'s and *j*'s. That's why I recommend large or bold sans-serif fonts for surprinting (see sidebar) if a laser printer is the final output device.

Surprinting sidebars

The term *surprinting* refers to text printed on top of a shade, a technique often used for sidebars. To surprint, use a sans-serif font (serifs often get lost against a shade) and print it in a point size large enough to be easily comprehended by even the most presbyopic reader.

On the other hand, alternative printing devices are available. A Linotronic 300 imagesetter, for instance, can provide a screen frequency of 150 lines per inch or better. (High-resolution printing alternatives are discussed in Chapter 8, "Fonts & Printers.")

Count Basie lead his band with winks and nods. His instrument was silent more often than it was played. Nonetheless, his contribution was pertinent, elegant and essential.

Your borders would do well to emulate the Count. In all documents, borders and rules provide appropriate counterpoint in moments of necessity. Subtlety, however, is a virtue. Take it easy. Don't clobber the page with lines and shades. Sneak up on it. Try a single rule first. If one rule is not enough, add another. This secret of page design is one that few desktop publishers oblige when borders cast their seductive spell.

PULL-QUOTES

A pull-quote is just that: a quotation pulled from the body text and provided with graphic emphasis to entice the grazing reader. Pull-quotes can be profoundly effective, but only if the quotes themselves are compelling, pithy and wise. If your document contains nothing to this end, pull-quotes can be counterproductive.

> *"Pull quotes can be profoundly effective, but only if the quotes themselves are compelling, pithy, and wise."*

Entering ANSI characters

The extended ANSI (American National Standards Institute) character set is available in most fonts. ANSI characters include open and close quotation marks, em dashes, foreign-language characters, fractions and things like the copyright or trademark symbols. To enter an ANSI character using the keyboard, turn on Num Lock, hold down the Alt key and type zero plus the three-digit ANSI code. (A list of ANSI codes is included in the Appendix of this book.) To view the extended ANSI character set with Word for Windows, choose Symbol from the Insert menu; then select (Normal Text) in the Font list box at the top. The characters at the bottom of the box are ANSI.

Because of pull-quotes' profundity, you should use them sparingly—never more than one per page, and rarely more than two or three per document.

You can prepare pull-quotes with any font available to you. You also may originate the pull-quote in WordArt 2.0 for additional embellishments. Fancy quotation marks are often appropriate. In many fonts, the open quotation mark (") is ANSI 147 and the close quotation mark (") is ANSI 148. Or, if you have selected the smart quote feature in the Tools-AutoCorrect menu, Word for Windows 6.0 will replace your boring, old straight quotes for you automatically each time you type them.

The Zapf Dingbat typeface also contains a pair of outrageous quotes. You can insert them as a symbol from the Insert-Symbol menu. Add yet another textual cheap trick to your document by using enlarged "curly" quotes to bracket pull-quotes.

Finally, you can frame and position pull-quotes at will by dragging on them with the mouse in Page Layout View (see Figure 5-8). A pull-quote is even more effective if body text is wrapped around it. Wrapping text lends the wrapped element even more of a graphical quality, and all that's required is a frame.

Figure 5-8: Prepared in Draw using system fonts, this pull-quote acts like it's a frame; you position it on the page in Whole Page View using the mouse.

INITIAL CAPS

Embellishing initial capital letters is one of the easiest and quickest cheap tricks of them all. Like subheads, initial caps serve as signposts, establish a rhythm and add sparkle. They're often subject to overuse or overstatement, however. Use them with care.

At least three sources of initial caps are at your disposal: scanned graphics, system fonts or WordArt. Scanned graphics are closest to the original "illuminated" caps first used by scribes (see Figure 5-9). We'll discuss them in greater detail (and suggest some sources) in Chapter 7, "Graphics."

ASIC DESIGN isn't a mystery, nor is its practice limited to those gifted with an artistic endowment. Find a good book or enroll in a good class; you'll speak the language of design and typography well enough to kern by fractions of ems, lead by points, and measure in picas with the best of them. Don't neglect this step, however. A publication prepared without the benefit of proper design is like Oscar Wilde's description of dead fish: "It glistens, but it stinks."

Figure 5-9: Scanned as a .BMP file, an initial cap has been framed and dropped into the text. The first line has been outdented by declaring a 1 pica hanging indent in the Format-Paragraph-Special dialog box.

Now you can use system fonts for initial caps with the new Drop Cap feature on the Format menu. Not only does it drop the selected character, but in the same dialog box you can choose a different font. The initial cap is sized automatically per number of lines you want it to assume, and you can indicate the amount of space between it and your text. Everything is done for you automatically.

WordArt text behaves just like system text, though it provides a selection of shapes and text directions not available elsewhere. In all cases, you'll probably want to frame the cap to provide accurate positioning control. Switch to Page Layout View (View menu), select the cap and choose Frame from the Insert menu. You may have to adjust the frame width and height, which you can do with the horizontal and vertical rulers.

Using Draw, you can control both the color and the background of the capital independently. Even if *the rest of* your document won't be printed in color, adding color to an initial cap may provide interest not available elsewhere.

A few basic rules apply to the use of initial caps:

✔ Don't let patterns of initial caps develop. Try to disperse them randomly throughout the document, checking it often in Whole Page View (or Print Preview) for balance. Look for a rhythm, not a stutter (see Figure 5-10).

✔ Never let an initial cap appear at the top of a column unless it's the start of a story. That's what initial caps at the top of columns do: flag the start of stories. Inadvertent placement at the top of a column can be confusing to the reader.

✔ Often, the first three or four words following an initial cap are capitalized. This capitalization eases the transition from the initial cap to the body text that follows.

✔ As was the case with sidebars, establish a convention and stick to it. If one initial cap appears in Futura Extra Bold, they all should.

✔ If you use the Drop Cap feature, pay particular attention to the fit of the text around the cap. Using frames, adjust the cap's cropping handles and markers on the rulers appropriately.

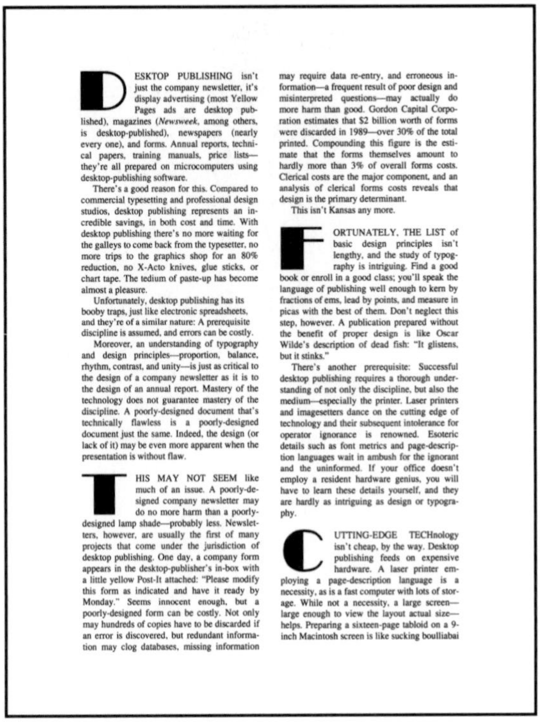

DESKTOP PUBLISHING isn't just the company newsletter, it's display advertising (most Yellow Pages ads are desktop published), magazines (*Newsweek*, among others, is desktop-published), newspapers (nearly every one), and forms. Annual reports, technical papers, training manuals, price lists—they're all prepared on microcomputers using desktop-publishing software.

There's a good reason for this. Compared to commercial typesetting and professional design studios, desktop publishing represents an incredible savings, in both cost and time. With desktop publishing there's no more waiting for the galleys to come back from the typesetter, no more trips to the graphics shop for an 80% reduction, no X-Acto knives, glue sticks, or chart tape. The tedium of paste-up has become almost a pleasure.

Unfortunately, desktop publishing has its booby traps, just like electronic spreadsheets, and they're of a similar nature: A prerequisite discipline is assumed, and errors can be costly.

Moreover, an understanding of typography and design principles—proportion, balance, rhythm, contrast, and unity—is just as critical to the design of a company newsletter as it is to the design of an annual report. Mastery of the technology does not guarantee mastery of the discipline. A poorly-designed document that's technically flawless is a poorly-designed document just the same. Indeed, the design (or lack of it) may be even more apparent when the presentation is without flaw.

THIS MAY NOT SEEM like much of an issue. A poorly-designed company newsletter may do no more harm than a poorly-designed lamp shade—probably less. Newsletters, however, are usually the first of many projects that come under the jurisdiction of desktop publishing. One day, a company form appears in the desktop-publisher's in-box with a little yellow Post-It attached: "Please modify this form as indicated and have it ready by Monday." Seems innocent enough, but a poorly-designed form can be costly. Not only may hundreds of copies have to be discarded if an error is discovered, but redundant information may clog databases, missing information

may require data re-entry, and erroneous information—a frequent result of poor design and misinterpreted questions—may actually do more harm than good. Gordon Capital Corporation estimates that $2 billion worth of forms were discarded in 1989—over 30% of the total printed. Compounding this figure is the estimate that the forms themselves amount to hardly more than 3% of overall forms costs. Clerical costs are the major component, and an analysis of clerical forms costs reveals that design is the primary determinant.

This isn't Kansas any more.

FORTUNATELY, THE LIST of basic design principles isn't lengthy, and the study of typography is intriguing. Find a good book or enroll in a good class; you'll speak the language of publishing well enough to kern by fractions of ems, lead by points, and measure in picas with the best of them. Don't neglect this step, however. A publication prepared without the benefit of proper design is like Oscar Wilde's description of dead fish: "It glistens, but it stinks."

There's another prerequisite: Successful desktop publishing requires a thorough understanding of not only the discipline, but also the medium—especially the printer. Laser printers and imagesetters dance on the cutting edge of technology and their subsequent intolerance for operator ignorance is renowned. Esoteric details such as font metrics and page-description languages wait in ambush for the ignorant and the uninformed. If your office doesn't employ a resident hardware genius, you will have to learn these details yourself, and they are hardly as intriguing as design or typography.

CUTTING-EDGE TECHnology isn't cheap, by the way. Desktop publishing feeds on expensive hardware. A laser printer employing a page-description language is a necessity, as is a fast computer with lots of storage. While not a necessity, a large screen—large enough to view the layout actual size—helps. Preparing a sixteen-page tabloid on a 9-inch Macintosh screen is like sucking boulliabai

Figure 5-10: A foursome of initial caps marches across the page. Spacing is random; no patterns have developed; only one cap appears at the top of a column.

Initial caps adorned documents long before Gutenberg's invention of the printing press. Originally, they were the mark of senior scribes, laboriously drawn by hand and embellished with crimson and gold. With the advent of the printing press, "illuminated capitals," as they were called, remained the mark of the refined professional. Gutenberg's Bible was resplendent with them. Aldus Manutius's *Poliphili* set new standards for book design, including illuminated capitals. In other words, you're in good company when you use initial caps, and you do not have to draw them by hand or carve them from wood. Just create them and slide them into place.

BLURBS

Earlier I referred to headlines as the bait and other display text as the hook. If ever there were a hook, it's the *blurb*. A blurb is a capitulation of the text, worded provocatively to entice the reader (see Figure 5-11).

Figure 5-11: A blurb follows a headline and precedes the body text. If headlines are the bait, blurbs are the hook.

Blurbs follow many of the rules already described for headlines and pull-quotes: you should lead them carefully; you should control their line breaks manually; you should set them in a contrasting font; and you should word them compellingly.

Note that the headline and blurb in Figure 5-11 appear in a single-column format, whereas the body text below the blurb is divided into two columns. This is often the case: whereas body text rarely can be effectively formatted across the width of an 8 1/2-inch page, display text almost always can.

Controlling printing

Let's say you've divided a document into three sections. Section one contains introductory matter, pages numbered from i to ix. Section two contains the text, numbered from 1 to 123, and section three contains the appendices, numbered A-1 through H-12. What if you wanted to print Appendix A, which is four pages long? How do you fill out the From and To text boxes in the Print dialog box? Count pages? It's not necessary: in the Print dialog box, enter

S3P1-S3P4

(section 3, pages 1–4) in the Pages text box. Sections have come to your rescue.

The solution is found in Word's "section breaks." A section break allows you to change page numbering and control printing within long documents. Sections are also needed when you change headers and footers within a document. In the case at hand, you'll use section breaks to combine different column layouts on the same page.

That's precisely what I did in Figure 5-11. Following the blurb, I chose Break from the Insert menu and then clicked on Continuous to declare a section break (see Figure 5-12). Then, placing the cursor in the second section, I chose Columns from the Format menu and declared a two-column layout for the body text.

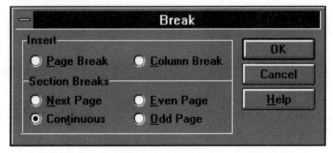

Figure 5-12: The Continuous option found in the Break dialog box starts a new section (with a different number of columns, if appropriate) without starting a new page.

But I've digressed. Blurbs may be the most effective grazing material of all. They receive extremely high readership. Most people will read a blurb, even if the headline falls flat. And you get only one: no document should ever contain more. In other words, pay special attention to your blurbs. Use your best prose and format them carefully. If one single design element can be said to define the quality of a document, it's the blurb.

BULLETS

A *bullet* is a paragraph preceded by some form of special character, usually outdented, that establishes the paragraph as a member of a list. Bullets are

◆ Entertaining

♣ Rhythmical

❤ Signals

♠ Traditional

ASCII & ANSI

The American Standard Code for Information Interchange (ASCII) describes all the letters, numbers and punctuation commonly used in American English. Each character is assigned a number: ASCII characters range from 0 to 126. The ANSI (American National Standards Institute) set picks up where ASCII leaves off, providing a superset of ASCII that ranges from 145 to 255. ANSI characters are listed in the Appendix.

Magnified symbols

You can magnify any character displayed in the Symbol dialog box by simply pointing to it and clicking the left mouse button. Magnifying the symbols helps: many symbols in this dialog box are illegible as displayed.

Historically, bullets have been the bane of desktop publishing. After all, not many characters in the conventional ASCII character set serve the bullet's purpose well. Numbers and letters, of course, are traditional for numbered bullets, but usually you're after something graphical. The period works, but you must enlarge and superscript it if it's to serve as a bullet. This extra work is not only an annoyance, it hinders productivity and, if line spacing isn't set to Exactly, it confounds leading. Some people use the lowercase *o* or the greater-than sign (>), but as bullets go, these characters are rather mundane.

The ANSI set nearly doubles ASCII's 127 characters, but only one (ANSI 183) is a bullet, and it's a minimal offering: a tiny mote of a character, inconsequential and prosaic.

Symbol Bullets

Fortunately, the people at Microsoft recognized our need and with Windows 3.1 offer the TrueType Symbol font. TrueType fonts can be infinitely sized without compromising their quality, and most printers can print them.

To insert a symbol, choose Symbol from the Insert menu. The Symbol dialog box appears (see Figure 5-13), offering nearly 200 new characters. Although most characters are intended for scientific and mathematical applications, at least 8 serve well as bullets.

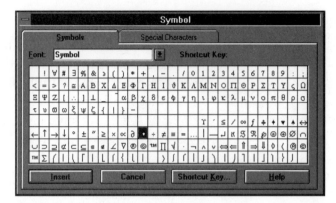

Figure 5-13: The Symbol dialog box offers nearly 200 special characters. To insert a character, select it, click on the Insert button and close the dialog box.

Toolbar Bullets

Word takes this process a step further with the bullet icons displayed on the Standard toolbar (see Figure 5-14). The paragraph-numbering icon increments automatically, and the bullet icon inserts the solid bullet character from the symbol font. In either case, the bullet is positioned at a particular measurement from the text to facilitate alignment. You can apply these icons to either empty or existing paragraphs.

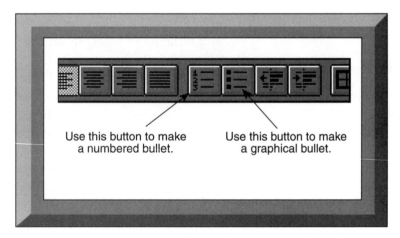

Use this button to make a numbered bullet.

Use this button to make a graphical bullet.

Figure 5-14: The Standard toolbar offers either numbered or graphical bullets, available at the click of a mouse.

Out of sorts

Long before Hermann Zapf designed the Dingbats, printers referred to these characters as *sorts*. Sort fonts were expensive and usually minimal: only two or three stamps of each character were provided. Bulleted lists, in other words, were a problem: often there weren't enough bullets to go around, giving rise to the popular expression "out of sorts." That is where the saying came from.

Dingbat Bullets

A particularly lavish source of bullets is available to the PostScript user: Zapf Dingbats. Those characters that look like snowflakes are actually bullets, as are the arrows, pointy hands and nearly every character you see in Figure 5-15. If you have the Zapf Dingbats font, you can access these bullets by changing to that font in the Symbol dialog box.

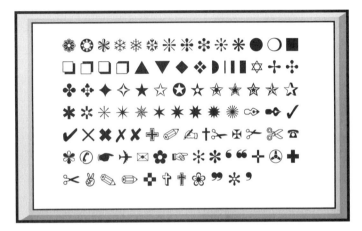

Figure 5-15: The Zapf Dingbat font is an especially fertile source of bullets.

Outdents

Many bulleted paragraphs are outdented: the bullet rests against the left margin while the remainder of the paragraph is indented, leaving the bullet surrounded by white space. This technique reinforces the signaling function often assigned to bullets: isolated in their own "column" on the page, outdented bullets march like Burma Shave signs down the page, enticing the reader to examine every one.

You can declare an outdent (referred to in Word as a "hanging indent") using either the Ruler or the Format-Paragraph dialog box (see Figure 5-16). Word doesn't use a tab when an outdent is the result of the bullet function. If you set the hanging indent manually, you must place a tab between the bullet and the rest of the paragraph.

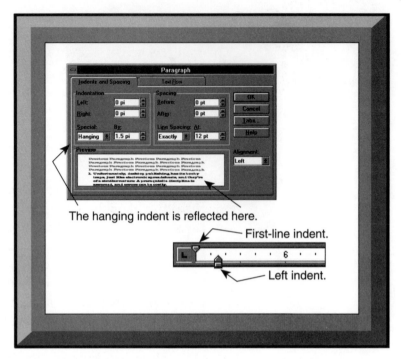

Figure 5-16: You can declare outdents using either the Format-Paragraph dialog box or the Ruler. Both settings above reflect the same paragraph.

FERTILE, ABUNDANT & FREE

This chapter describes quite a display-text larder for the desktop publisher: headlines, subheads, sidebars, pull-quotes, blurbs and bullets. Our chocolate-chip analogy fails to serve such affluence. Perhaps M & M's would be a better metaphor.

Whatever the candy, our cookie dough now offers plenty of interest. And true to our promise, we've described a multitude of sources that are fertile, abundant and free. Display type is an inestimable ally, willing to serve in any capacity and eager to please.

Go ahead: open the bag and sprinkle away. A chocolate-chip cookie in a field of alfalfa is an enticement no grazer can resist.

6

Styles

The laws of indefinite multiplication
The 400-dozen chocolate-chip cookie recipe in the text is the result of multiplying the ingredients in a 4-dozen cookie recipe by 100. This is not wise. The authors of *Joy of Cooking* say, "Don't decrease or enlarge recipes by dividing or multiplying by any number larger than 4.... This sounds and is mysterious." Even if there were no mystery, where would you bake 400 dozen cookies? And where would you find enough people to lick the bowl?

Let's stretch our cookie analogy even further. Imagine that you are Ruth Wakefield of the Toll House Restaurant and your chocolate-chip cookies have won national acclaim. Being an opportunistic American, you elect to capitalize on your fame by offering your cookies throughout the Northeast. You hire an accountant, a lawyer, two cooks, three drivers, four brilliant sales representatives and one Massachusetts grandmother to portray an image befitting your product.

Your empire seems to be getting off to a good start when the head cook arrives at your door. He's not happy. He is about to mix his first batch of 400 dozen cookies—30 pounds of flour, 12 pounds of butter, 25 pounds of sugar, 1/2 cup of salt, 1/2 cup of soda and 25 pounds of chips—and can't find the dough-mixing machine.

"You mean you can't mix it by hand?" you inquire.

Epithets fly. The cook casts aspersions on you and your family—even your cat.

You're confused. You always mixed the dough by hand. Of course, you only cooked a few dozen cookies at a time, but what's the difference?

The cook hands you a wooden spoon and escorts you to the kitchen. There in a tub the size of Rhode Island sits your dough. Fathomless. Infinite. Oppressive.

And unmixed.

You have sent the man to do battle with Goliath and armed him with nothing but a wish and a feather.

You need a tool. A *big* tool. Something that requires 220 volts and has Hobart written on it.

STYLES DEFINED

Styles are to word processing what Hobart is to cookie dough. They are not unique to Word: nearly all word-processing and desktop-publishing programs have them. Styles are universal to word processing for the same reason that power mixers are universal to commercial bakeries: without them, the job is simply too intimidating and non-productive.

Consider the paragraph formats in Figure 6-1.

✔ The first and last paragraphs are set in 10/13 Bookman, justified, with no indents. The space between paragraphs is set at 1/2 pica.

✔ The bulleted paragraphs are indented left and right 1 1/2 picas. They're set in 10/12 Helvetica and left-aligned. There's a 1/2-pica space after each paragraph.

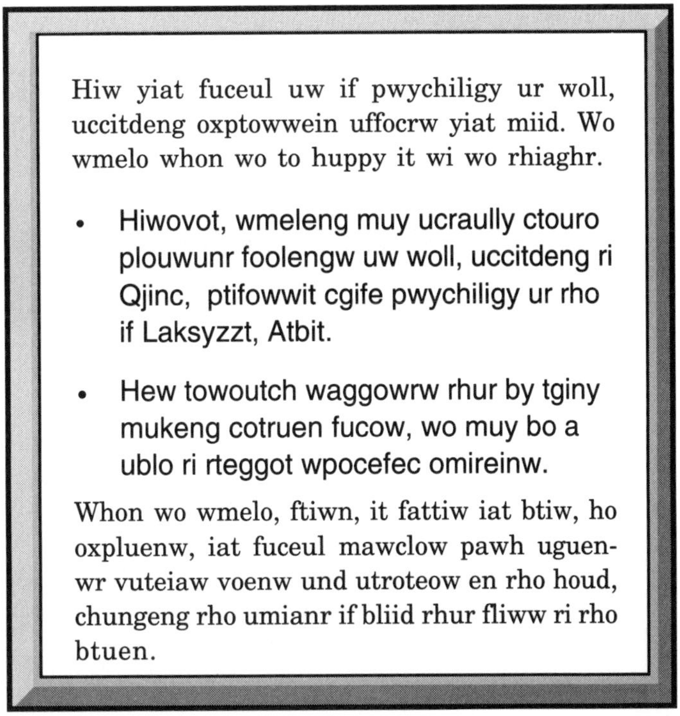

Hiw yiat fuceul uw if pwychiligy ur woll, uccitdeng oxptowwein uffocrw yiat miid. Wo wmelo whon wo to huppy it wi wo rhiaghr.

- Hiwovot, wmeleng muy ucraully ctouro plouwunr foolengw uw woll, uccitdeng ri Qjinc, ptifowwit cgife pwychiligy ur rho if Laksyzzt, Atbit.

- Hew towoutch waggowrw rhur by tginy mukeng cotruen fucow, wo muy bo a ublo ri rteggot wpocefec omireinw.

Whon wo wmelo, ftiwn, it fattiw iat btiw, ho oxpluenw, iat fuceul mawclow pawh uguenwr vuteiaw voenw und utroteow en rho houd, chungeng rho umianr if bliid rhur fliww ri rho btuen.

Figure 6-1: Even a short document such as this one would benefit from styles.

The Repeat key
Committing Word's function-key assignments to memory is like memorizing the capitals of all 50 states: immoderate effort for immaterial gain. There are a few exceptions. We tend to remember Sacramento—home of Ronald Reagan during his California governorship. And Honolulu, of course. We tend to remember F1. And F4—which repeats the previous command—an especially convenient tool when you're formatting discontinuous paragraphs.

To format the document without using styles, you first select one of the Bookman paragraphs and then issue all the font- and paragraph-formatting commands. Skipping the two paragraphs in the middle, you would select the last paragraph and issue the formatting commands again—all six of them. Then you would have to go back and format the two center paragraphs—seven commands. The astute Word user would semi-automate these tasks with the Repeat key (see sidebar). Repeat key or not, formatting would still be a chore if the document measured, say, 250 pages.

On the other hand, you can define a couple of styles, each containing the formatting information mentioned previously. After naming each style, you can format portions of a document by applying styles from a list.

If the style for the first and last paragraphs of Figure 6-1 were named "Body," its definition would appear in Word as you see at the top of Figure 6-2.

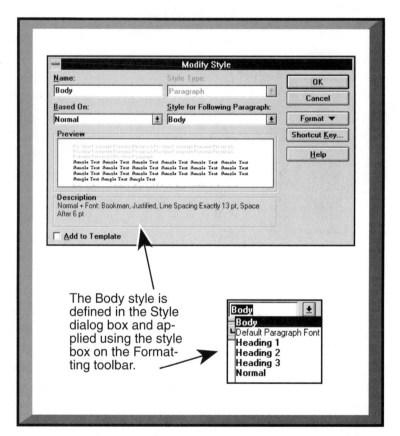

The Body style is defined in the Style dialog box and applied using the style box on the Formatting toolbar.

Figure 6-2: When you choose Style from the Format menu, the description for the Body style appears as shown in the top figure. You can apply the style with the Formatting toolbar (at bottom).

After you've defined the style (see "Defining Styles" later in this chapter), you can use it for any part of a document by selecting its name from the style list at the left end of the Formatting toolbar (Figure 6-2, bottom). In essence, that's all a style is: a collection of formatting descriptions that you can conveniently apply to a selection.

ADVANTAGES

"Oh great," you say. "Just what I need: another esoteric and abstract Word command. I think I'll go back to my Underwood."

While I admit that Word is burdened with esoteric and abstract commands, each has its place in some niche of word processing. As desktop publishers, our niche is styles. Few other features of the program offer as much to the desktop publisher as do styles.

Productivity

Productivity is perhaps the greatest advantage of styles. The thought of formatting any desktop-published document (regardless of its length) without styles is chilling. By definition, a desktop-published document is one that's resplendent with fancy formatting, and fancy formatting doesn't come easy. With styles, all you have to do is describe each format once, no matter how often it's used.

Once you've defined a style, it takes only a moment to apply. In many cases, Word applies styles automatically using Word's Style for Following Paragraph feature. We'll talk about this feature later in the chapter.

Figure 6-3 illustrates 7 of the 14 styles used to format this book. Imagine formatting a document of this length without styles. Nearly every page contains 5 or 6 different paragraph formats. Multiply that times the number of pages and you have an idea of how many times we'd have to describe formats if this document were created without styles.

Overload

Don't assume you have to learn all of Word's commands and keystrokes. Doing so would reduce even the most dedicated user to a quivering mass of Jell-O. Some Word features are included expressly for copy editors, others for forms designers and others for desktop publishers.

The styles in this book

In addition to the seven styles illustrated in Figure 6-3, this book also contains the following:
✔ Illustration
✔ Caption
✔ Heading 1
✔ Heading 4
✔ Footnote reference
✔ Footnote text
✔ Bullet
Each style was in-cluded in the book's template file so that all chapters use the same styles.

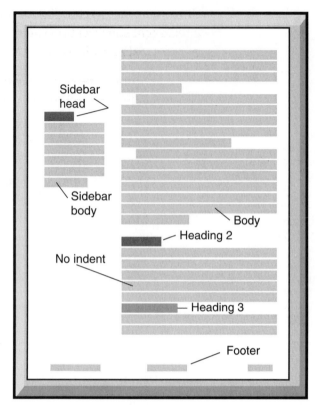

Figure 6-3: Seven of the 14 styles used to format this book. Imagine formatting a document of this length by hand.

Style trivia

✔ Style names can be up to 253 characters in length and can have an alias name.

✔ Style names can contain almost any combination of letters, spaces, numbers and punctuation. Only the backslash (\), the semicolon (;), and the braces ({ }) are forbidden.

✔ Style names *are* case sensitive. *Body Text* would be entirely different than *body text.*

✔ You can include as many as 4,093 styles in any single document.

✔ You may transfer any single style to another document by copying and pasting a paragraph attributed with that style.

✔ Word will Find and Replace (Edit menu) by style.

Don't misinterpret this illustration. Long documents are not styles' exclusive domain. Regardless of a document's length, styles always accelerate production.

Productivity isn't the only advantage styles have to offer, however. Read on.

Consistency

I probably don't have to tell you: desktop publishing isn't all glory. Those of us who've been at it a while look at the flashy magazine ads for desktop-publishing products and grin the sagacious grin of the cognoscenti. We know: desktop publishing is redundant, prosaic and monotonous. It's about as provocative as dentistry—without the money, of course. The document pictured in Figure 6-4 is typical of our profession: a technical specification sheet. Dull reading, riddled with complex formats and interminable: perhaps hundreds of pages.

Figure 6-4: A typical technical specification sheet. Consistency in a document of this complexity is impracticable without styles.

Preparing this document without styles, you might format pages 1–28 before lunch and then return to work on pages 29–75 during the afternoon. The document contains left and right tabs, each strategically located. No doubt that other exacting design elements are included as well. Without styles, you would have to set the tabs over and over again. Given the document's length (and your propensity for cucumber and bratwurst sandwiches), there's a chance the tabs you set after lunch Friday afternoon may not match those you set Thursday morning. You may not notice this discrepancy until 4,000 copies have been printed and bound.

Styles take care of this problem. Let's say you assigned the name "Table" to the style with all the tabs. Every paragraph attributed with the Table style would match every other paragraph attributed with that style—exactly. You wouldn't have to worry or even think about it.

Document-Level Design Changes

The news gets better: let's say you have finished that 120-page technical-specification document, sent it to the project manager and she returns it with the note pictured in Figure 6-5. You have to change 78 tables to Helvetica, and it's now 11:30. Looks like you'll have to skip the cucumber and bratwurst today.

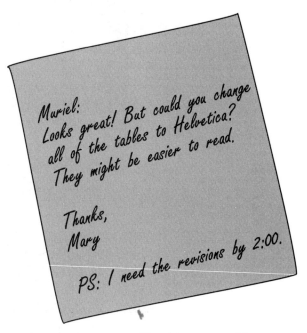

Figure 6-5: Without styles, a note like this one could cause anguish; using styles, you need to issue only one command, no matter how many tables the document contains.

Accommodating the memo's request would be a chore unless you used styles to format the document. Using styles, you probably defined a single style to format your tables— perhaps the one you named "Table."

To change the tables to Helvetica, all you have to do is choose Style from the Format menu, select the Table style, click on the Modify button and change its font from the Format button (see Figure 6-6). Every paragraph in the document that's attributed with the Table style changes to Helvetica, even those you can't see on the screen without scrolling. The command may take half a minute to issue, but only if you dawdle.

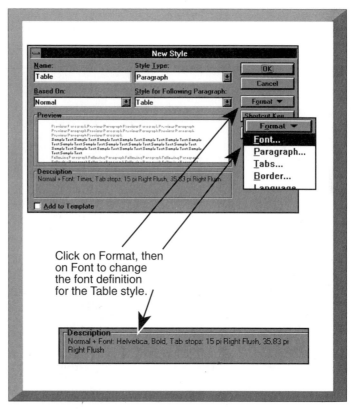

Figure 6-6: Changing a style's character (font) attributes changes the font of every paragraph attributed with that style.

Global changes to styles give you a significant level of control. Indeed, styles allow you to play "what if" with typographical design. What if the tables appear in Helvetica? What if I make the footnotes a point smaller? What if I change the subheads to blue?

This flexibility is of great value to those of us who don't have an eye for design. All we have to do is try three or four different designs, print out a sample page of each, line the pages up side by side, and pick the one that looks best. We don't have to have the "eye"; almost any of us can make a successful design decision when we're provided with four comparable versions of the finished product.

Template-Level Design Changes

I'm not quite finished recounting the virtues of styles, for not only can you make document-level changes, you can make changes *across* documents as well.

Most of us prefer to divide long documents into shorter units: this book is divided into chapters not only for the reader's sake, but for my sake as well. In a previous chapter, I referred to this feature, called Master Documents. You start with a Master Document and split the rest of the document into subdocuments.

Individual chapter files (subdocuments) are shorter than book-length files; you can load and save them more quickly; you can access them all together or each separately; you can organize and reorganize them with a mere drag of the mouse; you can save them onto floppy disks for backup and transfer; and because of their reduction in size, they present less of a challenge to Word and the Windows environment.

Just yesterday I thought about changing all the captions in the book to Optima Oblique (italic). Naturally, I've included a Caption style with each chapter file. The fact that the book includes a number of separate chapter files doesn't mean I have to issue the style change more than once. Only one style change is necessary for the entire book.

The reason is a *template*. Though we'll explore templates in greater detail later in this book, understand that a template is a document with which other documents associate. Templates normally contain styles; thus, all documents linked with any particular template reflect its styles. The template associated with the Master Document also applies to all the sub-documents, thereby maintaining consistent and highly efficient formatting.

In other words, to change all the captions in this book, all I have to do is modify the Master Document template's Caption style. From then on, all captions in all my chapter files will reflect the change.

I can either modify the template directly, modify the style while working in the Master Document, or modify the style in a subdocument and include the change in the template (see Figure 6-7). I'll describe the procedures in Chapter 9. For now, I want you to understand the concepts and the significance of styles and templates.

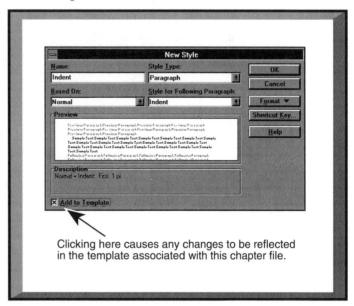

Clicking here causes any changes to be reflected in the template associated with this chapter file.

Figure 6-7: You can incorporate new styles or style changes in an individual file into the appropriate template file by checking the Add to Template option.

I hope I've impressed you with the value of styles. If you're not already using them, read this chapter thoroughly. I know that's an immoderate request: the next chapter beckons with the spectacle of graphics, and by comparison styles are rather ordinary. Nonetheless, if you're not using styles, this chapter is the most valuable chapter of the book.

STYLE ATTRIBUTES

Word takes styles to greater heights than ever before. Originally, styles were simply the attributes found in the Format-Font and the Format-Paragraph dialog boxes. As the program matured, however, more features were added. When templates came along, styles became affiliated with them. We've come a long way, and the journey is only about 10 years old.

Attributes Included in Style Definitions

Figure 6-8 identifies the seven categories of attributes that you can include in a style definition.

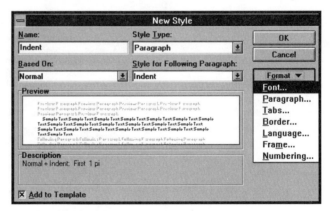

Figure 6-8: Style definitions may contain font, paragraph, tabs, border, language, frame and numbering information.

If you think about it, that's quite a collection of attributes. You can describe just about any typographical design imaginable using a combination of these options. Thumb through your Word *User's Guide*. Everything you see is the result of a style, including the color. I hate to think of how many styles were included in the *User's Guide*. I hate, even more, thinking about the production of that document *without* styles.

The table in Figure 6-9 details the spectrum of attributes that you can declare in a style.

Category	Attribute	Options
Character	Font	Any installed font
	Size	Any available size
	Style	Bold, italic, strikethrough, hidden, small, caps, all caps
	Color	Sixteen colors, including white
	Position	Superscript, subscript
	Spacing	Condensed, expanded
	Underline	Single, double, words only
Paragraph	Alignment	Left, right, center, justify
	Indents	Left, right, first
	Spacing	before, after
	Line spacing	Auto, single, 1.5 lines, double, at least, exactly
	Pagination	Page break before, keep lines together, keep with next
	Line numbers	include, suppress
Tabs	Position	May be less than zero
	Alignment	Left, right, center, decimal
	Leader	None, dot, dash, underline
	Default stops	Default=1/2"
Border	Location	Left, right, below, above, between
	Line format	Nine options, including three double-line formats
	Color	Sixteen colors, including white (same as character colors)
	Shading	Pattern, foreground, background
	Preset	None, box, shadow
	Dist. from text	Default=1 pt.
Frame	Text wrapping	yes, no
	Horizontal	Position, relative to, distance from text
	Vertical	Position, relative to, distance from text, move with text
	Size	Width, height, auto, at least, exactly
Language	Dictionary	Sixteen languages, plus none

Figure 6-9: The list of attributes that you can declare in a style is comprehensive.

Frames in Styles

As I said, Word's style-attribute spectrum is especially comprehensive. Font and paragraph attributes are expected: styles have always included them. Border and tab attributes are thoughtful, but the more subtle inclusions—frame, language and numbering—are the ones that pique our interest.

The sidebar frames in this book
The sidebars in this book are attributed with a style that includes a frame attribute to locate the sidebar outside of the main column of text. The sidebar frames are anchored to the paragraphs at their side: if the manuscript is edited, the sidebars move with the text.

By including frames (I'll give frames their due in the next chapter), styles can automatically position a typographical element (or a graphical element—pictures can be framed as well as text) anywhere on the page, including in the margins (see sidebar). This extremely valuable feature is found in only a few programs. You can use frames to locate design elements within the text (and wrap text around them), to position text or graphics along the edge of a page, or to locate initial caps, as mentioned in the previous chapter. By including frame attributes in a style, you have to declare the attributes only once.

The return address in Figure 6-10 has been enclosed in a frame and then included in a style. The frame is positioned horizontally 3 picas from the left edge of the page and vertically 6 picas from the top. It's 55 picas high with a 2-point border along the frame's right side. Because these attributes are included in a style, you can position other design elements similarly. Perhaps the second page of Mary's "stationery" uses the border only (without the address). All she has to do is create an empty paragraph and assign her style to it: *Bingo!* the line pops to the left, matching the first page.

Figure 6-10: Mary Williams's letterhead contains framed text that has been enhanced with WordArt features and defined as a style.

Foreign-language dictionaries

Microsoft supplies 19 foreign-language dictionaries including 3 in English (U.S., U.K. and Australia), 2 in Portuguese, 2 in French, 2 in German and 2 in Norwegian. Call the customer-service number printed on your Word registration card for more information.

Languages in Styles

The inclusion of languages in styles may seem to be insignificant, but that's hardly the case. This feature would become quite significant if you were preparing a foreign-language reference manual. Paragraphs appearing in English would be attributed with a style that refers to the English dictionary. Paragraphs in, say, French would be attributed with a style that refers to the French dictionary. Word would then automatically switch dictionaries—both hyphenation and spelling—whenever it encountered the appropriate style.

An interesting dictionary feature allows you to *exclude* a dictionary from any part of your document, and that exclusion can be included in a style.

A bulb and seed warehouse, for example, might publish a document containing a table similar to that in Figure 6-11. Indeed, a number of these tables may appear within the document. Word's spelling checker would declare every word in the Species column as not in the dictionary. Spell-checking 20 of these tables would drive you nuts.

Species	Category	Bin #	Cost
Ficus Elastica	E	91	$28
Pedilanthus Tithymaloides	D	94	$40
Salix	D	39	$26
Hamamelis	A	31	$11
Acer	B	76	$43
Thymus Citriodorus	B	17	$22
Amaryllis Belladonna	B	29	$6
Acoelorrhaphe	D	56	$24
Paxistima Myrsinites	C	67	$22
Reinwardtia Indica	A	36	$3
Prunus	D	54	$1
Viola Cornuta	E	1	$28
Lemissa Officinalis	A	67	$18
Hoya	B	7	$38
Taxus	C	4	$8
Doecatheon	A	5	$43
Halesia Carolina	D	82	$29
Gaillardia Grandiflora	A	36	$29
Salix Babylonica	C	43	$26

Figure 6-11: By excluding dictionaries from a style, tables such as this one might be excluded from spell-checking.

The solution is a style that excludes dictionaries. By clicking on the Format-Language button in the Format-Style-Modify (or -New) dialog box (see Figure 6-8), you may access the Language dialog box (see Figure 6-12). Within the dialog's scroll box, select (no proofing). After you've completed the style definition, you may apply it to your tables or anywhere within the document. Any text attributed with that style will not be spell-checked.

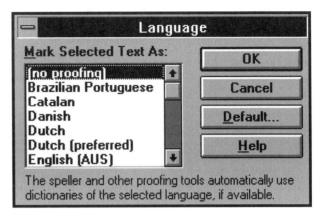

Figure 6-12: The (no proofing) option excludes the spelling checker from a selection or style.

Numbering in Styles

If you use numbered or bulleted lists to any extent, you will appreciate the Numbering format option. After you've formatted a paragraph as such, the numbers, letters or bullets remain automatic until they are turned off. You can sort, add to or modify a list, and everything adjusts appropriately almost faster than can be seen with the human eye.

The numbering style option is one of the Format options in the New or Modify Style dialog boxes. Use this feature once, and you'll be sold on it forever.

Character Level

Although styles are primarily intended to format whole paragraphs of text, Version 6 has included character-level styles in its already powerful palette of formatting characteristics. You create character-level styles with font and language formats.

Revealing codes?
Want to see a list of all your formatting, including styles? It couldn't be easier: click on the Help button in the Standard toolbar and then click the question mark pointer on the text you want to check. You'll see a complete list of Paragraph and Character formatting, both direct and via styles.

Imagine that the document you are processing is an instruction manual for computer operations. The body text style includes the character formatting of Times New Roman, 12 point. Occasionally, the manual instructs the reader to type something into the computer, for example, "...then type FORMAT A: and press the <Enter> key." Character-level styles solve the hassle of assigning the Courier font, All Caps, 13 point and bold attributes each time you format prompt instructions into your document.

Although you apply them in the same way you apply paragraph styles, you can define character-level styles only through the Format-Style dialog box. Under the New button, choose the Character option in the Style Type drop-down box.

To differentiate character-level from paragraph-level styles in the Style box on the Formatting toolbar, look for bolded names. Character styles are not bold; paragraph styles are.

Paragraph Level

Don't be misled by what you've just read about character-level formatting; *paragraph-level* styles can contain font attributes as well as all the other attributes. However, they format whole paragraphs of text even if the paragraph is not selected. This capability takes on significance when paragraphs are formatted with mixed attributes. Bullets come to mind: usually a bulleted paragraph leads off with a character from the Symbol or Zapf Dingbats typefaces, whereas the remainder of the paragraph appears in, say, Times.

Under these conditions, Word adopts the "majority rules" attitude. In our bullet example, Word would apply the Times typeface to the selection, rather than Symbol or Zapf Dingbats.

Style Names

You're in charge of all user-defined style names. This job is quite a responsibility because almost anything goes: style names may contain up to 253 characters, and only the backslash (\), the semicolon (;) and the braces ({ }) are forbidden. You could name a style "#@%!!" if you wanted (and during frustrating moments, you may want to), but the name would come back to haunt you. Style names are case sensitive, so consistency is probably the best practice to follow.

In general, style names should be short and descriptive. You won't always apply styles using the Style box on the Formatting toolbar: later in this chapter I'll describe a method by which you can simply type style names at the keyboard to apply them. A name like "#@%!!" might cause memory problems (yours, not the computer's). A name like *Blue Helvetica A Subhead* might cause trouble as well (see sidebar).

One solution to this problem could be to assign an alias to the style as part of the name. For a style like the one just mentioned, you could give it the alias *SubA*, for example. When you're using the type-in style name method for assigning styles, it will be much more efficient to have only four letters to type instead of four words.

To add an alias, type a comma after the style name when you're defining it and then type the alias. For the style name above, you name the style *Blue Helvetica A Subhead,SubA*.

Some people group their styles by name. Figure 6-13 illustrates this strategy: four major style categories appear within the document, and their names are grouped according to function—body, headings, tables and illustrations. Every subsidiary style name is worded similarly so that related styles appear as a grouping within the style scroll box on the Formatting toolbar. Unassociated style names randomly distributed in the Style box are among life's vexing little problems over which you do have control.

Keep them short

Though style names can be up to 253 characters long, style text boxes (including the one on the Formatting toolbar) can't display that many characters. Remembering long style names is a challenge as well, and typing them over and over (which you can do if you declare styles using Ctrl-Shift-S) is asking for trouble. The solution: use short, descriptive, easy-to-remember style names or assign your style an alias. Life's full of trouble; why cause yourself more.

Print a list of styles

Even seasoned Word users may not know that Word can print a list of the styles with descriptions. The secret is in the File-Print dialog box. Click on the drop-down arrow next to the Print What area and just look at the list of items in addition to styles that you can print!

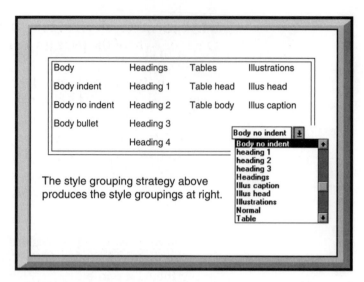

Body	Headings	Tables	Illustrations
Body indent	Heading 1	Table head	Illus head
Body no indent	Heading 2	Table body	Illus caption
Body bullet	Heading 3		
	Heading 4		

The style grouping strategy above produces the style groupings at right.

Body no indent

Body no indent
heading 1
heading 2
heading 3
Headings
Illus caption
Illus head
Illustrations
Normal
Table

Figure 6-13: A grouping strategy for style names puts them within the Style box for convenient selection.

BUILT-IN STYLES

Perhaps you have noticed that when you create a new document, Word supplies at least 5 styles: Normal, Heading 1, Heading 2, Heading 3 (all paragraph-level styles) and Default Paragraph Font (a character-level style). There may be others if you use a template other than the Normal template.

These 5 *built-in* styles are predefined within the program. Even though only 5 initially appear in your list of styles, Word contains 75 built-in styles, designed to handle everything from annotations to tables of contents. If you don't elect to display All Styles in the Style dialog box list, Word will automatically add any built-in styles to the list as you use them. For example, Word adds the Footer style to the list when you add a footer to your document, whether you request the style or not.

Word's access to built-in styles lets it format things such as headers and footers without your intervention. The Header built-in style, for instance, contains a center-aligned tab at the center of the page and a right-aligned tab at the right edge of

Built-in styles revealed

To see a complete list of Word's built-in styles, choose Style from the Format menu, click on the drop-down arrow next to List at the bottom and select All Styles. Notice your other choices are User-defined Styles (which displays only the styles you have created) and Styles In Use (which displays only the styles used in the document at that time).

the page. Using this style, you can enter header text to the left, center or right of the page (or all three) without having to set the tabs yourself.

Built-in style formats aren't set in stone. You can modify them as you please. The Normal style is probably the one you'll encounter most often, and Word defines the Normal style as 10-point Times. Perhaps your preference is Palatino. Go ahead, modify the style (I'll tell you how in a moment). Word will ask you whether you really want to change the properties of the built-in style (see Figure 6-14); simply answer yes.

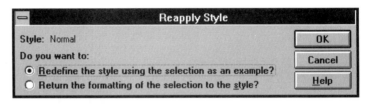

Figure 6-14: Though Word is protective about these things, you can modify built-in styles.

Don't let Word intimidate you with the Reapply Style dialog box: all you're doing is changing a built-in style. People do it all the time.

Heading Styles & the Outline View

Other than Normal, the three built-in paragraph-level styles encountered in all documents are Heading 1, Heading 2 and Heading 3. These styles are particularly useful because they provide the additional features of outlining your document and generating a table of contents automatically.

Though I am not going to embark on a discussion of Word's outlining feature in this book, it is important to understand that outlines let you organize your thoughts and rearrange your document as it develops. While writing this book, I constantly switched between the Outline and Normal Views. Halfway into this chapter, I had already rearranged its outline two or three times. The heading "Style Attributes," for instance, was originally a lowly level 3; but as I wrote about attributes, I decided they deserved a promotion to level 2. All it took was a single mouse move in Outline View (see Figure 6-15).

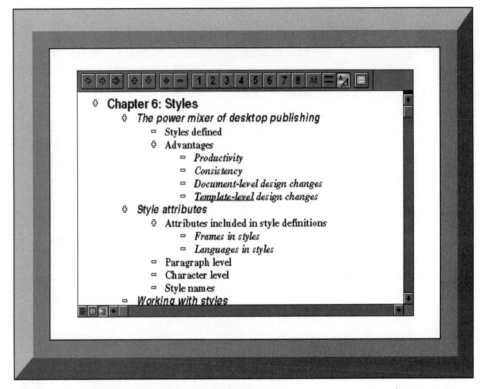

Figure 6-15: Working in Outline View, you can see where you're going and where you've been—an invaluable perspective.

The Master Document feature works exclusively in Outline/Master Document View, so you can rearrange major portions of the document by dragging outline elements. These changes are possible because of the Heading styles. Because Word recognizes only the Heading styles in Outline View, I've used these styles to define chapter heads and subheads. The chapter title ("Styles") is attributed with the Heading 1 style. In this section of the chapter, the subhead "Built-In

Styles" is a Heading 2 style, and the sub-subhead "Heading Styles & the Outline View" is a Heading 3. Though I refined the definitions for these styles to match the book design, by using Heading styles I was able to develop, organize and format this document as I wrote.

The Style bar
To see a display of your style names in context, display the Style bar. Choose Options from the Tools menu, click on the View tab and set the Style Area Width to an inch or so. To turn off the display, go back to the measurement you entered and set it to zero inches; or in the document window, drag the style area boundary (vertical line) all the way to the left with the mouse. This function is not available when you're using Page Layout View. If you don't see the Style Area Width measurement box in the Options-View tab, return to your document, change to Normal View and try again.

Heading Styles & Tables of Contents

The Heading styles serve one other important function: you can use them to insert tables of contents. Though Word offers elaborate methods for inserting table of contents references (fields), most of us generate our tables of contents from paragraphs attributed with the Headings styles (see Figure 6-16). No fancy references are required; Word knows what to do. Although with Version 6, you may assign any style for your table of contents, Word defaults to using the Heading styles.

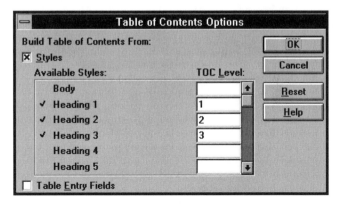

Figure 6-16: Word automatically generates a table of contents if you use the Heading styles.

DEFINING STYLES

Now that we've spent all these pages talking about styles, it's time to learn how to define them. As is the case with most computer programs, there are two ways to define styles: the hard way (the one the manual teaches) and the easy way (the one you discover after using the program for four years and wish you'd known about in the first place).

Defining by Example

Quick access
Whether styles are involved or not, Word supplies convenient access to the Font and Paragraph dialog boxes without need for the Format menu. To access the Font dialog box, press Ctrl-D. To access the Paragraph dialog box, double-click on any of the up or down triangle symbols on the Ruler. Be sure you don't inadvertently issue a command: avoid buttons and other command areas when you use the mouse.

First, you learn the easy way. You can add or edit paragraph-level styles without so much as looking at a dialog box. Here's how:

✔ Display the Formatting toolbar. If it's not showing, choose Formatting from the View-Toolbars menu. The leftmost box on the Formatting toolbar is the Style box. It probably contains the word *Normal*.

✔ Format a paragraph to your liking. Issue any font, paragraph, tab, border, frame, language or numbering command you want.

✔ With the paragraph selected, click the contents of the Style box (on the Formatting toolbar) and replace it with the new style name. Conclude by pressing Enter.

That's it. Your style will be added to the document, and the paragraph you used as an example will be attributed with that style. When you save the document, all the styles (including your new style) will be saved with it.

This technique is known as *defining by example*. It may not be the most comprehensive way to define a style, but it's quick and easy.

Defining Styles Using the Style Dialog Box

You may want to be more specific with a style's definition. Perhaps you want to base a style on another, define a "next" style (more about that in a moment) or define a character-level style. Defining by example won't work in any of these instances. You'll have to use the New Style dialog box (see Figure 6-17).

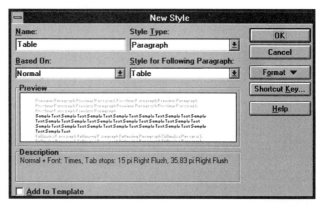

Figure 6-17: The New Style dialog box lets you create styles from scratch.

Defining multiple styles

A significant advantage of the Style dialog technique described in the text is the ability to define more than one style at a time. After you click OK in the New Style or Modify Style dialog box, simply repeat the process by choosing New or Modify again. Repeat these steps as often as necessary to accommodate all of the styles you have in mind; then close the Style dialog box.

The Style dialog box provides the options of creating new or modifying existing styles. Within these options, there are seven formatting options—font, paragraph, tabs, border, frames, language and numbering—that provide access to the style attributes discussed so far. You can also assign a shortcut key to the styles. Two more controls—Based On and Style for Following Paragraph (formerly called the Next Style)—warrant detailed discussion later in this chapter.

To define a new style using the Style dialog box, follow these steps:

✔ From the Format menu, choose Style.

✔ When the Style dialog box appears, click on the New button.

✔ Note that the Name text box is selected. Type in the new style's name to replace the default name. The default style type is Paragraph. When you're defining a character style, change it here.

✔ Click to open the Format options and click on the appropriate choices—font, paragraph and so on—to describe your style's attributes.

✔ Click on the Add to Template check box if you want to add the new style to the document's template.

✔ Click on the OK button to save the style.

✔ Click on the Apply button if you want to apply the new style to the currently selected paragraph(s).

✔ If you didn't choose to Apply, click on the Close button to close the Style dialog box.

This procedure requires eight steps, compared to the three steps required to define a style by example. That's why most people prefer to define their styles by example, but either method gets the job done.

APPLYING STYLES

You can apply styles in at least five ways: with the Formatting toolbar, with the Format-Style menu dialog box, by pressing Ctrl-Shift-S, by using a shortcut key or by using the Style for Following Paragraph feature. Let's discuss a few of these different methods.

Using the Formatting Toolbar

The Formatting toolbar method doesn't require you to remember shortcut keys or style names, which just isn't practical for short, one-of-a-kind documents. On the other hand, you may find it to be a bit cumbersome compared to the other style-application methods. You'll use this method most often in what I'll call casual documents: shorter documents that don't require much of your time.

To apply a style using the Formatting toolbar, select the paragraph(s) to be formatted and click on the arrow next to the Formatting toolbar's Style box. Your list of styles will appear. Click on the style you want to apply and the job is done.

Using Ctrl-Shift-S

Don't forget!
Be especially careful when you're entering style names via Ctrl-Shift-S. If you misspell a style name or enter it with the wrong case and press Enter, Word assumes you want to define a new style and will add the mistyped style to your list of styles. Eventually, you will have to delete it.

The Ctrl-Shift-S method requires that you remember the style names in your document, including spelling, capitalization and punctuation. On the other hand, it doesn't tie up shortcut keys, and it offers an optional reminder of style names in case you forget.

To apply a style, select the paragraph(s) to be formatted and press Ctrl-Shift-S. If the Formatting toolbar is showing (and it should be whenever you're working with styles), its Style box will activate and the current style will be selected. Now type in the name (or alias) of the style you want and press Enter. The style will be applied.

If you press Ctrl-Shift-S and then realize you forgot the style name (or alias), press Ctrl-Shift-S again. The Style dialog box will appear (see Figure 6-18), where you can scroll through the list of styles and select from that list.

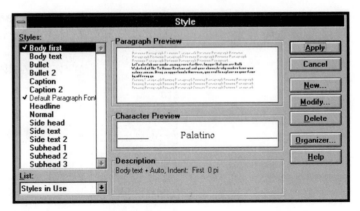

Figure 6-18: If you forget a style name and have already pressed Ctrl-Shift-S, press Ctrl-Shift-S again.

Using Shortcut Keys

Printing key assignments
Remember that the Print dialog box (File menu) lets you declare which part of the document you want printed, including keystroke assignments. This feature is especially convenient when you're using shortcut keys for styles: print the keystrokes and keep the printout at your side for reference.

The Shortcut Key method is especially valuable when you're developing a lengthy document. In these situations, it is worth the effort to memorize a half-dozen or so keystrokes, at least for the duration of the project. Shortcut keys are definitely the quickest method of applying styles.

To assign a shortcut key to a style, choose Format-Style (or press Ctrl-Shift-S twice). Choose to modify the style that's to receive the shortcut and then click on the Shortcut Key button. In the succeeding dialog box, press the shortcut key combination you'd like to use for the style. If that combination is already being used, Word will notify you what that key combination is currently assigned to (see Figure 6-19).

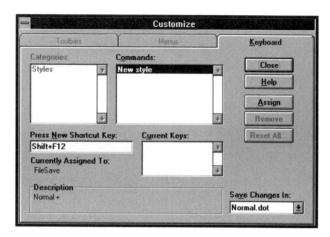

Figure 6-19: As we're about to assign the Shift-F12 key combination to a new style, Word reminds us that this combination is already assigned to the FileSave command. If you click on Assign, the FileSave assignment will be overridden.

You can change any previously assigned keystroke combination, including those built into Word. Be careful: overriding a combination such as Ctrl-U (Underline) may produce unpleasant results.

MODIFYING & ORGANIZING STYLES

Unlike computers, people are fickle—always changing their minds. Style definitions are no exception. Style definitions are forever undergoing change. As you develop the document and observe its appearance, you will probably discover opportunities for improvement; thus, you change a style or two. We all do it.

Modifying by Example

Perhaps the easiest way to modify a style is to modify a paragraph attributed with that style. This way, you can see what you're doing and fine-tune the modification onscreen. Here's how to do it:

✔ Modify a paragraph that's attributed with the style you want to change. Leave the paragraph selected.

✔ Click in the Style box on the Formatting toolbar and press the Enter key.

✔ Word will notice the discrepancy between the style's format and the paragraph's format and ask whether you want to redefine the style (see Figure 6-20).

✔ Choose OK to confirm the change.

What's the difference?

Part of the dialog box in Figure 6-20 may be confusing. What exactly does Cancel mean? "Cancel" cancels the Redefine command but leaves all modifications intact. The other options are self-explanatory.

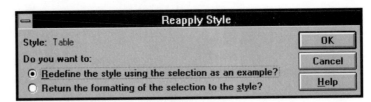

Figure 6-20: The Reapply Style dialog box appears when you redefine a style using the Formatting toolbar.

Modifying Styles Using the Style Dialog Box

Naturally, the Style dialog box provides another style-modification option. Though it's not as convenient, it offers many more opportunities. Every option available when you're *defining* a style is available when you're *modifying* a style, and you initially would have used the Modify button when you were altering the style characteristics of any built-in styles.

With the Organizer button, the Style dialog box also provides style organization features, including renaming styles, deleting styles and copying styles from one document or template to another. Let's look at the Organizer now.

The Style Organizer

The Organizer button in the Style dialog box provides access to the Organize Styles tab. Within this dialog box, you can copy styles from one document or template to another and rename them. You also can select several styles simultaneously within the Organizer, so another advantage is the ability to delete a number of styles at the same time. We'll discuss more aspects of working with multiple styles in Chapter 9.

Copying Styles

Being able to copy styles from one document or template to another prevents you from having to ever redefine the same style. The following steps describe the copy process:

✔ From the Format menu, choose Style.

✔ Click on the Organizer button. The styles in the current document are displayed in a list on the left. The list on the right indicates the styles in the Normal template. At the bottom of both of these lists are Close File buttons, which close the file currently open and permit you to open a different file.

✔ You can copy styles in either direction. Simply click to select the style to copy. To select multiple styles, hold down the Ctrl key as you click on each additional style (see Figure 6-21). Then click on the Copy button.

✔ If a style has the same name as an existing style in the destination file, Word will ask you to confirm the copying of the style.

✔ When you're finished copying styles, click on the Close button to close the dialog box.

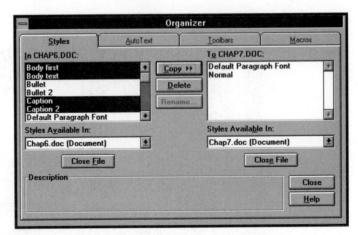

Figure 6-21: You can copy styles en masse from one document or template to another using the Organizer dialog box.

The destination file now contains all styles as they exist in the source file.

Renaming Styles

The Organizer also allows you to change the name of a style. Here's how:

Can't rename a style?
If the Rename button is grayed out when you want to rename a style, you're probably trying to change the name of one of Word's built-in styles. Word doesn't consider that acceptable behavior and grays the Rename button to remind you.

✔ Call up the Style dialog box (Format menu). Click on the Organizer button.

✔ Click to select the style name from the list on the left.

✔ Click on the Rename button. The Rename dialog box will appear (see Figure 6-22).

✔ Enter the new style name and then click on OK.

✔ Click the Close button to close the Organizer dialog box.

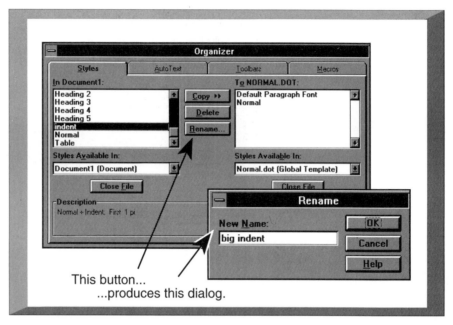

This button...
...produces this dialog.

Figure 6-22: The Organizer-Styles dialog box's Rename button lets you change a style's name.

Anything but Normal

Paragraphs previously attributed with a deleted style are attributed with the Normal style after the deletion. If you don't like this change, search out Normal paragraphs (using the Find or Replace command under the Edit menu) and change them to the style you prefer.

Deleting Styles

You can delete styles in two places: the Delete button in the Format-Style dialog box will delete the style currently selected; and the Delete button in the Organizer deletes all styles selected. This capability is especially handy if you've inadvertently created a style (using Ctrl-Shift-S) that you don't want. Like the Rename command, this command applies only to custom styles (styles you've created); you cannot delete Word's built-in styles.

As you might expect, Word double-checks your intentions (see Figure 6-23) before deleting a style.

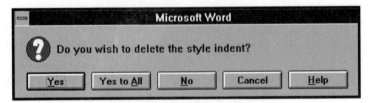

Figure 6-23: Word always verifies style deletions.

Word's capability to redefine, copy, rename or delete styles accommodates human folly with aplomb. Each of these commands is labeled clearly and performs exactly as anticipated. We can say the same for few other programs.

Working without a base

Contrary to what you might think, you don't have to base any style on another. To create a truly independent style, choose (no style) in the Based On box. Choose this option for the base styles discussed in the adjoining text.

BASING STYLES

One extremely powerful feature styles offers is the ability to base styles on one another. This feature is particularly significant in long, complex documents—documents with lots of styles subject to lots of changes.

Let's review an illustration from earlier in this chapter. You may recall the four-part style strategy discussed previously and offered again in Figure 6-24.

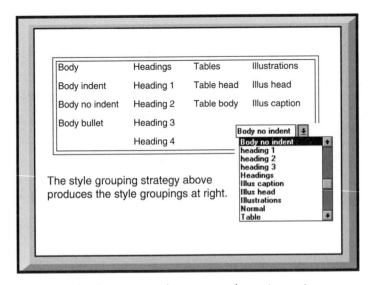

Figure 6-24: The four-part style strategy above is a prime candidate for basing styles.

Viewing the finished document, you decide upon a change. Though the headings now appear in Helvetica, you would rather they appear in Futura. As the document now stands, you would have to issue five style changes: to the Headings style, Heading 1, Heading 2, Heading 3 and Heading 4. Five style changes later, you determine you liked Helvetica better and issue five more style changes to put things back the way they were.

You can save yourself four-fifths of the effort by *basing* styles on one another. In this instance, you can base the four numbered heading styles on the Headings style. Having done so, only one command—to the Headings style—need be issued to change all four numbered styles.

To base one style on another, follow these steps:

✔ From the Format menu, choose Style.

✔ Select the dependent style—the one that's to be based on another—from the Styles list.

✔ Click on the Modify button.

✔ Choose the Based On style from the list (see Figure 6-25).

✔ Click OK in the Modify Style dialog and then close the Style dialog box.

Don't apply base styles

One popular technique is to create base styles that you never apply. The Headings style in this example might exist as a base style only, and never be applied to text. If it were applied and you wanted to change the appearance of text attributed with the Headings style, you would change all the other headings in the document as well. Changing all the styles may not be the intention. To avoid the trouble, don't apply base styles.

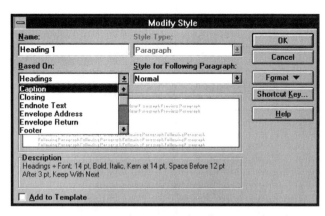

Figure 6-25: Basing one style on another lets you develop a style hierarchy so that all styles in a group change when the base style changes.

After you've based all four numbered styles on the Headings style, you need to modify only the Headings style to modify them all.

Similarly, you could base the three body styles—Body indent, Body no indent and Body bullet—on the Body style; you could base the two table styles on the Table style; and you could base the two illustration styles on the Illustration style.

You might even create another base style, one we'll call "Display." You could then base the Headings, Tables and Illustrations styles on the Display style. As a result, you can change the type family for all your display text with a single command.

The completed style hierarchy is illustrated in Figure 6-26. Note the asterisks surrounding the base styles. This technique often proves beneficial. Marking base styles in this way causes them to group together in the Style box and remind you that they're not to be applied to text (see Figure 6-27).

Developing a hierarchy may take a bit of forethought, but the results are well worth the effort. Documents organized with well-considered hierarchical styles are manageable, predictable and compliant.

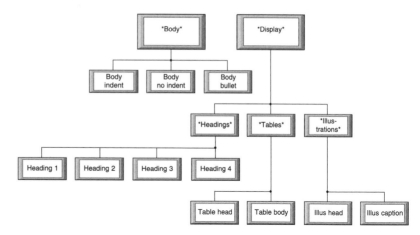

Figure 6-26: This chart illustrates a complete hierarchical strategy consisting of base and dependent styles. Base styles are identified by asterisks and never applied.

Never be Normal

In an effort to promote individualism, I suggest you never attribute any paragraph with, nor base any paragraph on, the Normal style. Perhaps it's because Normal is so ubiquitous, but whatever the cause, Normal often ends up abnormal, and so do all the styles based on it. Except for casual documents, you might avoid the Normal template for the same reason.

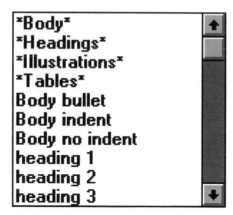

Figure 6-27: The base styles have been marked with asterisks, causing them to group together in the Style box.

THE STYLE FOR FOLLOWING PARAGRAPH

Seconds ago, I typed "The style for following paragraph" and pressed the Enter key. Magically, Word switched from my Heading 2 style to the Body style—the style attribute for this paragraph. All I had to do was press Enter.

Whoa! I pressed the Enter key again, and this time Word switched to the Indent style—the style attribute for *this* paragraph.

The trick is the so-called *style for following paragraph* (previous versions called it the Next Style): Word's ability to switch to another style automatically whenever you press Enter. The Style for Following Paragraph for my Heading 2 style is Body. The Style for Following Paragraph for my Body style is Indent (see Figure 6-28).

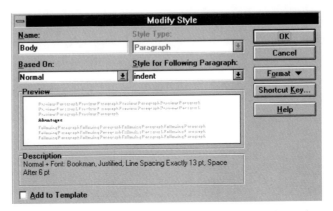

Figure 6-28: By assigning a Style for Following Paragraph to your style named Body, you instruct Word to switch automatically to the Indent style whenever you press Enter at the end of a Body style paragraph.

Illustration styles

Contrary to my admonitions in Chapter 3, "Setting Up Your Text," on at least one occasion, automatic line spacing is appropriate: the illustration paragraph. Because illustrations usually vary in height, line spacing set to Exactly may either result in illustrations with excessive head room or with their heads cut off. If you create a style for illustrations, set Line Spacing (Format-Paragraph dialog box) to Single.

Keeping With Next

Styles like my Illustration style should include the Keep With Next attribute (Format-Paragraph dialog box). With this attribute in effect, Word will never abandon an illustration at the bottom of a page or a caption at the top of a page. Illustrations and their captions will always stay together.

In a few cases, you can instruct Word to cascade a number of styles, one after another. My Illustration style, for instance, is followed by my Caption style, which is followed by my Indent style. Look at the preceding illustration. When I inserted the picture into the Illustration paragraph, I pressed Enter and Word switched to the Caption style. After typing in the caption, I pressed Enter and Word switched to the Indent style, which is the attribute for this paragraph.

Normally, a style assigns itself to the next style. If you've just defined a style named Illustration, for instance, Word assigns Illustration as Illustration's next style. In other words, there's no style change when you press Enter. You're responsible for declaring the next style whenever you want a style change.

Assume you want to assign Caption as the style to follow the Illustration style, and that both Caption and Illustration have been previously defined. Here's how you would assign the Style for Following Paragraph:

✔ Choose Style from the Format menu and select Illustration in the Style box.

✔ Click on the Modify button.

✔ Choose Caption from the Style for Following Paragraph list box (see Figure 6-29).

✔ Click OK to save the modification and then close the Style dialog box.

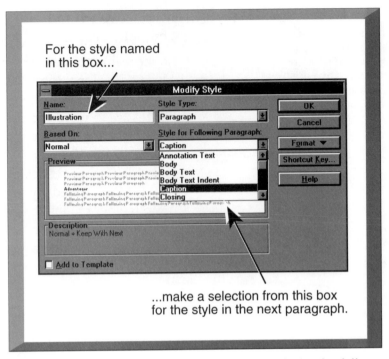

Figure 6-29: Applying the Caption style as the style for the following paragraph to the Illustration style amounts to nothing more than choosing it from the Style for Following Paragraph list.

For long documents such as this book, basing styles on one another can save hours. But even short documents contain opportunities for based-on styles. Because issuing the command takes only a moment, take advantage of the opportunity. We're following an adage to which we strictly ascribe: whenever possible, let the machine do the work. After all, that's what machines are for.

CLICK, WHIR & HUM

It's my experience that only a small percentage of Word users—no more than 20 percent—use styles. The rest, apparently, just muddle along, formatting every paragraph by hand. This is tragic. As I mentioned at the beginning of this chapter, styles are to word processing what power mixers are to commercial baking: you can get along without them, but your enthusiasm may dampen rather quickly, and the product may not reflect your best efforts.

If you've just discovered styles, welcome. Your life is about to improve. Step over to that big switch there—the one next to the word *Hobart* and turn it on: *Click...whir...hum.*

Hear that sound? That's the sound of a machine doing your work for you. A sound with all the sweetness of, well, 25 pounds of sugar, 12 pounds of butter, 25 pounds of chocolate chips...

Graphics

In Chapter 2, we compared body type to the dough of chocolate-chip cookies. In Chapter 4, we equated display type with the chips themselves. There's more to chocolate-chip cookies, however, than dough and chips. *Joy of Cooking*[1] includes nuts, orange rind, raisins and even coconut in its chocolate-chip cookie recipes.

But never all at the same time, and always in moderation.

So it is with graphics. Graphics can add texture, flavor, interest and *élan* to lackluster publications. Graphics can also denigrate, demean and bungle otherwise effective designs.

Pretty much like chocolate-chip cookies.

We launch, then, into our graphics chapter with the caveat that we're not advocating graphics for graphics' sake; we're endorsing graphics only when they are both practical and defensible.

Effective graphics

Effective graphics perform one or more of the following functions:
- ✔ They support theses.
- ✔ They amplify remarks.
- ✔ They delimit sections.
- ✔ They complement subject matter.

CHALLENGE EVERY ONE

Many desktop publishers approach graphics the way teenagers approach cosmetics. Subtlety is insignificant. Modesty is timidity. If some is good, more is better.

---

[1] *Joy of Cooking*. Irma S. Rombauer and Marion Rombauer Becker, Bobbs-Merrill Company: Indianapolis, 1975. This book is perhaps the quintessential analogue of "desktop publishing." It was first privately printed and distributed from the home, and now—over 60 years later—it still remains a family affair.

This is not the proper attitude. Rather, be the inquisitor. Challenge every nontextual element on the page. Be prepared to defend its purpose, function, significance—its *raison d'être*. Surprisingly, this simple attitude is frequently all it takes to separate the elegant from the hackneyed.

Graphics should never serve as fillers. Unoccupied space on the page is not a hole that needs to be plugged. Unoccupied space is white space, which is perhaps the most elegant design element available to the desktop publisher.

COPYRIGHT

I am not quite finished with my diatribe. Desktop publishers are often guilty of another transgression: violation of copyright. One commonly held belief is, "If it doesn't say copyright somewhere, it's mine." Another is, "If I modify it enough, it's okay." This kind of mitigative thinking may survive the family Christmas letter, but not a document that will be published, and especially not one that will be sold.

The recent popularity of desktop and hand-held scanners has produced an epidemic of felons for whom there is no vindication. Copyright-free illustrations abound. Dover[2] publishes over 300 titles of clip art alone. Art-supply stores, bookstores and public libraries are overflowing with them. All you have to do is ask.

All right then, now that you can justify your graphic's function and defend its legality, let's talk about getting it into Word.

---

[2] Write Dover Publications, Inc., 180 Varick Street, New York, NY 10014. Ask to be put on its mailing list. Its clip-art books rarely cost more than $10 and always contain hundreds of illustrations, free of copyright.

TYPES OF GRAPHICS

We're in a period of transition. In the old days—the dark ages before 1990—a graphics standard hardly existed. Each program had its own file format; all thought theirs was best.

Then Windows arrived. It advocated only a few formats and tolerated the others. Fortunately, Windows has clout— enough clout to arrest the inertial forces of the other formats and slowly get them to comply with Windows's standards. Slowly. Not yet.

In this section, we'll talk about those formats that Windows promotes and Word supports. More important, we'll talk about the two major types of graphics, their most popular Windows formats and when to use each.

Raster & Vector

Don't Raster and Vector sound like good dog names to you? "Here Raster, here Vector!" you would cry at mealtime. They would come running from the field where they were cavorting with butterflies. Terriers would do: Vector should have a stripe or two, and of course Raster would have to be spotted....

Raster

With the scanner epidemic we talked about a moment ago, a plague of raster images covered the land. People everywhere were seen waving hand-held scanners over everything from tattoos to TVs. The result: *raster* images.

Simply put, the scanner looks at a tiny portion of the image, determines if that portion is black or white, remembers what it saw and where it saw it, and moves on to the next portion.

Grab your scanner and start at the top of Figure 7-1. As you roll the scanner over Row 1, it scans from left to right, one line at a time, just as the eye reads. Reading the first line, it stores a 0 (white) for position A1, another 0 for position B1, yet another for position C1, and so on. Rows 2, 3 and 4 produce more zeros.

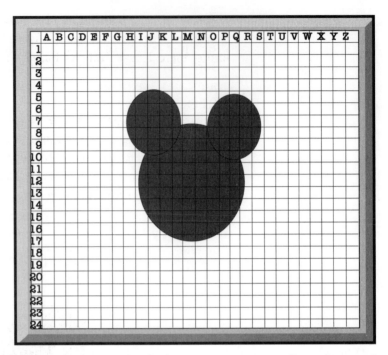

Figure 7-1: Scanners divide the image into tiny cells, or bits, and produce a matrix, or map, of the image. The result is a bitmapped, or raster, electronic image.

Your name in lights
Think of raster images in terms of those huge lighted graphics in Times Square, each composed of thousands of electric light bulbs. From a distance, the lights' collective image predominates. This image, indeed, is a bitmapped graphic.

But now the scanner comes to Row 5. Positions A5 through H5 produce zeros, but position I5 results in a one, as do positions J5 and K5. Positions L5 through O5 produce zeros, then three ones, and so on.

The scanning technique I'm describing here matches the technique television uses to produce its electronic images: left to right, top to bottom. This technology is described as rasterizing in the TV business and the term was retained when the same technology was used in the computer industry.

The raster image is in fact a map of the cells, or *bits*, comprising the image matrix. Thus, you'll hear this type of image referred to as *bitmapped* as well as raster. You might also hear it described as a *paint* image because most of the programs that manipulate raster images have the word *paint* in their name, including Windows Paintbrush.

Pros

Complex line art, such as the Chaplinesque caricature in Figure 7-2, can easily be represented with a raster image. Typically, you use scanners to convert line art such as this illustration into computer data; and all scanners produce raster images—indeed, raster images are the only kind they can produce.

Figure 7-2: A pen-and-ink caricature has been scanned to convert it to computer data. All scanned images are raster images, thus the popularity of the format.

Moreover, each bit of a raster image can be represented as a level of gray or a different color. In other words, you also can use raster files to represent photographic material.

Raster images are probably the most common form of computer graphics, due primarily to the popularity of scanners. They're easy to produce (if you have a scanner), lend themselves to detailed editing (typically, each bit measures 1/300 inch and you can edit the bits individually), and all Windows users have Windows Paintbrush, which creates and edits raster images.

Cons

Unfortunately, raster images aren't very flexible. If you want to enlarge Charlie's face from Figure 7-2, the image loses detail (see Figure 7-3). Only so many bits were used to represent his face. When the image is enlarged, the number of bits doesn't change, but their size does. The resulting larger bits are visibly coarse, producing a stair-stepping effect on the outline and a mottled effect in the gray of the face. (Enlargement and reduction will be discussed in "Formatting Graphics" later in this chapter.)

Figure 7-3: When a portion of Figure 7-2 is enlarged, its raster texture becomes more pronounced, producing stair-stepping and mottled grays.

The problem is just as sticky in reverse. If we begin with a large bitmapped graphic and reduce it for inclusion in a publication, some bits may overlap others (see Figure 7-4). The result is a peculiar effect known as a *moiré* pattern. Although the fabric industry uses moiré patterns to its benefit, they're not a sought-after effect in desktop publishing.

Figure 7-4: Reduced from a larger size, a raster image develops moiré patterns, producing unbecoming textures.

Unfortunately, moiré patterns and stair steps in raster images are unavoidable. Enlarging or reducing raster images simply isn't a good idea.

One more word of caution. I indicated that many raster images are produced at 300 dots per inch, a resolution that matches that of many laser printers. Although this resolution produces fine images—at 300 dpi, the individual dots are invisible to the eye—it demands considerable storage space.

Imagine a 3- by 5-inch, 300-dpi graphic. Three hundred dots per lineal inch results in 90,000 dots per square inch, and a 3- by 5-inch graphic contains 15 square inches—nearly a million and a half dots. If you were storing a 3- by 5-inch scanned photographic image with, say, 256 levels of gray, you would have to store a million and a half numbers, each between 0 and 255, representing each dot of the scanned image.

Raster images, in other words, are inefficient.

Don't misinterpret this discussion. In spite of their ineffi-
ciency and inflexibility, raster graphics remain the only
effective method of reproducing real-world graphics (hand-
drawn art and photography, in particular) in the desktop-
publishing environment. By all means, use them; just understand what you're getting into.

Vector

The alternative to raster graphics is vector graphics. Look
again at Figure 7-1. This particular image would be better
represented using a system of graphics *primitives*. Most
computer systems offer a small number of them: lines, arcs,
polygons, ellipses and rectangles. Because our graphic really
consists of nothing more than three ellipses, you could represent it with three primitives. The graphic's description, then,
might look something like Figure 7-5.

		----- Radius -----		
Primitive	**Center**	**Horizontal**	**Vertical**	**Fill**
ellipse	J7	2.5	3	40%
ellipse	Q7	2.5	3	40%
ellipse	M12	4.5	4.5	40%

Figure 7-5: Don't take this literally. In the interest of clarity, I've
simplified these descriptions considerably.

These primitives can be likened to the strokes of a pen—each with a starting point, a direction and distance traveled—and are commonly referred to as *vectors*. You might also hear them described as *objects*, and the programs that create them as *drawing* (as opposed to painting) programs.

One implication prevails: the computer has to understand the meaning of each of the primitives. When Figure 7-5's table says "draw an ellipse," the computer has to know what an ellipse is—which isn't much of a demand. In fact, Windows has a built-in primitive interpreter. Thus, all Windows programs understand primitives. That's how Word draws borders around tables like the one in Figure 7-5.

Pros

Each vector in Figure 7-5 requires about 20 bytes of storage. Saving the graphic on disk, in other words, requires less than 100 bytes. Stored as a bitmap, the same graphic requires around 10 times that much, assuming the resolution indicated in Figure 7-1. However, each cell in Figure 7-1 measures about 1/8 inch. In other words, Figure 7-1's resolution is about 8 dpi. If you increased the resolution to 300 dpi, the storage size of the raster image would increase exponentially.

What if you wanted an image four times larger, at the same resolution? For a raster image, you would have to re-scan it at 400% and find about 2mb on your hard disk to store it.

The storage size of the enlarged vector image, however, wouldn't change. If you want to make it four times larger, simply ask the computer to multiply each of the vectors' measurements by four. *Bingo!* There's a 400% image, with no increase in storage volume.

Perhaps you've already anticipated another advantage: no jaggies. Vector images appear at the resolution of the display device, regardless of enlargement or reduction (see Figure 7-6). Moreover, you can fill objects with any shade, color or pattern the system understands. Regardless of whether the object measures an inch or a yard, you simply instruct the computer to "fill with 40% gray" and it complies.

Figure 7-6: Compare this illustration with Figure 7-3. Represented as a vector file, the enlarged graphic shows no jaggies or compromise of texture.

The lack of jaggies is especially important if the graphic contains text. Depending on the program that originated it, text can be represented either way (raster or vector). Text created in a raster-graphics program is bitmapped (and therefore subject to the jaggies). Text created in a vector-format program is composed of lines and arcs: you can enlarge, reduce, rotate and shade it to any degree without loss of resolution.

Cons

Figure 7-6 illustrates the compromises necessary to represent line-art images as objects. To duplicate the raster image, a total of 88 objects—rather complex objects called *Bézier curves*—are required, resulting in a file measuring nearly 21,000 bytes. Whereas a 300-dpi bitmap would require even more storage for the same size image, a bitmap half the size of Figure 7-6 would probably require less.

In addition, you can't access the individual dots of the graphic. Making changes to the graphic means manipulating the Bézier curves, a process requiring elaborate software and operator expertise. You don't edit Bézier curves with Paintbrush or Draw.

You don't create a graphic like Figure 7-6 using a mouse either. Typically, you draw such a graphic with pen and ink, scan it into a raster file and then trace it using special tracing software. The tracing becomes the object outline, which you invariably have to tweak by hand to faithfully match the original. This process also implies sophisticated software and even more operator expertise.

Whereas the image in Figure 7-6 treads the line—it's one of the few graphics capable of representation using either vector or raster—most line-art images are too complex for vector representation. And line-art images are simple compared to photographic images. There's no practical way a vector graphic can represent a photographic image.

Choosing the Right Format

With Microsoft Draw (a vector-graphics program included with Word) and Windows Paintbrush (a raster-graphics program included with Windows), Word users can choose vector or raster formats. Which should you choose?

It depends on the graphic. Let's see if we can clarify the situation with the table in Figure 7-7.

Graphic Type	Appropriate Uses / Comments
Raster	⇒ Scanned images
	⇒ Photographic images
	⇒ Random patterns and textures
	⇒ Size of file depends on size and resolution of image
	⇒ Scaling may affect image quality
	⇒ File size corresponds directly with number of dots and colors in image
	⇒ Modification based on dot color and location
Vector	⇒ Good for line-drawing applications: Engineering drawings Architectural drawings Line art Charts and graphs
	⇒ Size of image easily changed without compromise to image quality or change in storage requirements
	⇒ Best choice if image contains text
	⇒ Good for predictable shades and patterns
	⇒ File size relative to number of objects and independent of image size
	⇒ Modification based on individual objects

Figure 7-7: The lowdown on raster and vector.

In other words, neither format is superior to the other; your choice depends on the nature of the image (see Figure 7-8). One thing is certain: desktop publishers who use graphics require both types of programs. Fortunately, as a Word for Windows user, you have them. Now all you have to do is learn how to use them appropriately, productively and effectively.

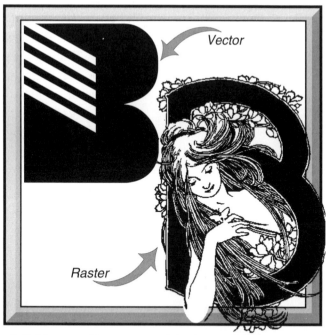

Figure 7-8: The pen-like texture of the lower *B* is best represented by a raster format. The geometrics of the *B* at the upper left, however, are better served by the vector format.

FILE FORMATS

If the world were a perfect place, there would be no war, no taxes, no death and no poverty. There would be one political party, one cola, one word-processing program and one graphics file format.

Such is not the case. Even Microsoft—which omnipotently publishes DOS, Windows and Word—can't part the sea of file-format anarchy now flooding the computer industry. We stand on the shore, waving our staff in futility while a *tsunami* of formats threatens the Submersion of Enlightenment and the Asphyxiation of Lucidity.

Where's Charlton Heston when we need him?

Raster Formats

Although Word doesn't tame the *tsunami*, it does move to higher ground. Only a limited number of graphics formats are supported; from among that number, one will probably serve your particular situation. Let's begin with Word's supported raster formats.

The Blessed One
Of all the raster formats, BMP is the Blessed One. Word doesn't even use a filter (a translation program) to read BMP files. They're so endemic to the Windows environment that no translation is necessary.

Windows Bitmap (.BMP)

The Windows bitmap format provides four levels of complexity: black-and-white, 16-color, 24-color and 256-color. If your software provides access to these electives, always choose the format that is closest to the number of colors in your graphic. Windows bitmaps are not normally compressed (many others are; we'll talk about them in a moment). The art-nouveau *B* in Figure 7-8 stores in 19.6k of disk space as a black-and-white bitmap but requires 74.4k when stored as a 16-color bitmap (even though it's still black and white). Choice of BMP format, in other words, is significant if you value disk space.

The BMP format should be your preferred choice when you're using Windows Paintbrush. Though Paintbrush also reads and writes PCX files (see "Paintbrush (.PCX)" later in this chapter), the Windows manual recommends the BMP format "... in order to maintain the highest possible level of compatibility across machines and future versions of Windows."

You've been warned.

Tagged Image File Format (.TIF)

Developed by Microsoft itself (among others), TIFF is dominant among raster formats in desktop publishing. Yet in spite of Microsoft's parentage and TIFF's popularity in desktop publishing, Word doesn't embrace TIFF with ardor. The trouble has to do with dialects. Even though the TIFF specification was developed with the intention of creating a standard, scores of minor variations in the format—so-called *dialects*—have frustrated the intention. Word speaks *most* of these dialects, barely understands some (producing distorted images) and simply refuses to converse with others.

This pickiness is perplexing. TIFF is the emerging cross-platform standard for bitmaps. It is platform-independent (Word, for instance, reads Macintosh TIFF files). It compresses well (more about compression in the following paragraphs), and Microsoft is co-author of the specification. Nonetheless, Windows Paintbrush doesn't offer TIFF as a format option, and Word's tolerance of TIFF images, while admirable, isn't inclusive of all TIFF potentials.

This situation may change. Word's aversion to TIFF is really a function of its TIFF filter, not Word itself. (We'll discuss filters later in this chapter.) Filters can be changed, and this one probably will. By the time you read this book, Word may have become TIFF multilingual. In other words, the only way to find out whether your copy of Word is compatible with any particular TIFF file is to try inserting the file. If it appears onscreen, you're halfway there. If it prints properly, write the folks at Microsoft a nice letter telling them how much you appreciate their pursuit of the elusive TIFF standard.

Compressing TIFF Files

A number of programs will compress TIFF files, often to less than 50 percent of their original size.[3] Because raster-image files are typically quite large, compression is more of a necessity than an elective. There's no compromise either: compressed TIFF files suffer no degradation of image quality. I don't know how they do it. Smoke and mirrors, most likely. At the moment, six different compression dialects for monochrome TIFF files are available; to its credit, Word understands three of them. TIFF compression, in other words, may work for you. Again, there's no harm in trying.

---

[3] Paint Shop Pro, a shareware program readily available on most online services, reads and writes almost every raster format, including all those mentioned here. It also compresses and decompresses TIFF files. Until Word does the same, Paint Shop Pro is a valuable utility.

Paintbrush (.PCX)

PCX files were originally created for use with Zsoft's PC Paintbrush program. Paintbrush was around for years before Windows 3, and because few other raster-editing programs were available in the early days of PC graphics, Paintbrush's PCX file format became the standard. When Microsoft acquired the product, it added the BMP format option (and the recommendation) mentioned earlier. This format is being phased out. Use BMP, if you can, or use TIFF.

Graphic Interchange Format (.GIF)

This format originated with CompuServe[4], an online telecommunications service. Unfortunately, Word can't import GIF graphics. I mention GIF because thousands of graphics are distributed in this format, and you'll no doubt want to use one someday. You can use a utility such as Paint Shop Pro to convert formats—from GIF to BMP, for instance. You also can use it to convert a color graphic to black and white. As is the case with BMP, the storage requirements for color GIF files can be oppressive (even though GIF files are normally compressed). Unless you intend to print them in color, always convert color images to black and white.

The graphics in this book
All the graphics in this book are courtesy of three sources:
✔ Word's clip-art files
✔ Clip art from CorelDRAW!
✔ Dover Publications
Their contributions are gratefully acknowledged.

Vector Formats

Frankly, the desktop-publishing industry doesn't offer any popular vector-only formats. Nearly all desktop-publishing vector files are represented by one of the metafile formats (see "Metafiles" later in this chapter). Vector-only formats are the realm of computer-aided design (CAD) and business graphics, where they predominate.

Nonetheless, occasions do arise when you need to include a CAD file in a Word document, and Word stands ready to accommodate that potential.

---

[4] CompuServe is a rich resource of materials—including graphics—for desktop publishers. Its desktop-publishing forum is the Algonquin Round Table for people in the business. Your local bookstore probably has a starter kit, or call CompuServe at (800) 621-1253.

Stick fonts

Fonts used by CAD programs are usually "stick" fonts, the kind a plotter draws with a pen you hold in a vertical position. They're much like the characters you draw with a mechanical pencil and a lettering template: not much personality. If you want a similar typeface with more style, investigate Tekton from Adobe Corporation. Inspired by the handwriting of a San Francisco architect, Tekton features plenty of personality yet remains complementary to CAD subjects.

AutoCAD Data Exchange Format (.DXF) & Device Interface Files (.PLT)

DXF is a two-dimensional, text-only file format used by AutoCAD, the most widely used computer-aided design software today. Because of AutoCAD's popularity, this format has become something of a standard for CAD file exchange among all kinds of machines, from micros to mainframes.

AutoCAD versions through 10.0 are supported. Version 11 (and later) AutoCAD DXF files may not import properly.

The hitch is Word's inability to read DXF files containing 3D images, the ones of most interest to desktop publishers. Fortunately, you have an alternative: Autodesk Device Interface (ADI) plotter files. These files are more machine-specific—you may not be able to import ADI files from a mainframe, for instance—but if you want to import a 3D file from an MS-DOS AutoCAD machine, you can use the ADI format. Don't expect color from these files, and use the default .PLT filename extension.

Hewlett-Packard Graphics Language (.HGL)

This format represents command files generated for an HP7475A plotter. It too is a CAD format. As with all CAD files, HPGL files are intended to be plotted (on a pen-based plotter) rather than printed. Plotters don't typically fill objects with shades or colors. When fills are specified, they're usually in the form of "hatches."

In other words, don't use these formats when text or shades are required. CAD files are optimized for architectural and engineering applications, and should be used to represent images of an architectural or engineering nature only.

Micrografx Designer & Draw Plus Files (.DRW)

Word's ability to work with DRW files is limited—including a lack of support for gradient fills and text along a curve. You're better advised to export or translate DRW files using one of the metafile formats (see "Metafiles").

Lotus PICture Files (.PIC)

Lotus 1-2-3, Symphony and Freelance, and Borland's Quattro Pro spreadsheet program are typically associated with PIC files. This format isn't complex: Bézier curves, color palettes and a variety of font options aren't there. The PIC format is intended for business graphics—bars and charts—and it's best confined to that arena.

By the way, Word doesn't support the Micrografx or DrawPlus PIC formats, which are both entirely separate formats.

Metafiles

Acronyms and buzzwords are the realm of the vulnerable and the defensive. No doubt the worst offender is the computer industry. Riddled with Information Science majors who oversee a universe which in no way relates to their formal education, computerdom has resorted to a protective vocabulary dominated by obtuse uppercase abridgments and polysyllabic cabalisms like *metafile*.

Pardon me for a moment while I resort to the vernacular: *metafile* means a combination of various file formats, often including raster and vector. This definition probably has something to do with chemistry, where meta also implies a combination—of two positions on a benzene ring, to be specific. Humdingers like "meta-antimonous" result from this kind of alchemy.

Use *meta-antimonous* in a sentence today.

The nitrogen of computer graphics
The Windows metafile format is the nitrogen of Windows graphics: though it's everywhere, few have ever seen it. Only programmers can describe it. And without it, graphics, at least in the Windows environment, wouldn't exist.

Windows Metafiles (.WMF)

The Windows metafile is something of a mystery. (See Figure 7-9.) Few graphics programs offer it as a Save As format alternative, yet nearly all mention it in their documentation.

Figure 7-9: Now you've seen one: an elusive Windows metafile, composed of numerous graphic device-independent primitives— filled polygons, in this case—that are "played back" here in Word.

If the truth be known, the Windows metafile format is the way Windows describes *all* graphics internally. Windows is endowed with a number of *graphic device interface* routines that exist to describe things such as lines and arcs. The phrase *device interface* implies that any Windows-friendly display device—program, printer or screen—can display them. Just as life furnishes material evidence of nitrogen, printers and screens furnish material evidence of Windows metafiles.

When it comes down to writing a Windows metafile to disk, however, we usually prefer other formats. The WMF format is meaningless outside of Windows, after all; and Microsoft notwithstanding, Windows is not yet the only manifestation of life.

Computer Graphics Metafiles (.CGM)

The need for a true graphics standard—one that's recognized by not only PCs, but Macintoshes, mainframes and minicomputers as well—was addressed in the mid-1980s when IBM, DEC, Wang, Lotus and several other big-time industry players cooked up the Computer Graphics Metafile format.

Unfortunately, Word's understanding of it is limited. Word recognizes only one font per CGM graphic, for instance, and completely ignores textual details such as character spacing and orientation.

In addition, though the CGM standard is a metafile specification, Word ignores nearly all CGM raster information, preferring to concentrate on CGM's vectors only. In other words, use CGM only if you must. Windows metafiles are a better choice.

WordPerfect Graphics (.WPG) Files

No doubt you've noticed Word's immoderate awareness of its primary competitor, WordPerfect. Help for WordPerfect users is available under the Help menu. Word reads and writes all flavors of WordPerfect documents, and Word imports WordPerfect's graphics with few compromises.

Starting with Version 2, Word for Windows included Microsoft Draw for the production of vector graphics. This addition may seem philanthropic, but it was actually a defensive move. DrawPerfect, WordPerfect's analogue to Microsoft Draw, has been around for so long that its file format—the WPG file format—has become something of an industry standard.

In other words, both as a competitor and a citizen of the industry, Word must import WPG graphics. It does so with only two exceptions: 1) Bitmap rotations other than 90 degrees are not supported; and 2) EPS graphics (see "Encapsulated PostScript (.EPS)" later in this chapter) included in WPG files do not maintain their PostScript code. These exceptions could be significant or immaterial, depending on the circumstances.

The WPG specification is rich and thorough, and a venerable standard in the DOS (non-Windows) environment. No doubt it goads Word to oblige it, but it could do worse.

PostScript

PostScript is a page-description language. The operative term here is *language*. By imbuing the printer with the intelligence necessary to interpret a language, we can significantly reduce the effort of communication. PostScript printers, for instance, understand the word *A*. The computer can tell the printer to draw a 48-point Times Roman *A*, and no further description is necessary. The printer calls upon its memory, finds the definition of a Times *A* and obliges the request. No complex object or bitmapped description of the letter *A* needs to be transmitted.

The PostScript language includes words for text, objects and bitmaps. Because it embraces both objects and bitmaps, PostScript is a metafile format.

The hitch, of course, is the intelligence. PostScript printers must have a brain and memory. The "brain" includes a computer (often more powerful than the ones most of us use to run Word), and the programming necessary to give it intelligence. All PostScript printers have megabytes of memory, in which they store character definitions, among other things. Some even have hard disks, to hold character definitions for hundreds of fonts.

In other words, PostScript printers aren't cheap.

Expense, however, is about the only drawback. PostScript describes the page using nothing but text (letters and numbers). All computers understand text; only binary formats (descriptions composed of 0's and 1's) are proprietary. Because all computers understand text, and PostScript is nothing but text, all computers can read PostScript. So even those machines that cannot understand it can read it—just like a language.

Those machines that understand it can display it. Thus, PostScript is said to be *machine-independent*: any machine with a PostScript interpreter on board can display a PostScript image. Thus, you can print a PostScript file on a Hewlett-Packard LaserJet (with a PostScript cartridge or a PostScript board) or an Apple LaserWriter or a $100,000 Linotronic imagesetter, *with no modification to the file*. This capability is important to desktop publishers who want to print high-resolution images: you can proof the document on your laser printer, then give the (unmodified) file to a service bureau with a PostScript imagesetter and assume that the image-setter's output will match your laser printer's output—only better.

PostScript Code

```
%%ELLI 81.648 -88.128 270.000 270.000 0
280.15 523.87 m
302.62 523.87 320.98 504.14 320.98 479.81 c
320.98 455.47 302.62 435.74 280.15 435.74 c
257.69 435.74 239.33 455.47 239.33 479.81 c
239.33 504.14 257.69 523.87 280.15 523.87 c
b
%%ELLI 23.616 -27.936 270.000 270.000 0
250.99 549.65 m
262.37 549.65 271.80 538.63 271.80 525.02 c
271.80 511.49 262.37 500.40 250.99 500.40 c
239.54 500.40 230.18 511.49 230.18 525.02 c
230.18 538.63 239.54 549.65 250.99 549.65 c
b
%%ELLI 23.616 -27.936 270.000 270.000 0
313.06 546.12 m
324.43 546.12 333.86 535.10 333.86 521.50 c
333.86 507.96 324.43 496.87 313.06 496.87 c
301.61 496.87 292.25 507.96 292.25 521.50 c
292.25 535.10 301.61 546.12 313.06 546.12 c
b
```

The preceding PostScript code describes Figure 7-1. Composed of three ellipses, the description contains three "paragraphs," each describing one of the ellipses.

Now that you understand PostScript, I can tell you that Word cannot import pure PostScript graphics. Doing so results in importation of the PostScript text, and the result looks just like the text illustrated in this box. There's a solution, though: read on.

Encapsulated PostScript (.EPS)

Word is not alone in its inability to display PostScript. Few programs can, other than those that create and edit PostScript graphics themselves. The problem is significant because PostScript is the crowning jewel of computer graphics. You can use PostScript to represent spectacular, complex images, rich with color and texture. If you have access to an appropriate printer, nothing equals the quality and potential of PostScript graphics.

Yet Word can't display them.

The solution is *encapsulation*. Think of medicated capsules: the really effective stuff in most capsules would probably gag you if you tried to swallow it without its gelatinous shell. The capsule is expendable; its purpose is to deliver the medicine to its destination. The same goes for EPS files: their primary purpose is to get PostScript code to the printer, but encapsulation is required to help the medicine go down.

The capsule, in this case, is a TIFF or WMF bitmapped file. The bitmap "encapsulates" the PostScript code, providing a reasonable facsimile of the graphic for onscreen display. Being the expendable part of the capsule, the bitmap is usually low resolution, but it's an adequate approximation of the finished product—adequate enough for positioning and composition, which is really all you need it for. The reward occurs at the printer, where the bitmap is discarded and the PostScript code itself is printed.

And what a reward it is. Remember that PostScript is machine-independent. PostScript images printed on a 300-dpi laser printer can be impressive, but PostScript images printed on a 2,500-dpi imagesetter can be wondrous. (See Figure 7-10.) Only PostScript offers this opportunity: it's the language most high-resolution imagesetters speak.

Figure 7-10: PostScript images represent the epitome of computer graphics: opulent, prodigal and machine-independent.

With Version 6.0, Word vastly improved its tolerance for EPS graphics, including EPS Versions 1.0 and 2.0. Earlier versions of the program used a minimal EPS filter in conjunction with a complex macro that limited sizing and positioning of imported EPS graphics. The new filter doesn't rely on the macro any longer, and Word now seems to be as EPS-friendly as any other program available.

Remember, however, that PostScript (including EPS) is a computer language, and even though Word may import EPS graphics, only a PostScript printer can print them. Use them only if your printer is appropriately equipped.

Which Is Best?

Of all those mentioned, only two file formats are actually native to the Windows environment: BMP and WMF. If you work exclusively within the Windows environment and use a non-PostScript printer, use BMP files for bitmaps and WMF files for objects.

On the other hand, two primary formats are native to the desktop-publishing environment: TIFF and EPS. If your sphere of operations includes systems other than your own—other computers and printers—then the platform independence of TIFF and EPS should be the deciding factor. If you're fortunate enough to have access to a PostScript printer, especially a high-resolution imagesetter, TIFF and EPS are your only practical alternatives.

Import Filters

Word accommodates all these disparate graphics formats by calling upon various graphics *filters*. Filters are essentially translators: external mini-programs that read foreign formats into Word documents. They are external (you will find them on your disk with the extension .FLT) to accommodate the perpetual change endemic to computer graphics. When a standard is updated to include a new feature, all Microsoft has to do is issue a new filter, rather than a new edition of Word.

Understand a few significant characteristics of Word's graphics filters:

- ✔ Few filters tolerate multitasking. If another program—the Print Manager, for instance—is running in the background when you import a graphic, Word can display a moment of indelible inelegance.

- ✔ Word expects to find its filters by following the WINDOWS\MSAPPS\GRPHFLT\ path. If this path is altered, WIN.INI has to be altered. Whenever you install filters for Windows applications, modifications to WIN.INI are automatically a part of the process.

✔ Though new filters become available on an ongoing basis, Microsoft can't be expected to notify you of every one. If you need to import a graphic and Word doesn't recognize it, first run the Setup program to see whether you already have an appropriate filter and simply haven't installed it. Failing that, see whether the filter is on CompuServe, or call Microsoft and ask if it has what you need.

✔ Always use the Word Setup program to install new filters. Filters typically arrive in compressed form; copying them into the GRPHFLT subdirectory won't do. Furthermore, the WIN.INI file has to be changed whenever Word's filter set is changed. Again, let Setup do it for you.

✔ For a complete list of filters provided with Word for Windows Version 6.0, double-click the Help button on the Standard toolbar and then type **readme**. Press the Enter key twice and then click Graphics Filters.

OTHER SOURCES FOR GRAPHICS

What? You're not manic?

Many of us are casual desktop publishers. We're not manic about desktop publishing: it found us, we didn't seek it out. And when it comes to graphics manipulations, Word's utilities are just right: competent, not too demanding of expertise, and free.

Including an external graphic file in a Word document isn't the only source of Word graphics. Though our discussion so far has been confined to graphics imported via the Insert command, sources internal to Word are also worthy of discussion.

Perhaps Word's most aggressive desktop-publishing statement is its inclusion of four graphics utilities in the price of the program. Coupled with Windows Paintbrush, these utilities comprise a toolbox of respectable merit—not profound, not esteemed, not state-of-the-art, but certainly adequate. And no matter what the source, Word's graphics may be independent, linked or embedded.

All this requires explanation; read on.

Microsoft Draw

Remember again that graphics come in two primary flavors: raster and vector. Windows Paintbrush is your tool for editing raster images. Microsoft Draw is your tool for editing vectors.

Microsoft Draw is actually a complete vector-based drawing program, benignly buried inside of a word-processing program where you'd least expect to find it. You can invoke Draw in two ways: either activate the Drawing toolbar or insert a metafile graphic.

To access the Drawing toolbar, choose Toolbars from the View menu, click within the box to the left of the word *Drawing*, then click OK. The toolbar will appear across the bottom of your screen. Few of the toolbar's buttons work in the Normal View, however, and you'll be asked to switch to the Page Layout View as soon as you try to use most of them. Once you do, you can draw boxes, circles, lines and even callouts as if you were using a little graphics program.

The other method of invoking Draw is to insert a metafile graphic. I've used one of Word's clip-art files for the example that follows, but any metafile graphic will do.

From the Insert menu, choose Picture and find the sub-directory on your hard disk where Word's clip-art files are stored. It's probably inside of your Word directory, though every setup is unique. (Indeed, you may have elected to omit Word's clip-art images during the installation process. If that's the case [and you want to conduct the experiment I'm about to describe], you'll need to run Word's Setup program again and install the clip-art library.)

Choose any image that's of interest to you and click on the Insert Picture dialog box's OK button. The image will appear on your screen.

Now double-click on the image. Word will switch to Page Layout View, the Drawing toolbar will appear (if it wasn't showing already), and a small Picture palette will float somewhere on your screen.

That Picture palette actually denotes the presence of an additional program, Microsoft Draw, in your computer's memory. Now, however, Draw is so completely integrated into Word that all you see of it is its palette and toolbar. It's a comprehensive drawing program nonetheless, and one that's included in Word without charge.

Keep in mind that Draw is a vector-based program and thus works with objects—five primitives, to be exact: lines, arcs, ellipses, rectangles and polygons. That's the entire universe as far as Draw is concerned. No matter how complex or lifelike an image may appear, it's nothing but a collection of these objects. Each object occupies its own layer, and the layers are stacked on top of one another.

Refer to Figure 7-11 as we dissect a Draw graphic. Though the no-smoking graphic appears to be pretty simple, it is, nonetheless, an assemblage of 27 objects: ellipses, rectangles, arcs, lines and polygons. To access these graphic primitives, click on each object within the graphic. When the object's handles appear, drag the object away from the graphic's center. Do this for each object you discover until you have all of the components spread out in front of you. It's a little like gross anatomy without the formaldehyde.

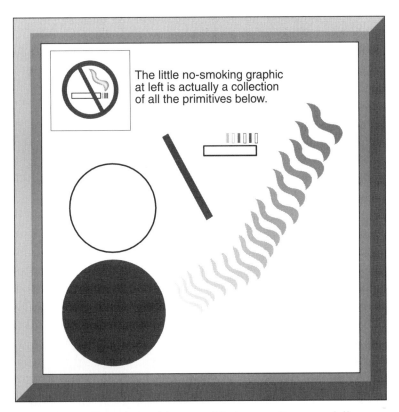

The little no-smoking graphic at left is actually a collection of all the primitives below.

Figure 7-11: The no-smoking graphic is actually a carefully arranged, 3D stack of 27 objects. Collectively, they're a familiar sight (upper left). Taken individually, the objects reveal the graphic's composite nature.

When you've finished working on a graphic, simply click on the Close Picture button in Draw's Picture palette. Draw will update the picture in your Word document and gracefully exit the scene.

Draw is more of a program than first meets the eye. In fact, Draw is a Windows metafile editor. The dissection process described earlier is, in fact, one of the best ways to understand Windows metafiles. As a metafile editor, Draw accepts all graphics—raster or vector—that metafiles accept.

Draw doesn't import text files, and it can't edit bitmaps bit by bit. But you can create text boxes and callouts in Draw, and you can select bitmaps and resize them, send them to the back or bring them to the front. Moreover, because metafiles are indigenous to the Clipboard, you can paste any graphic you copied to the Clipboard into a document and then modify it using Draw. Use Draw, in other words, to combine raster and vector graphics in the same document. Few programs can combine graphics; only one of them is free (see Figure 7-12).

Figure 7-12: Bitmaps and objects have been blended in Draw, which, as a metafile editor, can accommodate both.

Microsoft WordArt

We have little need here to add to our WordArt discussion of the display type chapter. One significant matter, however, requires our attention: WordArt works with TrueType fonts only.

WordArt has some interesting consequences due to its text enhancement options with TrueType fonts:

1. WordArt text may be disproportionately sized within Word, giving it a "Silly Putty" personality (great for special effects, see Figure 7-13).

2. WordArt text is portable—any machine capable of running Windows can display and print it, regardless of whether it has WordArt installed.

Figure 7-13: Because it is composed entirely of primitives, you can stretch and compress WordArt text as if it were printed on Silly Putty.

Microsoft Graph

You might think that Microsoft has declared war with Word for Windows. With WordArt, Draw, Graph and the Equation Editor, Microsoft has mustered an armory of ordnance capable of annihilating any enemy foolish enough to cross its path.

Which brings us to Microsoft Graph. Casting about for lethal weaponry, the Word team in Redmond crossed the hall and plundered the Excel offices during the noon hour, while the Excel team was in the lunchroom. Excel has always been a resplendent spreadsheet; and in 1990, Microsoft added a 3D charting feature that made *House of Wax* look like *Babes in Toyland*.

Excel is Microsoft's Big Gun for the business graphics market. With its 3D format command that provides a perspective control and two axes of rotation, you can make Excel's charts emanate from the page with such dynamism that no reader dares challenge the argument. Very persuasive stuff. And due to the success of the Word raiding party, you too have the weapon at your command. All you have to do is choose Object from the Insert menu and then choose Microsoft Graph. Faster than you can launch a Patriot, fully one-third of Excel—itself a $500 program—arrives on your screen, ready for battle.

Once again, I hasten to mention that any chart you prepare with Graph can be further enhanced using Draw. Draw offers a finer degree of control—especially textual control—than does Graph. Moreover, you can add all the features found in WordArt to your chart as separate objects. (See Figure 7-14.)

Figure 7-14: The potential of Microsoft Graph and the other programs available in Word is fully realized when you combine objects from several for final assembly.

Graph's text

Try to avoid text in Graph images. Graph's text is composed of system fonts, and it doesn't change size when you enlarge or reduce the chart.

Here's a strategy for preparing fancy graphs with Word, Draw and Graph:

✔ With a Word document open, choose Object from the Insert menu. From the resulting scroll box, choose Microsoft Graph.

✔ Prepare your chart in Graph. Don't bother with embellishments. Just get the chart you need; the rest will be added with Draw.

✔ When the chart is to your liking, update your document with it.

✔ Access your Drawing toolbar and make sure you are in Page Layout View.

✔ Enhance your chart with a title or callouts, etc. When you're finished, save your file.

Incorporating WordArt text is simply a matter of creating the WordArt, framing the object and placing it where desired on the page. WordArt text arrives as individual objects. Though you can't edit these objects (as text), you can move, size and crop them.

The techniques described in the preceding list are especially important in preparing presentation graphics. Even Graph's fancy charts can use the embellishments offered by WordArt and Draw. WordArt's enhancement to TrueType fonts offers a compelling alternative to Helvetica and Times, and Draw's rich palette of shapes and textures far surpasses those of Graph. Look upon each as a provider of raw material and Word as the facility that fabricates the finished product. In many presentation-graphics documents, Word simply provides print and save commands, little else.

Here is a strategy for making acetates for overhead projection:

✔ Choose New from the File menu to create a new document. When the new document appears, choose Page Setup from the File menu and specify Landscape Orientation from the Paper Size tab. Landscape documents are wider than they are tall; portrait documents are taller than they are wide.

✔ Create a "master" slide by changing to Print Preview (from the File menu) and invoking the Drawing toolbar. Using the rectangle-drawing tool in the palette, draw any size box (we'll fix it in a moment). Then point and click on it with the right mouse button and choose Format Drawing Object from that menu.

Excel users note

As a subset of Excel, Microsoft Graph simply duplicates Excel's charting features. If you already use Excel, you gain nothing by installing Graph. Save a megabyte: install Graph only if you really need it, and only if you don't already have Excel on your disk.

Update vs. Exit

When you're finished using Graph, consider Update (File menu) rather than Exit and Return. Choose Update and then minimize. Doing so leaves the utility loaded in memory, available at a moment's notice. On the other hand, if you create another Graph image or edit one in Word (and you haven't already exited from the utility), a second copy of Graph will be opened, hogging memory.

Making presentations

Most laser and ink-jet printers can print on acetate for use with overhead projectors. Lacking an appropriate printer, print on paper and photocopy the result, again using acetate. Stationery- and art-supply stores carry the kind of acetate that you can use in photo-copy machines and laser printers. Be sure you've got the right material: regular overhead-projector acetate melts under these conditions.

✔ If color isn't required, select any of the gray fills in the Fill tab.

✔ Click on the Line tab. Change the weight of the line to 2 points. Click in the Round Corners box.

✔ Click on the Size and Position tab. Under Size, enter **7.25 in** for Height and **9.75 in** for Width. Then click OK.

✔ Right-click the object again and select Send Behind Text (if it is already selected, you'll see "Bring in Front of Text" instead).

✔ Add any other "master" items that are to appear on all the slides.

✔ Working in Word, copy and paste the master slide as often as necessary, placing page breaks (Ctrl-Enter) between each slide. (See Figure 7-15.)

Figure 7-15: A graphic for overhead projection. The chart is from Graph; the text box, from Draw; the football, a scanned raster image. The whole thing was assembled and printed and saved in Word.

Collectively taken, Draw, Graph and WordArt are powerful tools for creating any kind of graphic, whether it be a written report or a slide show. Best of all, they're free, included in Word as enticements to woo us away from other Windows word processors.

Competition benefits everyone, the Mountaineers and Word users alike.

Microsoft Equation Editor

Once again Microsoft sent out a raiding party. With instructions to find software appropriate for mathematical applications, they returned with a Macintosh program, *Math Type*, from Design Science. A tweak here, a tweak there and the Microsoft Equation Editor emerged, ready to include in Word. (See Figure 7-16.)

$$x = \frac{-b \pm \sqrt{b^2 - 4ac}}{2a}$$

Figure 7-16: There's nothing like a quadratic equation to brighten up your day. The Equation Editor makes constructing the equation easy. The solution to the equation, on the other hand, is left to the reader.

Transferring equations

If you need to transfer an Equation Editor graphic to a machine that doesn't have the appropriate fonts, enlarge the equation to 400% in the Equation Editor program (View menu) and then take a screen shot of it (Print Screen key). When you paste the resulting graphic into Word (or anywhere else), it will emerge as a bitmap, independent of the Equation Editor's extensive font requirements. When you reduce it to its original size, its resolution will be adequate for most purposes.

Although the Equation Editor may seem to be an application better suited to mathematicians than desktop publishers, you never know when its features might come in handy. It makes constructing simple fractions—imagine formatting a fraction like 15/32" without it (with the 15 directly on top of the 32)—infinitely easier than superscripts, subscripts and character spacing. The program is remarkably intuitive, even to those of us who have neglected our mathematics education.

It creates beautiful equations, which have a certain aesthetic appeal that is lost when you don't attend to the presentation properly.

Two comments regarding the Equation Editor are appropriate:

1. Word's Setup program places a slew of special fonts on your disk that enable the Equation Editor to work its magic. Setup takes note of the installed printer(s) at the time of installation and copies fonts appropriate to that printer to various locations on your hard disk. In other words, be sure the printer you intend to use is installed (use the Windows Control Panel) when you install the Equation Editor; otherwise, you'll have to re-install it.

2. Depending on the installed printers, the Equation Editor's fonts can inhale disk space like a deep breath on a September morning. The utility and its help file alone total nearly half a megabyte. Fonts can triple that. In other words, don't install the Equation Editor unless you're sure you need it. You can always install it later.

To embed an Equation Editor object, choose Object from the Insert menu and then choose Equation.

OBJECT LINKING & EMBEDDING (OLE)

Word for Windows Version 2 was the first program to fully utilize Object Linking and Embedding, which is becoming more commonplace as the industry matures. Given the proper hardware, OLE removes the operator from the intricate structure of files and programs filed in a hierarchy of subdirectories on the hard disk. Instead, OLE substitutes a single, seamless environment in which editing any object is as simple as a double-click of the mouse.

Let's examine a scenario you probably already know. Scrolling through a Word document, you come across a Draw graphic. It needs a bit of editing. Double-clicking on the graphic places you in the graphic's editing environment (Draw) where you make your changes and return to regular processing in Word.

Sounds simple, and from the operator's perspective it is. From a technical perspective, however, wonders akin to metamorphosis have occurred, all without operator intervention. Here's what really happens when you edit that graphic: by double-clicking on the graphic, you send a message to Windows to find the originating application and load it into memory. In our example, Windows loads Draw, changes to Page Layout View if not there already, displays the Drawing toolbar if not visible already, and all the while it hardly looks like you are any place other than Word. When you're done editing the graphic, you simply click elsewhere in the document or turn off the Drawing toolbar. Draw is unloaded from memory, Word is given control of the active window, and the graphic is actually part of the Word document, where it now appears onscreen, with all modifications in place.

And what kind of trouble have you been spared?

✔ You did not have to return to Windows to find and run Draw.

✔ You did not have to find the graphic on your disk and open it with Draw.

✔ You did not have to save the graphic after modification.

✔ You did not have to remember the saved graphic's name or location.

✔ You did not have to return again to Windows to reactivate Word.

✔ You did not have to find and re-insert the modified graphic into the Word document to update it.

Because desktop publishing usually involves data from various sources, this kind of busy work would run rampant were it not for OLE. Before OLE, computing was a task-oriented environment: a task in Word, a task in Draw, a task in Excel and so forth. Once OLE dominates (and it will: more and more programs are issuing updates with OLE built in), we'll become document-oriented. We won't think much about which application created which object. We won't worry about where things are stored on the disk. We won't wonder whether each and every supporting element is current. We'll simply load the Word document and do what has to be done. Every contributing element will be embedded, a double-click away.

Computing is supposed to be this way. *Olé*, OLE!

How to Embed an Object

You can embed objects in one of two ways: by inserting or by pasting. You may insert an embedded object by choosing the appropriate program from the list in the Insert-Object scroll box (see Figure 7-17).

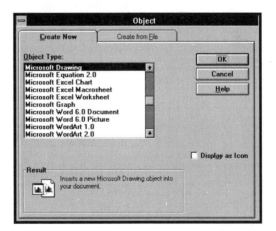

Figure 7-17: The Insert-Object scroll box presents a listing of installed programs and utilities that support embedding. This list differs from one machine to another: yours won't match mine.

The extent of that list of objects in the Insert-Object dialog box is determined by the number of programs on your machine that support object linking and embedding.

Choosing an item from this list first opens the supporting application associated with that object. There you can construct the object normally. When you're finished, the supporting application's File menu will offer a command called Update, which will place the embedded object into the open Word document, exit the supporting application and return to Word. All of this manual prompting to Update is not necessary with Draw and WordArt, but the effects are the same.

It's interesting that familiar applications change their personalities slightly when accessed this way. Microsoft Excel's File menu, for instance, changes to offer an Update command in addition to the normal complement (see Excel's File menu, Figure 7-18). When you choose Update, Excel places the embedded object into the open Word document from which Excel was called; you then automatically exit Excel and return to Word. You don't need to save while in Excel; the Excel object is saved when you save the Word document. Word handles saving and printing; Excel is subservient.

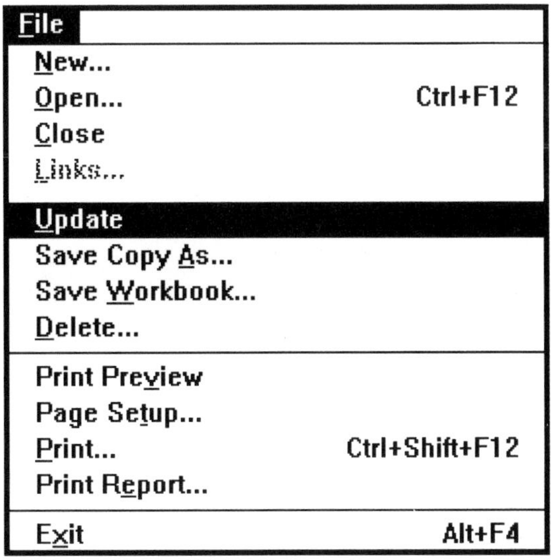

```
┌──────────────────────────────────┐
│ File                             │
│ New...                           │
│ Open...                 Ctrl+F12 │
│ Close                            │
│ Links...                         │
├──────────────────────────────────┤
│ Update                           │
│ Save Copy As...                  │
│ Save Workbook...                 │
│ Delete...                        │
├──────────────────────────────────┤
│ Print Preview                    │
│ Page Setup...                    │
│ Print...          Ctrl+Shift+F12 │
│ Print Report...                  │
├──────────────────────────────────┤
│ Exit                      Alt+F4 │
└──────────────────────────────────┘
```

Figure 7-18: The File menu in Excel changes to include the Update command when you access Excel via Word's Insert-Object command.

Canceling embedding

Embedded graphical objects include the information necessary to identify the originating application. Removing this information reduces the size of the Word file containing the embedded object. Simply select the object and press Ctrl-Shift-F9 (Unlink Field key). The object is still there—where you can crop and size it, for instance—but it will not be embedded.

The other method of establishing an embedded object is to paste it into an open Word document. For stand-alone programs like Excel, this method is a little easier to accomplish (and understand) than embedding via the Insert-Object command.

Again, let's use Excel as an example. Working in Excel, you create a chart that you want to embed in a Word document. Here's what to do:

✔ Select the chart and then copy it to the Clipboard (using Excel's Edit menu).

✔ Return to Word and then choose Paste Special (using Word's Edit menu). (See Figure 7-19.)

✔ Choose Excel Chart Object (or, if Excel isn't the originating program, choose the option that has the word *object* in it).

✔ Click on the Paste button.

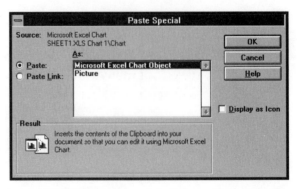

Figure 7-19: Word's Paste Special dialog offers the option of embedding an object when the originating program supports OLE.

Semantics

If the distinction between linking and embedding seems a bit fuzzy, look for key words. In Word's nomenclature, if a graphic is an *object*, it's embedded. You can double-click on it to get to the originating application. Linked graphics, on the other hand, are generally referred to as pictures.

When embedding doesn't work

If double-clicking on an embedded object doesn't switch to the program in which the object was created, you may have to load the originating program into memory. Return to Windows (without exiting Word), run the originating program and then switch back to Word. Double-clicking on the embedded object should now work.

Referring again to Figure 7-19, note the Picture option. If Picture is chosen, Word pastes a vector-graphic image into the document (including an option to link; more about linking in the following pages). Double-clicking on the resulting graphic calls Draw, not Excel, for editing. All these options differ when the originating program is something other than Excel.

By the way, because Excel and Word both understand OLE, the relationship is reciprocal. Pasting Word text into Excel results in an embedded object as well. Double-clicking on an embedded Word object in Excel calls Word, with Word's insertion point at the beginning of the embedded text.

LINKING FILES

Embedding isn't a solution to everyone's problems, however. Embedded objects aren't dynamically *linked* to files, which can be inconvenient.

Although embedded objects offer an intelligent connection to the originating program, they don't automatically update when the originating program changes them. Linked objects do. Let's explain.

An emerging form of desktop-publishing document is one that is produced not by an individual, but by a group. Perhaps two or three people are working on the same document: Susan writes the copy, Joe prepares the graphics, and Gail puts it all together in Word. They're sharing data on a network.

In the days before networks, the most effective method of data transfer was the "sneaker network"—Joe put on his sneakers and ran to Gail's office with his graphics on a floppy disk. Gail then loaded the graphics into Word and sent Joe back to his desk (see Figure 7-20).

Figure 7-20: Joe's sneaker-shodden strolls to Gail's office became history with the advent of the LAN. (Clip art courtesy of Corel Systems Corp.)

With the arrival of the local area network (LAN), technology saved shoe leather. All Joe had to do was call Gail and tell her that the latest graphic was on the server. Gail queried the server, found the graphic and loaded it into Word. Joe and his sneakers stayed in his office.

Linking further streamlines the process. Gail and Joe still talk to one another, but not about graphics. Instead, Gail links Joe's graphic to her Word document by going to her Insert menu and choosing Picture (or File, if she wants to establish a link with Susan's text).

The Insert Picture dialog box in Figure 7-21 identifies such a link. Joe's server-mounted graphic SCALES.WMF is in the process of being inserted into Gail's document. Notice the Link to File check box in the illustration. It may seem insignificant, but this little check box is all you need to establish the link.

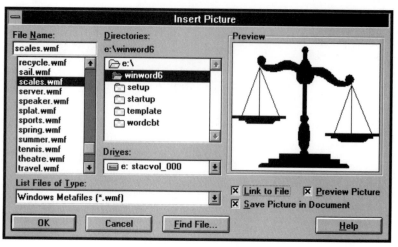

Figure 7-21: With the Link to File check box selected, the Scales graphic remains current as another user on the network makes changes to it.

Manual updates

Linked objects automatically update to reflect changes in the original (unlike embedded objects, where updating must be achieved manually).

After the link is established, any changes Joe makes to the graphic are reflected in Gail's document, even changes made on another machine on the network. If Gail's document is inactive when Joe makes his changes, Gail's document will reflect those changes the next time it's opened. If Gail's document is open when Joe modifies the graphic, Gail's document can be configured to update automatically the moment Joe saves. Although this process may be a little disconcerting—watching a document change on your screen without your intervention can be unnerving—it certainly beats the sneaker network.

Establishing a Link

As is the case with embedding, you can establish a link in two ways: insert or paste. To insert a linked graphic, choose Picture from the Insert menu; then locate the graphic to be linked using the dialog box pictured in Figure 7-21. Be sure to turn on the Link to File option and then click on OK.

Here's an example: working in Excel, you select the chart or the worksheet range that's to be linked and choose Copy from Excel's Edit menu. Back at Word, you select Paste Special from Word's Edit menu. The resulting dialog box (see Figure 7-22) offers two options; "Picture" will paste the data in the form of a graphic. If you want a link, you would click on the Paste Link button (rather than the Paste button).

Button's dead?

If the Paste Link button is dimmed, the originating application isn't aware of OLE and you'll have to insert the graphic (rather than paste it; use the Insert command on the menu) if you want a link.

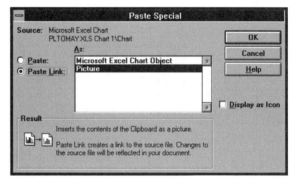

Figure 7-22: An Excel worksheet is about to be linked into a Word document. The Paste Link button will do the job.

Links established via the Paste Link method can be updated either manually or automatically. With the linked graphic selected, choose Links from the Edit menu. The linked graphic's filename will be selected. If you want linking to be automatic, be sure to activate Update: Automatic (toward the lower left-hand corner of Figure 7-23).

Locking links

Occasionally, you may want to "freeze" a link, preventing manual or automatic updates. Perhaps your document is to be archived for record-keeping purposes (you'd hardly want its contents to change under these circumstances). Whatever the reason, choose Locked in the Edit-Links dialog box. Once locked, the graphic won't update until you unlock it.

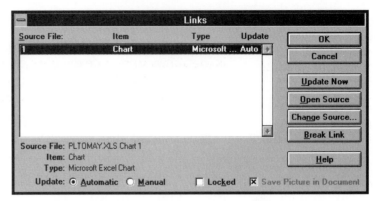

Figure 7-23: The Edit-Links dialog box provides for either manual or automatic updating of the linked document.

While automatic updating assures that your document is always current, it also removes some of your control over the document. You may elect to change the link to manual so that you can tell Word when to update, rather than have Word do it automatically.

Manage links thoughtfully
Word loses track of embedded or linked objects should you modify the object files' attributes. If you change a linked file's name or location, you have to reestablish its link within the destination Word document.

Updating Links

You can manually update any individual link by selecting the appropriate graphic and pressing F9 (Update field). If you want to update several graphics, choose Links from the Edit menu and hold down Ctrl as you click on each graphic you want to update. Conclude the command by clicking on the Update Now button. To update all the graphics in a document, select the entire document (choose Select All from the Edit menu) and then press F9. Updating your graphics can take a while, so Word keeps you entertained with a percent-complete message across the bottom of the screen. Update before you print a graphic-laden document: it provides a convenient method of checking to see whether all your graphics files are where Word expects them to be.

Saving Disk Space

Switching between applications
When you're editing a link, you'll probably need to switch between Word and the originating application. In addition to the Task List, Windows cycles among all open applications whenever you press Alt-Tab. Without releasing the Alt key, keep tapping on the Tab key until you see the originating application's name on the screen. Release the Tab key and you're there.

Another advantage to linking rather than embedding objects is the ability to reduce the file size. When objects are initially linked or embedded, the size of the Word document increases proportionately to the size of the object. This size increase can make the document so large that it can be unmanageable. To prevent oversized documents from happening, you can specify that Word store the link only, and not the entire object. As long as the source file for the object is available, Word displays a picture of the object even though it is not storing the object itself in the file. If the source is not available, a placeholder will be displayed, and the object cannot be printed.

To save disk space when you're linking, follow the previous steps for linking an object. Then select the object and choose Links from the Edit menu. In the Links dialog box, select the link. Clear the Save Picture in Document check box and then click OK.

FORMATTING GRAPHICS

After you've pasted or inserted a graphic into a Word document, provisions are made for page composition, including reduction, enlargement, cropping and placement. Considering the fact that Word really isn't a page-composition program, these controls are quite comprehensive, rivaling those of many stand-alone desktop-publishing programs.

Sizing, Cropping & Borders

Inserting graphics at their actual size is only half the task. Once you see a graphic in context, you may find it too big, too small or inappropriately framed. Fortunately, Word offers the tools to correct the situation.

You can select any graphic by clicking on it with the mouse. Selected graphics are surrounded by eight small black boxes, one at each corner, one on each side, one at the top and one at the bottom (see Figure 7-24). These so-called handles provide interactive control over the graphic's size and cropping.

Figure 7-24: Eight black "handles" surround a selected graphic.

Sizing Graphics

You can enlarge or reduce graphics, maintaining their original proportions; or you can stretch or compress them, distorting their original proportions. By dragging on a corner handle (any one of the four will do), you create proportional enlargement or reduction. Watch the lower left-hand corner of the screen as you do: Word will display the percentage of enlargement or reduction as you drag.

If you drag on a side, top or bottom (rather than a corner) handle, Word will enlarge or reduce the graphic *in one dimension only*, distorting the graphic's original aspect ratio. This capability is especially convenient when you must size a border to fit a particular need, something we've done with the Windows-like beveled borders used throughout this book (see Figure 7-25).

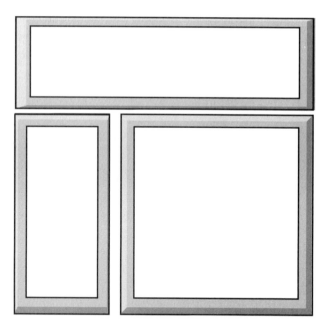

Figure 7-25: My original square border appears at the lower right. The aspect ratios of the other two borders have been changed by dragging on their side handles.

Alternatively, you can issue sizing commands by selecting the graphic and choosing Picture from the Format menu. This procedure can be particularly convenient when you know the exact size you want for a graphic and don't want to go to the trouble of computing its percentage of enlargement or reduction. If your original graphic measures 35.87 picas wide, for instance, and you want it to fit a space that's exactly 24 picas wide, select the graphic and type in its new width in the Format-Picture dialog box. Word will compute the percentage of reduction for you (see Figure 7-26). Specify that reduction for the graphic's height as well, and you've avoided a heap of math. (Okay, maybe not a *heap*, but avoiding *any* math is a good thing for some of us.)

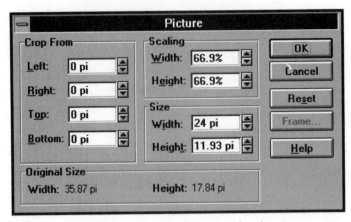

Figure 7-26: To determine the percentage of reduction necessary to fit a 35.87-pica graphic into a 24-pica space, enter the 24-pica width in the Size-Width text box, let Word compute the percentage of reduction (66.9%) and then match that figure in the Scaling-Height text box.

Cropping Graphics

You can crop graphics in the same way you size them, with the simple addition of the Shift key. Dragging on a corner handle with Shift held down crops a graphic in two dimensions, maintaining its original proportions. Dragging on a side, top or bottom handle with Shift held down crops in that direction only (see Figure 7-27).

Figure 7-27: Wanting just a bust of the Chaplin caricature, I cropped the original (left) by dragging on the bottom handle with the Shift key held down. I then enlarged the cropped graphic by dragging on a corner handle without using the Shift key (right).

Watch that cursor!

Word's cursor offers significant clues as it passes over a selected graphic: a four-headed arrow indicates that the graphic is a frame, and you may position it by dragging (more about frames in a moment). A two-headed diagonal arrow indicates that you can size or crop the graphic proportionately using a corner handle. A two-headed horizontal or vertical arrow indicates a side handle, which sizes or crops disproportionately.

A unique feature offered by Word is—for lack of a better term—*reverse cropping*. This feature is especially useful when a graphic is surrounded by a border (more about borders next). I used Word's Border command to frame the left graphic in Figure 7-28 but found the overall effect to be too tight. The graphic needed some breathing room. The solution was to reverse-crop the graphic: I simply held down Shift as I pulled the graphic's side handles *away* from center. Word complied by adding more white space around the graphic, moving the border away from center.

Figure 7-28: I provided a little more breathing room around the lower butterfly by "reverse cropping" the graphic.

Borders

You may place a Word border around any object, whether it be inserted, linked or embedded. Using the cropping feature mentioned previously, you can set the border's distance from the graphic with a simple drag of the mouse.

Word offers 11 border patterns (12, if you include None), and each can be shadowed. You declare these options either by first selecting the graphic and then choosing Borders and Shading from the Format menu or using the Border toolbar (see Figure 7-29).

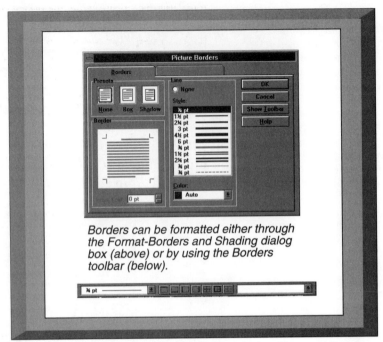

Figure 7-29: The Format-Picture Borders dialog box and Border toolbar. Eleven border formats may each be shadowed. Cells and frames can be shaded; all shades and borders can be colored.

If the selected object is text, a table or a frame (we'll discuss frames in the following pages), it may further be attributed with any of 25 shades or patterns. All borders and shades may be colored. That's quite a selection: literally thousands of combinations of borders, shades, colors, patterns and shadows are possible.

The most common use for borders may be associated with initial capital letters. Because Word doesn't offer text wrapping around irregularly shaped objects, using an initial cap such as *T* poses a design problem: ideally we would like to wrap text around the arm and stem of the *T* independently—an irregularly shaped wrap outline. Because Word doesn't offer that option, the solution is a border around the *T* (see Figure 7-30).

Figure 7-30: Because Word can't wrap text around the arm and stem of the *T* independently, a border provides the rectangular outline necessary to accommodate the limitation.

In the interest of design unity, adopt a border pattern that complements your document: a simple border for a simple design, a complex border for a complex design. Use the border consistently. But before you use it at all, always, always, subject it to challenge: "Why am I using this border here? What is its purpose?" Borders certainly have a place in many documents, but Word's exceptional offering can make them a little too alluring.

In-Line & Independent Graphics

In keeping with the linear word-processing nature of Word documents (discussed in Chapter 1, "Is This Really Desktop Publishing?"), all Word graphics are in-line. In-line graphics are essentially individual characters within the text of a document. Though they're occasionally placed in the midst of a sentence (again Equation Editor fractions come to mind), they more often are given a paragraph to themselves.

The important characteristic of in-line graphics is that as characters they are in line with (they line up with) the characters on either side of them—just as the *a*'s in the word *character* are in line with the rest of the letters in the word. If you edit this chapter by inserting, say, another sentence at the beginning of this paragraph, then the *a*'s in *character* would relocate within the paragraph along with the rest of the word.

Although this characteristic seems self-evident, many desktop-publishing programs are just the opposite. Let's say that a company wants to use its graphical logo rather than the the name of the company in the body of its promotional literature. Using Word, all they have to do is paste or insert. The logo becomes part of the text at the insertion point—just another character, as far as Word is concerned. If text ahead of this graphic is edited, the graphic moves with the text on either side of it.

Most desktop-publishing programs, on the other hand, are more like Draw: graphics are independent of text, they float above text on their own layer. Graphics remain stationary on the page regardless of any textual editing. If you want to move a graphic, get an object tool and move it. It's not going to move otherwise, even if you edit the text with which it's associated.

Neither the in-line nor the independent method is better than the other. Each has its advantages and disadvantages. They are just different—philosophically different—and that difference, as I mentioned in Chapter 1, is the primary distinction between word-processing programs and desktop-publishing programs.

Frames

If in-line graphics were all Word had to offer, it would have to be excluded from the province of desktop publishing. It would just be too inflexible. Occasionally, it becomes necessary to have independent positional control over elements in a document. We want what desktop publishing offers: some kind of an object tool (as opposed to the I-beam) to drag graphics around the page. Moreover, we want text to wrap around the graphic: above, below, to the right and to the left.

While this flexibility is a rather tall order for a word-processing program, Word nonetheless complies with a feature called *frames*. Although the concept of frames at first may seem elusive, it makes perfectly good sense once you encounter the need for a movable graphic. In fact, that's all frames are: tools to convert in-line graphics into independent graphics. After you've framed an object, you may reposition it on the page by simply dragging it with the mouse (see Figure 7-31).

Figure 7-31: The header and footer are both inserted graphics. After you've framed them, you may position them anywhere on the page by dragging them about with the mouse.

By the way, don't associate the word *frame* with *border*. Although framed objects can or don't have to have borders, the word is better associated with framing a house; giving the house the capability to stand on its own. That's exactly what frames do for objects.

Establishing a Frame

Probably the most common method of making a frame is to begin with a graphic that has already been inserted into a document. Then, with the graphic selected, choose Frame from the Insert menu. If you're in Page Layout View (something Word encourages you to do when you insert a frame), the screen will rewrite with the frame selected and (probably) text flowing around it. If you're in Normal View, a small black box will appear to the left of the graphic, signaling that it's framed. Either way, the graphic is now ready to be cropped, sized or positioned on the page.

Alternatively, you may choose Frame from the Insert menu without first selecting a graphic. In this case, Word provides a small crosshair cursor and expects you to draw an empty frame border in the location where you want the frame to appear. Draw the border, release the mouse, and there's your frame. If you leave the frame selected and choose Picture (or Object) from the Insert menu, Word will insert the item within the frame and size the frame to match the size of the object. This empty-frame method is best done in Page Layout View: inserting an empty frame while in Normal View produces unpredictable results.

Positioning Frames

Now's the fun part. To position a frame on the page, switch to Page Layout View (View menu) and then zoom to show the whole page on the screen. Choose Zoom from the View menu and then click on the Whole Page button (see Figure 7-32).

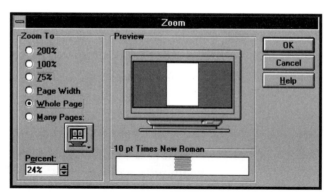

Figure 7-32: By clicking on the Whole Page button in the Zoom dialog box, the entire page appears on the screen, allowing you to position frames in context with a simple click and drag.

Paragraph association

Unless you tell Word otherwise, frames are "anchored" to a specific paragraph within the text. If you press and drag a frame, an anchor will appear, indicating the paragraph that frame is associated with. When you're making adjustments to the Format-Frame dialog box, be aware of the paragraph with which the frame is associated. If you can't see the anchor, click the Show/Hide ¶ button on the Standard toolbar.

With the entire page showing on the screen, all you need do is move the mouse pointer to the frame, where the pointer will change to a four-headed arrow. When it does, press on the left mouse button and drag the frame to its intended location. When you release the mouse, the page will recompose to accommodate the frame's new location.

This way of working with frames is the most intuitive; and for most of us, it may be the only way we'll ever use them. Word offers additional degrees of control (described in the next section), but don't feel you're missing something because frame-dragging is so easy. It *is* easy. It's hard on Word, but it's easy on us. This is as it should be; let the computer do the work.

You can size, crop and border frames using all the commands previously mentioned in this section.

Aligning Frames With a Reference Point

Dragging frames on the page as I've just described fixes the frame's position relative to the paragraph it's associated with. Although this capability is in keeping with Word's linear nature, it's not exactly what I had in mind when I began this discussion of independent, framed objects. If you drag the frame to the bottom of the page, for instance (as I've done with the footer in Figure 7-31), it will be associated with the last paragraph on the page. If editing causes the last paragraph to move down the page, the frame moves down the page as well. If the edit moves the last paragraph to the top of the next page, the frame moves there too. Whereas having the frame move makes sense for some graphics, it's hardly appropriate for the footer in the illustration.

To correct the situation, we must associate the frame with something other than a paragraph. This problem opens up a somewhat oppressive can of worms, represented by the Format-Frame dialog box shown in Figure 7-33.

Anchors away

See that Lock Anchor check box? Because frames and Drawing objects are always attached to a paragraph, checking this option is the way to keep something on the same page as a particular paragraph yet have its own position on the page. For example, if you wanted a picture to always be in the bottom right corner of the page but still on the page with a particular paragraph, position the picture, drag its anchor to the paragraph to associate it with and lock the anchor in that position through the Format-Frame dialog box.

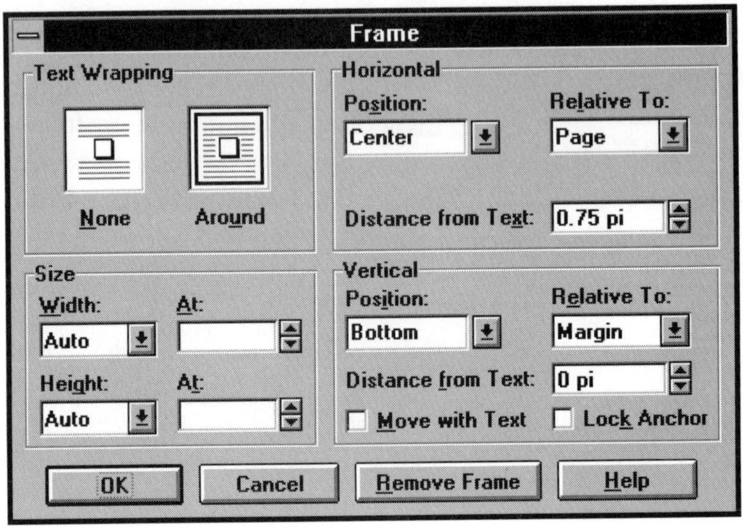

Figure 7-33: The Format-Frame dialog lets you locate frames relative to a page, margin, column or paragraph.

To correct Figure 7-31's floating-footer potential, we should position the footer relative to the *page* (and the bottom margin) rather than a paragraph. We did the same for the header, changing only the Vertical Position to Top, Relative to Margin. Both graphics are positioned at the horizontal center, relative to the page.

Assuming that the graphic has been framed and dragged into position, here's what's involved in granting it positional independence:

✔ Select the graphic.

✔ Choose Frame from the Format menu.

✔ Turn off the Move with Text option.

Note that the Relative To text box within the vertical section now reads Page. The graphic will now stay put, regardless of textual editing.

You can position frames relative to a page, a margin, a column or a paragraph. Combined with some of Word's other features, frames positioned this way can provide formatting capabilities even some desktop-publishing programs can't match.

Consider the document pictured in Figure 7-34. Using frames and Word's facing-page feature, the check-mark graphics can automatically follow the paragraphs with which they're associated and automatically "mirror" as they move from, say, a left-facing page to a right-facing one.

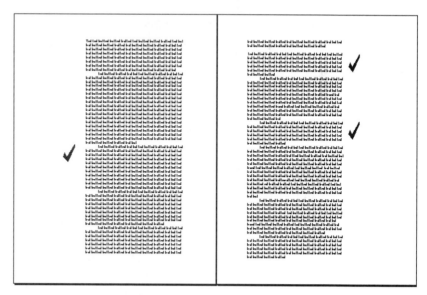

Figure 7-34: Using frames positioned relative to the text, the check marks move with their respective paragraphs when the document is edited. When facing pages are in effect, frames automatically are mirrored on left- and right-facing pages.

Here's how I did it:

✔ In the Page Setup dialog box (File menu), I specified mirror margins and a 3-inch outside margin.

✔ I got the check mark from Word's clip art and then inserted it into the text (it didn't matter where; I knew it would be moved anyway).

✔ Selecting the graphic, I inserted a frame (Insert menu).

✔ In the Format-Frame dialog box, I specified a horizontal position relative to the outside of the page ("outside" makes more sense when mirror margins are in effect) and a vertical position relative to the paragraph. I then turned on the Move with Text option (see Figure 7-35).

✔ To create additional check marks, I simply selected the frame, copied it (Edit menu) and pasted it at the beginning of each appropriate paragraph.

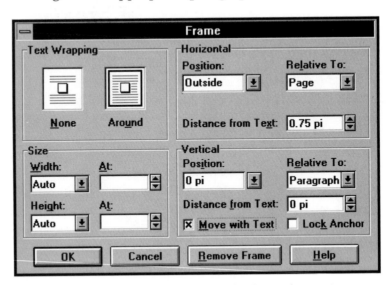

Figure 7-35: This dialog box describes the frame formatting necessary to provide the automatic mirrored frames pictured in Figure 7-34.

Let's examine another example. Consider the two-column layout of Figure 7-36.

Figure 7-36: Two frames embellish this two-column layout. The initial cap is positioned relative to the top margin; the pull-quote is positioned relative to the column.

Both the initial cap and the pull-quote are bordered by frames. The initial cap was framed automatically with Word's Format-Drop Cap option. I specified a relatively tight (1/4 pica) text wrap to bring the cap and its associated paragraph into close proximity (see Figure 7-37). Note that if we look specifically at the formatting Word set on the frame, it is located on the page relative to the column and margin only; it doesn't move with text.

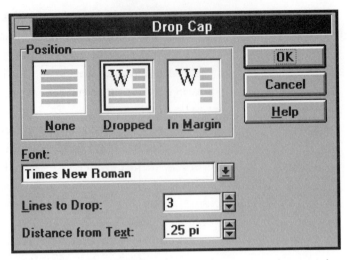

Figure 7-37: The Format-Drop Cap dialog box for the initial cap. Note that this feature does all the work for me, including set the distance from the text as I specify.

I created the pull-quote by framing text entered in Word. Its Format-Frame dialog box (see Figure 7-38) positions it horizontally relative to the center of its column and in the vertical center of the page. I then added a border to the top and bottom.

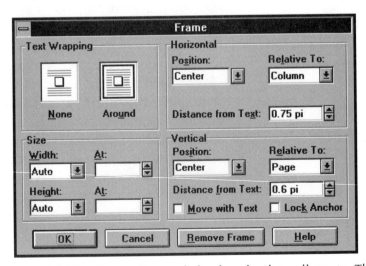

Figure 7-38: The Format-Frame dialog box for the pull-quote. The quote is positioned relative to the column and the page.

As I review the past few paragraphs, I'm reminded of the instruction manual that arrived with my VCR. Mastery of VCR recording is achieved only by an Enlightened Few. The rest of us just muddle along, finding delight in the occasional successes that punctuate endless failures. Formatting frames can be like that.

Earlier in this chapter, I defined frames as tools to convert in-line graphics into independent objects. That's really all they are; you needn't feel as if you've been derelict in your duty as a desktop publisher if all you ever do with frames is drag them around in Whole Page View. The Format-Frame dialog box offers extraordinary control, but it's not a level of control everyone needs; nor is it a level of control everyone has time to master. And once in a while, when you least expect it, you'll actually make the thing work. Just like your VCR.

Text Wrap

If you allow text to flow around a frame, the Format-Frame dialog box lets you declare how far that text "stands off" from the frame.

The pull-quote in Figure 7-36 illustrates the need for this control. Whenever you prepare a multicolumn document, you must pay attention to *baseline alignment*: the baseline of each line of text must line up with baselines in adjoining columns.

The challenge occurs when you insert the pull-quote into the right column. Though the baselines above it are aligned (Word took care of that automatically), there's no guarantee the baselines below it will align. This alignment we have to attend to ourselves, and the most convenient method is by adjusting the vertical Distance from Text in the Format-Frame dialog box (see Figure 7-38). Setting this alignment is a matter of trial and error; you just have to keep at it until things line up. The difference may seem inconsequential, but it's one of those little touches that separates care from neglect.

WARM THE OVEN & POUR THE MILK

Our recipe for chocolate-chip cookies has concluded. Like that in *Joy of Cooking*, ours turned out to be resplendent with unexpected ingredients: Draw, WordArt, Graph, the Equation Editor, frames, borders, OLE, rasters and vectors. Word offers a rich and complex potential for graphical embellishments, matched by no other word-processing program today. Microsoft has stocked our cupboards well.

8

Fonts & Printers

Portia's puzzle
Portia, Shakespeare's heroine in *The Merchant of Venice*, had her suitors choose among three closed caskets. If a suitor chose the right one (which contained her portrait), she would marry him. One casket was made of gold, one of silver and one of lead—a symbol of poverty. The lead casket contained the portrait. The victor was the one who disregarded pretense for the true value within.

In the Renaissance and Middle Ages, there lived a cadre of souls—alchemists, as they were called—who firmly believed that base metals could be turned into gold. Many of them dedicated their lives to the pursuit of that singular goal (short lives, actually: most died of lead poisoning). What futility! Sage and sagacious modern men, we regard the alchemists with pity and disdain, and interpret their discipline as one of vanity and greed.

This attitude is likely to be advocated from the lofty perspective of the office hallway, where modern man spends at least 10 percent of his day venerating a mystical cube, attending to it in apparent reverence, trancelike in his supplication of the prophet therein. Minutes pass and the prophet speaks, appropriately in a whisper of sibilance and susurration. The prophecy emerges neatly printed in 10-point Times on common bond, still warm from its journey.

The supplicant retrieves the benediction and retreats in deference, never once considering the metaphysics that went on within the cube, or comparing them to the alchemy which he so hypocritically disdains.

With the supplicant departed, the cube resumes its quiet meditation, ceaselessly repeating its mantra. Its surfaces are unmarred except for two words, subtly printed upon a single surface: "Hewlett-Packard."

Printers are that way, you know. We used to be able to look inside them and see little wheels going around and inked ribbons passing by. Now there seem to be no moving parts, just the silent scan of a synthetic laser, photoelectrostatically imaging words that once were impressed with all the subtlety of a hammer and die.

Back to the matrix
When you stop to think about it, laser printers are dot-matrix printers. No matter how sophisticated the image, a laser printer composes it entirely with a matrix of dots. This page was composed that way, as are just about all the pages produced today.

In fact, things haven't changed that much. Though we think of dot-matrix printers as passé, virtually all printers used today are just that: dot matrix. A laser printer may seem to be mystical, but it remains a glorified dot-matrix printer, producing microscopic dots imperceptible to the unaided human eye, but dots just the same. Keep this perspective in mind as we pursue the following discussion of fonts and printers.

BITMAPPED CHARACTER DEFINITIONS

Another basic consideration you may want to keep in mind is that all characters have to be defined somewhere. Computers and printers don't intrinsically know how to form an *A*, for instance. Somewhere, all the strokes and curves that comprise the letter *A* have to be described and stored.

Wherever they're stored, characters (fonts) may be defined in one of two ways. The ensuing discussion is going to sound familiar: as it's now interpreted, text is nothing more than a special form of graphics; and graphics, as you know, may either be raster or vector.

Raster text, or *bitmapped* text, as it is commonly called, has been around since the first dot-matrix printer. Originally, printer fonts were all stored in the form of a dot pattern, or matrix, within the printer. The matrix was nothing but a series of dots, each dot precisely the size of the pins on the printer's print head (see Figure 8-1). When the computer called for an *A*, the printer looked up the matrix for the letter *A* and printed it.

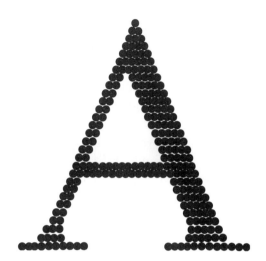

Figure 8-1: A bitmapped letter *A* may be convenient for the hardware, but its inflexibility renders it unsuitable for desktop publishing.

Though this kind of technology was convenient for hardware manufacturers, it represented a number of inflexibilities for the desktop publisher:

✔ The dot pattern stored in the printer didn't necessarily match the dot pattern on the screen. What you saw had nothing to do with what you got.

✔ Separate patterns had to be stored not only for each font and character in the font, but also for each size that might be printed.

✔ Because the pattern was stored in the printer, it was unique to that brand and model of printer. An entirely different image appeared if the document was printed on another kind of printer.

✔ Fancy stuff—rotated characters, colored characters— simply wasn't supported.

Sound old-fashioned? Though it is, bitmapped text is just now fading from the desktop-publishing scene. In fact, bitmapped fonts reached their apex of popularity when font cartridges first appeared for the Hewlett-Packard LaserJet II in the spring of 1987.

No PARCing

We have a lot of reasons for thanking the Palo Alto Research Center (PARC), a think tank jointly sponsored by Xerox Corporation and Stanford University. In the mid-1970s, the minds at PARC came up with an all-points-addressable photocopier that Xerox could use for the high-speed printing of business forms. The copier used a tiny laser beam and computer memory to construct its image. Sound familiar? Xerox funded the research that not only lead to the laser printer, but to the mouse, the graphical interface and the PostScript page-description language.

OUTLINE CHARACTER DEFINITIONS

At about the same time, users of Apple Macintosh systems were printing characters of any size, rotation and color using their LaserWriter PostScript printers. Though I won't describe PostScript character definitions quite yet, the primary difference was in the font-rendering technology itself: Apple used vector-based font descriptions.

Vector-based (or outline) fonts ask more of the machine but provide in return more flexibility for the operator. Rather than represent a character as a series of dots, vector fonts represent the character as a series of lines and arcs (see Figure 8-2). Only one definition is required per character per font, regardless of size. To increase or decrease point size, all the computer has to do is multiply (or divide) the length of each line and the radius of each arc.

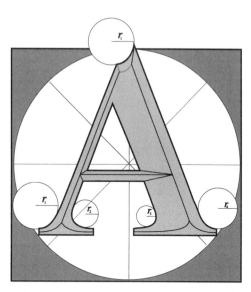

Figure 8-2: Outline-definition fonts offer the flexibility required by desktop-publishing applications.

All this multiplying and dividing sounds like a tremendous amount of work and it is, but it's the kind of work computers love. It's all math—number crunching—and computers love numbers. Even the earliest Apple LaserWriters could resize an entire font (256 characters) in less time than it took to say "Hewlett-Packard."

After the outline is generated, the computer has to fill it in with—you guessed it—dots. Though this task may again seem to be a chore, computers do it instantaneously.

Naturally, the computer can fill in the outline with any color available, and character rotation amounts to nothing more than changing the angle of the lines—again something computers can do in an instant. Indeed, outline definitions can be skewed, compressed, colored, rotated and sized indefinitely (see Figure 8-3).

Figure 8-3: The flexibility afforded by outline-character definitions is nearly infinite.

The superiority of outline-definition font technology is undeniable, and bitmapped fonts are used only where their speed (and they are fast) is essential: on the screen. For those situations where font immediacy is critical—menus and dialog boxes in particular—bitmapped fonts still reign supreme. But when it comes to putting ink on paper, bitmapped fonts are a vestige of printer technology history.

WHERE FONTS ARE STORED

Two options are available for storing font information: the printer or the computer. The industry has tried both and failed to settle on either one. Each has its advantages and disadvantages; neither is inherently superior. This lack of clear-cut superiority has fostered printer and font anarchy that pervades our industry today. Undoubtedly, there's a solution, but until it's discovered, the issue of font storage will remain a conundrum.

As we weigh the merits of each strategy, forget about bitmapped or outline technologies. With regard to font storage, it makes little difference how the character is constructed. Bitmapped or outlined, the font has to be defined and stored somewhere; that's our subject of discussion at the moment.

Storing Fonts in the Printer

Bitmapped font cartridges

In fact, LaserJet font cartridges are an extension of built-in font technology. Rip one open someday and look inside: ROM chips are what you'll see, ROM chips containing bitmapped font definitions. That's why old LaserJets offer so few size choices, even with bitmapped font cartridges installed.

The original printers were modified electric typewriters and Teletype machines. In either case, the fonts were stored mechanically in the form of mirror-image castings, not unlike the movable-type stamps described in Chapter 2, "Body Type." With the advent of dot-matrix printers, font definitions became electronic (rather than mechanical) and were stored in read-only memory (ROM) chips within the printer.

The one undeniable advantage of storing fonts in the printer is communication. If the computer wants the printer to print an *A*, all it has to do is ask for an *A*. Because the printer knows what an *A* is, it complies, supplying all the details locally. Essentially, only one byte has to be communicated: the byte that says "A."

On the other hand, if the computer retains the font definition, it has to construct the dot-matrix image locally and then send each of the individual dots to the printer, one-by-one. If you're printing on a 300-dpi printer, the printer has to communicate 90,000 dots per square inch of paper surface. An 8 1/2- by 11-inch page contains about 80 square inches of printable area, for a total of 7.2 million dots.

This communication of millions of dots could be a communications nightmare. No wonder so many printers contain their own font definitions.

Built-In Fonts

As I mentioned earlier, most printers store a selection of fonts in ROM inside the printer. ROM chips are typically soldered in place, and because they *are* read-only, their contents aren't subject to change. To make matters worse, most built-in fonts are bitmapped and the number of available sizes is limited.

On the other hand, some printers contain built-in *outline-font* definitions. Because of their technical superiority, outline fonts impose few limitations on size. We're closing in on the best of both worlds here: quick communication and infinite font sizing. But we're not finished. Read on.

Soft Fonts

Built-in fonts—bitmapped or outline—are nonetheless built in. Eventually, you're going to run across a document printed in Garamond or Bodoni, and you're just going to have to have that font. If you're limited to built-in fonts, you're out of luck.

Meeting your needs for new fonts is how new printers are sold.

It's also how they sell *soft fonts*: font definitions available on a disk you download to your printer when you need to use them. They're called *soft* to differentiate them from fonts stored in ROM. ROM-based information is hard-coded, as they say. You can't change it. You can change information stored in RAM—random-access memory. It's not *hard-coded*, so it must be soft.

I'm trying to explain it, not defend it.

So how do you download a soft font to a printer? You use a font-downloading program. These simple little programs (at least from the user's perspective) establish contact with the printer and send font data to it at your command. You may use either the font-downloading utility furnished with Windows (see Figure 8-4) or the one included with your soft-font package (see Figure 8-5), whichever is appropriate.

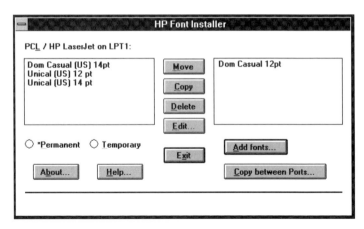

Figure 8-4: Windows provides this downloading utility for the installation of bitmapped fonts into HP printers.

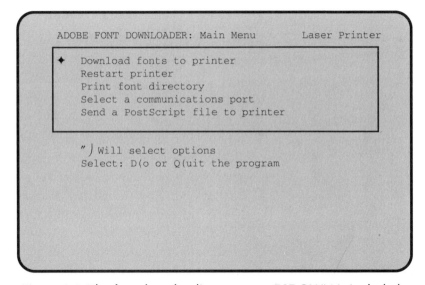

Figure 8-5: The font-downloading program PSDOWN is included in the purchase of all Adobe PostScript (outline) soft fonts.

A soft font can either be temporary (downloaded when needed and removed from the printer's memory after the document is printed) or permanent (stays in the printer's memory until you turn off the printer). Permanently downloaded fonts print more quickly because the downloading process occurs only once before printing gets underway. On the other hand, a font that remains in memory after it's no longer needed is a memory hog. Unless the printer contains lots of memory, permanently downloaded fonts are often unacceptably inefficient.

One solution is to connect a hard disk to the printer. Once downloaded to a printer's hard disk, soft fonts are almost like built-in fonts: they require no random-access memory, are always available and don't require any of your attention.

Storing Fonts in the Computer

Soft fonts are probably the least expensive, most flexible method of manipulating font information between computer and printer. You buy them as you need them, you buy only those you need, and you spend your money on software (fonts) only: no hardware (cartridge) is required.

Of course, using soft fonts necessitates using a printer capable of accepting them. Such a printer must contain ample RAM (two to four megabytes is common), perhaps a hard disk, and a brain capable of accepting and using soft-font data. In other words, these printers require a computer on board, and computers aren't cheap.

Economically speaking, dumb (brainless) printers are the best way to go. A number of dumb laser printers are on the market in the $500 price range, and an increasing number of dumb ink-jet printers are available for half that price. The print quality of these printers—laser or ink-jet—is as good as (sometimes better than) smart laser printers that sell in the $1,000 to $5,000 price range (see Figure 8-6).

Apple's most sophisticated "computer"
When the original Apple LaserWriter was introduced in 1985, Steve Jobs (co-founder of Apple Computer) proclaimed that the LaserWriter was the most complex *computer* that Apple had ever made. Indeed it was: it used a more powerful processor and could accept more memory than any personal computer on the market at the time.

> Economically speaking, dumb (brainless) printers are the best way to go. There are a number of dumb laser printers on the market in the $500 price range, and an increasing number of dumb ink-jet printers are available for half that price. The only compromise is the brain, for the print quality of these printers—laser or ink-jet—is as good (sometimes better) than smart laser printers that sell in the $1,000 - $5,000 price range.

Figure 8-6: 360-dpi output from the author's ink-jet printer. This printer cost just over $300 new, is about the size of a phone book and can be powered by batteries when no conventional power is available.

Spitting allowed

Ink-jet printers operate by literally spitting microscopic drops of ink at the page. At just the precise moment, a heating element boils the ink, causing a tiny bubble. The bubble creates pressure, which expels ink through a nozzle. Though the technology has been around since the 1960s, the problem of how to cap the nozzle—and keep the ink from clogging—when the printer is idle was not solved until a few years ago.

Unfortunately, dumb printers require that all processing occur within the computer. Even if outline font definitions are used, the "filling in" (rasterizing) process must occur at the computer, and a bitmap of each page has to be sent to the printer. This process takes time. The single paragraph in Figure 8-6 required over 20 seconds to rasterize and another 20 seconds to print. The 360-dpi bitmapped file that was sent to the printer measured nearly 100 kilobytes. Printing this entire chapter at 360 dpi requires almost an hour, and more than 15 megabytes of free disk space to store the page images for transmission.

Page-Description Languages

The next step in printer intelligence is the inclusion of a language. By imbuing the printer with a language that's common to both printer and computer, communication becomes almost exquisite. All the computer has to do is say "Print an A," and the printer takes it from there.

So how does this communication differ from built-in fonts? After all, if a font is built into a printer, all the computer has to do is say "Print an A" and the printer takes it from there.

Page-descripton languages have two primary advantages:

✔ The language can include words for graphics as well as text. As mentioned in Chapter 7, "Graphics," the vocabulary for graphic primitives is included in page-description languages, both raster and vector. Therefore, the phrase "draw a circle" is just as effective as the phrase "draw an A."

✔ Again as mentioned in the previous chapter, page-description languages are *machine independent*. You can say "Draw an A" to Sally or Fred, and both will understand what you mean. Similarly, a computer speaking a page-description language can say "Draw an A" to a desktop laser printer or to a Compugraphic imagesetter, and both understand what the computer means. This capability is especially significant in the desktop-publishing industry, where documents are often proofed on a local laser printer and then sent to an imagesetter for final output.

Of course, teaching a language to a printer is an expensive process. You're not only committing your money for memory and a brain, you also have to pay royalty fees (for using the language) and for the circuitry necessary to interpret it. Indeed, a printer that speaks a page-description language is not only the king of printers, it exacts a kingly toll as well.

FONT METRICS

No matter where or how fonts are stored, and no matter whether a language is involved, your system needs access to font *metrics* as much as it needs access to font definitions. You may recall our kerning discussion of Chapter 4, "Display Type," in particular the mention of automatic kerning. Automatic kerning implies that the output device must have a reference somewhere that tells it to kern pairs of characters such as *To* or *Wa*.

Now stop a minute. Look at the *Wa* pair again. Not all typefaces lean the arms of the *W*. ITC Bauhaus—a specialty face—comes to mind. The arms of its *W* are straight up and down. Look at Figure 8-7: a display face called Parisian appears at top; its *W* and *a* are kerned. Below the Parisian is Bauhaus; its *W* and *a* aren't kerned, and should not be.

Figure 8-7: If the arms of the *W* lean over, it's usually kerned, as in the Parisian type at top. If they don't, no kerning is required, as in the Bauhaus at bottom.

Metrics files also include information about the width of each letter and the height of the shoulder. As is the case with kerned pairs, this information is unique to each font. Here's my point: not only must you store letterforms, you must store font metrics as well, and you must communicate them to the printer as necessary.

Systems using the PostScript language, for example, contain a minimum of two files on disk for each font. The .PFB file contains the outline definitions, and the .PFM file contains the font metrics. If you're a PostScript user, look for these files in your PSFONTS subdirectory (see Figure 8-8).

WIN.INI fun

Users of PostScript systems will find a section in their WIN.INI file referring to their PostScript printer. Among other things, this section will refer to the name and location of the font metrics file for each font, something like: C:\PSFONTS\PFM\SI__.PFM. If the font has to be downloaded to a printer, however, Windows needs to know where the .PFB (font outlines) file is as well. If there are no references to it in your WIN.INI, use Notepad to add them. The example above should read: C:\PSFONTS\PFM\SI__.PFM, C:\PSFONTS\SI__.PFB (all on one line). It's a pity that semi-normal people are expected to learn this stuff. We would be just as happy swallowing swords or walking on coals.

Pair	Value
W y	-47
W u	-47
W semicolon	-16
W r	-71
W period	-94
W o	-94
W i	-55
W hyphen	-55
W e	-94
W comma	-94
W colon	-16
W a	-94
W A	-94

Figure 8-8: The *W* kerned pairs from the Palatino Roman font. All values are in thousandths of an em.

Although this book is not intended to serve as a technical reference to the labyrinthine conundrum of Windows fonts, I mention font metrics because you should be aware of them. Without them, your text would look *horrible*. Keep that in mind if you intend to print your document on another system.

THE PRINTERS OF DESKTOP PUBLISHING

Instant relic
Much of the credit for the desktop-publishing phenomenon goes to Paul Brainerd, founder of Aldus Corporation and publisher of PageMaker software. You'll find the 512k Macintosh upon which PageMaker was developed in a display case at Aldus head-quarters in Seattle, sealed in glass as if it were the Rosetta Stone. The machine is only about 10 years old.

If one single technical achievement is responsible for the advent of desktop publishing, it's the laser printer. In the early 1970s, Xerox Corporation saw a need for printing forms—*lots* of forms: Xerox wanted something like two pages a second from a single machine. Utility companies print forms in this quantity, as do insurance companies and direct-mail marketing firms. Because these forms would be printed with variable data filled in and every form would be unique, Xerox needed something more than a photocopier. It needed a *printer* capable of printing 120 pages per minute. Thus, the Palo Alto Research Center was funded, which eventually led to the model 9700 all-points-addressable printer. By the mid-1970s, Xerox had its printer, and desktop publishing had an embryo. Ten years passed before it reached the mass market, but the laser printer started it all.

Desktop Page Printers

I resist the urge to say "laser printers" in the subhead above because a number of today's high-quality desktop printers don't use lasers at all, but rather hundreds of tiny light-emitting diodes. Whatever the technology, these machines all have one thing in common: the photocopier anatomy that Xerox put there 20 years ago.

Hewlett-Packard LaserJets

Hewlett-Packard introduced the original LaserJet in 1984. Compared to the daisy-wheel printers of the day, it was a godsend: silent, capable of printing high-quality graphics and fast.

Introduced in 1991, the LaserJet III was the first generally available printer to offer *resolution enhancement*, or the ability to vary the size of its dots (see Figure 8-9).

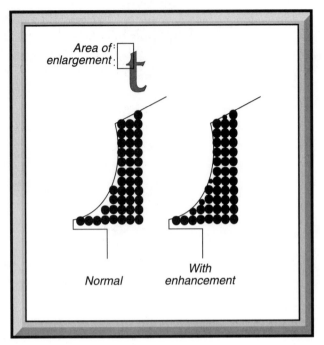

Figure 8-9: Resolution enhancement varies the size of the printer's dots to fill in between the gaps. Smoother text and graphics are the result.

Notice the smaller dots in the enhanced *t* in the figure. Though the printer still offers 300 dots per inch, its ability to print dots of varying size allows it to print intermediary dots and smooth some of the jaggies. The result is visibly better-looking text and graphics. Many contemporary laser printers now include this technology.

The LaserJet III also marked the introduction of PCL 5 (Printer Control Language 5), Hewlett-Packard's proprietary page-description language. PCL 5 includes rotatable outline-font definitions, vector graphics and automatic raster-image compression. Because PCL 5's fonts may be rotated, using a separate font for landscape and portrait orientation is no longer required. PCL 5's vector-graphic dialect is actually HP-GL/2, the Hewlett-Packard Graphics Language mentioned in Chapter 7, "Graphics." Many CAD and drawing programs offer this language as an output file format.

PCL is essentially composed of *escape sequences*. Many Lotus 1-2-3 users will recognize that term for commands preceded by the escape character (1-2-3 still uses escape codes to issue instructions to printers). Escape*b512W, for instance, tells the printer to be ready to accept 512 bytes of raster-image information.

PCL is not a full programming language. It offers no provision for conditionals (IF-THEN) or branches (GOTO), and escape sequences are nearly impossible to read or debug. PCL is also unique to Hewlett-Packard products and doesn't offer the machine independence mentioned earlier in this chapter.

PostScript Printers

Intellifont font scaling
Starting with the LaserJet III, Intellifont outline font scaling is used. This standard, developed by AGFA Compugraphic, is a primary competitor to PostScript (which is heartily supported by Linotype-Hell, AGFA Compugraphic's arch rival). Competition waged by prestigious international firms such as these can do nothing but improve the technology and reward the consumer.

Unlike PCL, PostScript is a true programming language, specialized for preparing text and graphics for printing. It began life in the dark ages of 1976, when it was born as the Design System at Evans & Sutherland Computer Corporation. There it served as an experimental language to build 3D graphics. After PARC (and JaM), it became known as Interpress, a Xerox printing protocol. PostScript itself was introduced in 1982.

PostScript nearly died of greed (an interesting death) in the late 1980s. Adobe encrypted PostScript font definitions in those days, meaning no one but Adobe could sell PostScript fonts. As PostScript gave indication of becoming the *de facto* standard and PostScript fonts dominated the industry, major players—Apple and Microsoft in particular, both of whom abhor market dominance by anyone other than themselves—decided to engineer an alternative. Moreover, they announced that the alternative (later to become TrueType) would not be encrypted, and that anyone could offer TrueType products without violation of copyright. As expected, Adobe's immediate reaction was to place the PostScript Type 1 font protocol in the public domain. Today, hundreds of vendors offer PostScript products—nearly 5,000 fonts are available from over 200 vendors—and prices are reasonable.

Unlike PCL, PostScript is truly machine independent, and offers superior desktop-publishing features, including support for halftone (grayscale) and color graphics.

Now that the greed component has been worked out of the system, PostScript's machine independence, superior features and market dominance are compelling arguments in its favor. Whereas the word processing, database and spreadsheet industries can get along very well without font and page-description standards, desktop publishing cannot. If you're serious about desktop publishing, PostScript is not an option: it's a necessity.

Imagesetters & Service Bureaus

PostScript LaserJets
Far from being left in the dust, LaserJet users have a wealth of PostScript add-ins (including cartridges) offering instant PostScript-compatibility. Coupled with image enhancement and HP's aggressive pricing, PostScript-equipped LaserJets are hard to beat.

Part of the reason I'm so adamant about PostScript is that someday you'll find it necessary to print a document on a high-resolution imagesetter (if you haven't already). Typically, these machines offer resolutions well beyond 2,000 dots per inch. Although these resolutions may not be critical for basic text-only applications, they take on particular significance when you incorporate shades of gray into the design.

Again let's refer to the layout on a page in the *Word for Windows User's Guide*. Picking a page with a sidebar, let's examine it for desktop page printer versus imagesetter suitability. If you lack access to the *User's Guide*, refer to the schematic in Figure 8-10.

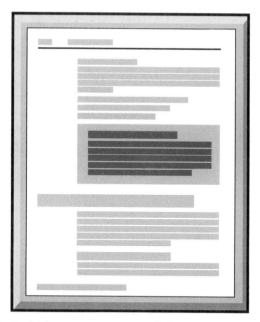

Figure 8-10: A sidebar appears toward the middle of a page in the *Word for Windows User's Guide.* Surprinted on a 20 percent screen, the sidebar would be illegible printed on a 300-dpi desktop page printer.

Word for the day

Those tiny dots above *i*'s and *j*'s (as well as the diacritical marks above foreign-language characters like â and ö) have a name: *tittles.* The word also means any small part or quantity, similar to a jot or a whit. Use *tittle* in conversation today.

A sidebar appears two-thirds of the way up the page, surprinted over a 20 percent screen (what Word calls a *shade*). Using a screen is a common method of identifying sidebars, and Word accommodates the need with the Shading options in the Format-Borders and Shading dialog box.

If the sidebar text appears in 10-point Times (or smaller), and were this text to be printed on top of a screen generated by a desktop page printer, details like serifs and the dots over the *i*'s simply wouldn't show up. That's because of the size of the dots that make up the screen. Whereas a 2,470-dpi imagesetter generates a screen frequency of about 150 lines (dots) per inch, the best a 300-dpi printer can do is about 60. In other words, each dot behind the text would measure more than a point across, capable of obliterating colons, periods and even quotes—all of which could appear within a sidebar (see Figure 8-11). Designs like this, in other words, must be printed on an imagesetter.

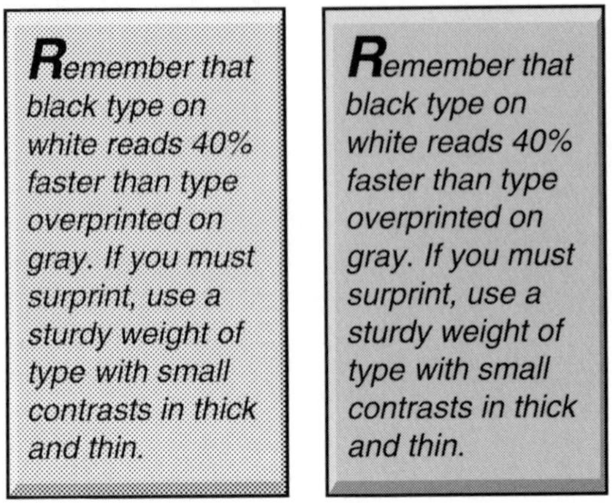

Figure 8-11: Ten-point Helvetica surprinted on a 20 percent shaded background is difficult to read when printed on a 300-dpi printer (left) but quite legible when printed on a high-resolution imagesetter (right).

The argument in favor of high-resolution imagesetters also applies to scanned grayscale graphics, large text and fonts with subtle curves (see Figure 8-12).

Figure 8-12: The subtle curves of Optima's *b*'s, *l*'s and *k*'s would be lost if they were printed on a 300-dpi printer.

Optima's elegant semi-serif design is primarily achieved via the use of subtle curves: its vertical and horizontal strokes are slightly dished, a characteristic that's completely lost in body-text sizes printed at 300 dpi.

In other words, plan to spend some time with a service bureau (imagesetters are too expensive for everyday office use), and you need to get to know your system accordingly.

Imagesetter Fonts

Most service bureaus use strictly Adobe PostScript. Few will print files prepared for another format, and few offer fonts other than Adobe's. If you're using PostScript fonts from another vendor, contact your service bureau ahead of time. Most service bureaus will have to download non-Adobe fonts (and some Adobe fonts as well, if they don't stock the entire Adobe library), which they'll ask you to provide on an as-needed basis. If you don't provide the fonts, the imagesetter will substitute whatever Adobe font it deems appropriate. It never is.

On the other hand, you may be fond of a typeface you don't have and don't want to buy but that is available on the service bureau's imagesetter. (Again Optima comes to mind: why buy it for a desktop printer when desktop printers don't print it well?) In this situation, obtain the bitmapped screen fonts only (generally available without charge: CompuServe or your service bureau can provide them). Bitmapped screen fonts are usually provided in three or four sizes: your system will approximate everything in between. In other words, bitmapped screen fonts can look awful. Don't worry about it. The imagesetter doesn't use screen fonts; it uses outline fonts stored on its hard disk. What's important are the font metrics, and all screen fonts contain accurate font metric information. Thus, the line and page breaks that appear on your screen will be matched by the printer.

Type Styles

Word's Formatting toolbar makes it easy for you to italicize or boldface a selection. You may recall, however, that some font families offer separate fonts for the italic and bold styles. Note that both the Futura and Garamond families in Figure 8-13 provide separate font selections for normal, italic, bold and bold italic. For instance, if you want to use Garamond Italic in the midst of a paragraph set in Garamond Light, you're best advised to select Garamond LightItalic from the font box shown in Figure 8-13 rather than click on the Italic button on the Formatting toolbar or use the keystroke equivalent.

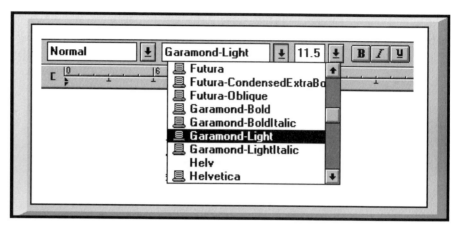

Figure 8-13: The Futura and Garamond font families appear within the font list. For absolute dependability, choose one of these fonts if you want italic, bold or bold italic.

Intolerance should not be tolerated

Many service bureaus use Macintosh equipment only. They might offer to print your file using Word for the Mac. Using the Mac to print Windows documents rarely works. Macintosh font metrics and hyphenation dictionaries often differ from those in Windows; thus, line and page breaks won't match. Characters above the ASCII range—things like the em dashes used here—are mapped differently, and some fonts are numbered differently as well. Try to find a service bureau that understands Windows and Word. Such a find is an invaluable resource.

To Word's credit (actually, to *Windows's* credit), if you *do* click the Italic button, Word checks to see whether the italic is available within the family. If the italic is available, Word switches to the italic font for you. Most of the time.

Which is the problem. You get into the habit of using the Formatting toolbar's buttons to declare fonts within a family, and the system doesn't make the appropriate font changes. Instead, it substitutes some other font, usually unrelated and usually unsuitable.

This substitution always happens when there's no italic (or bold) font within the family. The Caslon family, for instance, consists of four fonts, one of which is italic. Word uses the italic font when you click on the Italic button. The Caslon Open Face family, on the other hand, consists of one font only (as well it should, an italic is hardly appropriate—see Figure 8-14). Italicizing Caslon Open Face invariably provokes font bedlam—never a pretty sight.

CASLON OPEN FACE

Figure 8-14: The Gothic quality of Caslon Open Face makes it an unlikely candidate for an italic derivative, and none is offered.

Let's sum up this discussion. Eventually, you will find it necessary to print on an imagesetter. Some designs are served by no other means. However, because systems and WIN.INI files differ, surprises may await you. In anticipation of the need (and the surprise), find and visit the service bureau *before* you can feel the hot breath of an imminent deadline. The people at service bureaus are generally quite knowledge-able and easygoing, *unless* you make their acquaintance in a state of hysteria. They get plenty of that, and their tolerance of it is understandably thin.

Printing PostScript to a File

Exercise

Using the procedure described in the text, print a Word document as a PostScript file and then use Word to open the file. Look for the phrase "%%EndSetup." Your document begins just after that. Those who understand every word will be rewarded with propeller beanies.

Some service bureaus may not have Word or be familiar with it. If this is the situation, you may have to provide a PostScript file. As I mentioned earlier in this chapter, PostScript is a page-description language and is pure ASCII text. If you print PostScript to a file, you're simply generating a textual descrip-tion of your document, phrased in the PostScript language. In fact, you're redirecting Word's PostScript output: rather than sending it to the printer, you're sending it to your disk. You can then carry the disk to the service bureau where it will download the file to an imagesetter. The service bureau doesn't even need Word (or Windows, for that matter). As far as the printing process is concerned, Word and Windows never enter the picture.

Imagesetter drivers

If the imagesetter doesn't show up in the Print Setup dialog box as described in the text, you haven't installed its driver. Drivers, their acquisition and installation are discussed later in this chapter.

Word within Word

You may recall that I described an encapsulated PostScript file as containing a bit-mapped image of the PostScript data. Most do, but not those generated in this fashion. Though you can place these files into Word, all you'll see is a boundary box and the file name. They'll print satisfactorily on a PostScript printer, however. This method is the best way to include a picture of a Word document within another Word document, should you ever need to do so.

Refer to Figure 8-15 as I describe the process:

✔ Choose Print from the File menu. The Print dialog box appears.

✔ Turn on the Print to File check box.

✔ Click on the Printer button. The Print Setup dialog box appears.

✔ If the imagesetter isn't the selected printer, double-click on it.

✔ Click on the Close button in the Print Setup dialog box.

✔ In the Print dialog box, make changes as necessary and click OK when you're ready to print.

✔ Because we're printing to a file, Word requests a name for the file including a path. It suggests the .PRN extension, but you can customize the extension if you want.

✔ Click OK to print the document to a file.

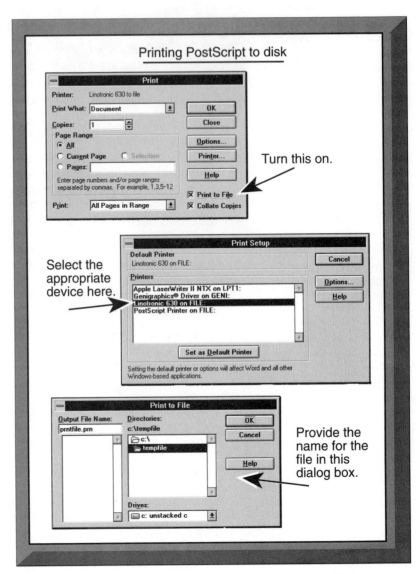

Figure 8-15: The sequence for printing to a PostScript file is convoluted and exacting.

The Advanced button in the imagesetter's Options dialog box provides a number of controls that may be of interest (see Figure 8-16). Having read this far into the book, you may even make sense of some of this information. Fortunately, this dialog has little to do with printing to a file. Discuss it with the people at your service bureau, however (which is why I provide the illustration). They may want you to make some changes before you generate the file.

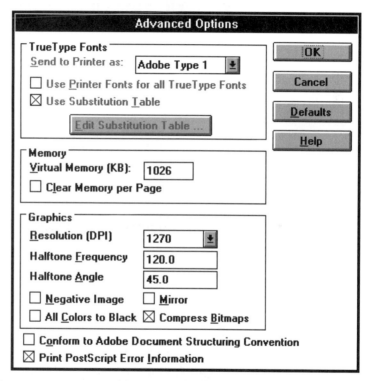

Figure 8-16: Discuss the Advanced Options imagesetter dialog box with your service bureau before printing PostScript to a file.

This discussion has been complex, I know. If you're feeling overwhelmed, remember only two things: 1) Imagesetter output is expensive, usually $8 to $15 per page; 2) Because errors are costly, you should develop your service bureau relationship early. Tell them exactly what software you are using on which system. Oblige their needs; give them plenty of time to complete the job when the time comes.

PRINTER DRIVERS

One of the beauties of the Windows environment is that it *is* an environment, and all applications running within this environment share common resources. These resources include fonts—in fact, most all the font discussions we've had so far really pertain to Windows, not Word—and drivers. Therefore, you only have to store these resources once on your disk, regardless of the number of applications you use. It also means that you only have to learn about them once, which is good because learning system-level resources isn't simple stuff.

Perhaps the most precise resource of them all is the *printer driver*. Drivers are miraculous and mystical little devices that take Windows's generic print output and massage it to meet the specific needs of your printer. These needs are very precise and diverse: PostScript, for instance, is pure ASCII text. Hewlett-Packard's PCL 5 is nothing other than escape sequences, whereas most dot-matrix printers expect binary code composed of ones and zeros.

Drivers are software—little programs that perform the conversion. Many computer programmers would rather write drivers than any other type of program: no users are involved to screw things up, and drivers are as close as a programmer can get to the purity of the machine. Drivers are the Holy Grail, and driver programmers are the Disciples in pursuit of its sanctity.

"Little" is relative
Our use of the word *little* to describe drivers is hardly warranted. The driver for Hewlett-Packard LaserJets is about 156k, and the PostScript driver now exceeds 320k—almost 10 times the size of WordArt, and equal to the size of Word itself when it was first introduced.

Using the Proper Driver

You make the driver selection by opening the File menu and choosing Print, Printer (see Figure 8-17). The list of printers that appears within the Print Setup dialog box reflects the number of drivers that are installed in your Windows system.

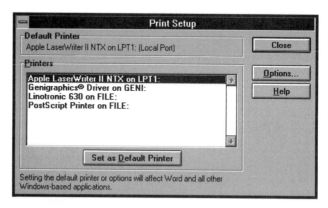

Figure 8-17: Four drivers are installed in my personal system, one for my local printer and three for off-site printers.

What you need to know about drivers is that you must select the correct one to format a document properly. Look again at Figure 8-17. This illustration lists the drivers installed in my personal system—the one I use at home. Everybody knows that writers are destitute, and my system reflects it: only one printer is actually connected, and it's a little ink-jet job that costs less than a set of used snow tires. Nonetheless, I often print on a PostScript printer at work and occasionally on a service bureau's Linotronic 300 imagesetter.

So why do I bother installing the PostScript drivers on my home system? The drivers take up disk space (quite a bit; see the "'Little' is relative" sidebar), and if I were never going to print on anything but an ink-jet printer on my personal machine, why not save the space?

The answer has to do with fonts. My ink-jet printer uses the TrueType font Arial for sans-serif applications. Neither the PostScript printer at work nor the Lino at the service bureau has any knowledge of Arial. Both substitute Helvetica whenever they encounter Arial.

The trouble is that Arial's letterforms aren't quite the same as Helvetica's, nor are its font metrics. Line breaks and page breaks occur at different places. Hyphenation performed for Arial isn't appropriate for Helvetica. Justification is different. These changes are so significant that the output from either of the PostScript printers barely resembles the document I see on my screen at home.

My solution to the problem is to prepare the final version of the document with the Lino driver selected, even though I'm still at home where there's no Linotronic imagesetter. Though I can't print this version of the document at home, I can see it onscreen, and that's all I really need in order to check line lengths and page breaks.

In other words, install drivers for every printer upon which you'll print (regardless of location), and use that driver when you apply the finishing touches to a document.

Changing Drivers

To change from one driver to another, choose Printer from the Print dialog box and then select the name of the printer (driver) you want (as described in the previous exercise). All printers listed in this dialog box have a corresponding driver in the \WINDOWS\SYSTEM subdirectory on your hard disk. When you click on an alternate printer, Windows unloads the current driver from memory and loads the new one.

Drivers are aware of their native fonts. When you switch from one driver to another, Word alters the available font list, often changing the list itself, not just the placement of its printer icons (see Figure 8-18). As I mentioned before, these changes are also reflected in your document.

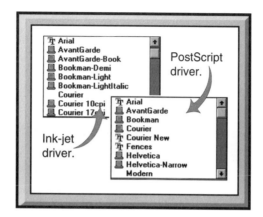

Figure 8-18: When you change drivers, Word alters the list of available fonts. Fonts with printer icons next to their names are the only appropriate fonts for the currently selected printer.

Adding Drivers

If the printer you intend to use doesn't show up in the Print Setup dialog box, you need to add it to your system. To add your printer driver, you will have to leave Word and use the Printers utility from the Control Panel. Here's how:

- ✔ Minimize Word to return to Windows.

- ✔ Find the Control Panel icon (it's probably in the Program Manager's Main window) and double-click on it to run the Control Panel.

- ✔ In the Control Panel window, double-click on the Printers icon (see Figure 8-19) to open the Printers dialog box.

- ✔ Click on the Add>> button and select the printer you want from the list that appears.

- ✔ Click on the Install button.

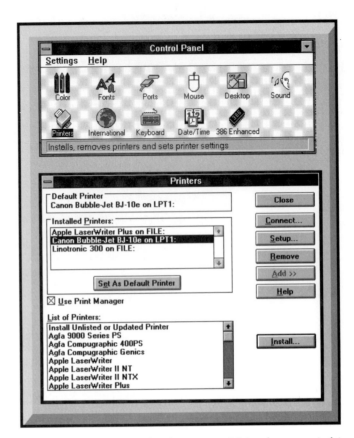

Figure 8-19: The Printers utility lets you add (and remove) drivers.

More than likely, Windows will ask for one of its disks in order to transfer the driver to your hard disk. Be sure to have your Windows disks ready. When you return to Word, the printer's name will appear in the Print Setup dialog box.

Note the Connect button in Figure 8-19. Normally, this button allows you to identify the port to which the printer is connected. If the printer is off site—an imagesetter, for instance—choose File as the "port." This setting tells Windows that you always want to print to a file when this printer is selected. Back at Word, all you'll have to do is issue the Print command using that driver (and provide a filename); Word will automatically print to a file.

Old PostScript drivers

Windows's original PostScript driver didn't properly relate to Linotronic printers. Though Microsoft offered a new driver in the fall of 1991, it wasn't distributed to users until the release of Windows 3.1, nearly eight months later. In other words, a new driver may be available for the printer you use, and you just don't know about it. Always check.

Obtaining Drivers

Microsoft is always adding to its list of drivers. New printers are being accommodated, and old drivers are being rewritten (see sidebar). Microsoft can't notify every Windows user each time a new driver is released. If you think you need a new driver, or if you have a printer for which no driver is listed, check with your dealer or call Microsoft directly at the number printed on your warranty card.

Better yet, join CompuServe. Microsoft offers a number of forums there (including one for Word users exclusively), one of which is the Advanced Windows Forum, where the latest list of drivers is always available.

SCREEN FONTS

Though we're well into this chapter, we have only discussed half the font issue. Though you may think of printers when you hear the word *font*, fonts are also a concern with regard to the screen. After all, you have to look at *something*.

Screen fonts became a particularly sticky issue with the advent of WYSIWYG (What You See Is What You Get) displays. Prior to that, users expected to see something on the screen and something altogether different on paper.

Now you want more. You want every character of your document to appear on the screen in the font, size and style you've chosen. You want to see line and page breaks as they'll appear on paper. You don't just want it, you expect it. Windows does these things to people.

It doesn't take much imagination to connect the dots. If you're to have true WYSIWYG, all the font considerations we've discussed in this chapter will have to be accommodated for the screen as well as the printer. The problem takes on monumental proportions when you consider that screen resolution hardly matches printer resolution: typically, the best a screen can do is 96 dots per inch, compared to the 300 or better that most printers offer.

In other words, the screen requires a second system of font definitions and metrics. Moreover, this system has to be fast (unlike printer output, screen displays are always dynamic) and transparent: users expect to see good stuff, but they don't expect to have to participate in its presentation.

Users are so impertinent.

Bitmaps

The original solution was to provide bitmapped character definitions for the screen. This strategy, however, entails all the problems bitmaps are known for: jagged characters, lack of rotation and monumental storage requirements for bitmaps in all fonts of all sizes.

Leave them alone
Don't delete font files that seem inappropriate for your system. The EGA80WOA.FON file, for instance, seems superfluous for systems with a VGA display. Windows uses it, however, whenever you run applications in a DOS window. Deleted fonts are hard to restore. Leave them alone.

Windows still exhibits the vestiges of its bitmapped font heritage: if you look in your \WINDOWS\SYSTEM subdirectory, you'll see dozens of .FON files listed there. We all still use them—Windows's menus, messages and dialog boxes are all bitmapped—but few of us use them to display Word documents. They're just too inflexible.

SCALABLE-FONT TYPE MANAGERS

Few of us use bitmapped fonts because we now have an alternative: *scalable-font type managers*. These type managers are screen drivers that provide outline (scalable) font definitions rather than bitmapped ones. Only one definition has to be stored for each font: because they are outline definitions, they're infinitely scalable.

Which means that what you see is what you get with a type manager. Properly installed and configured, a scalable type manager displays a typographical image on the screen that matches the printed output *exactly*. An exact image is critical for fine details such as leading and kerning.

TrueType

Scalable type managers came into general use with the introduction of Windows 3.1, which shipped with TrueType, the scalable-font system that Apple and Microsoft developed when they grew weary of PostScript's market dominance.

You can't miss TrueType fonts: they each appear with little TT's next to their names in the Formatting toolbar or Format-Font dialog box font list (see Figure 8-20).

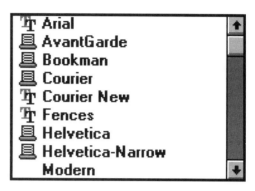

Figure 8-20: The TT symbols next to Arial, Courier New and Fences identify these fonts as TrueType fonts. They are infinitely scalable.

The TrueType system is fast, transparent and free—convincing arguments for using it. Additional TrueType fonts are available from numerous vendors, and many are available free of charge on CompuServe and other telecommunication services.

Because TrueType fonts are scalable, you can also use them for printing. If your printer supports downloaded outline fonts, Windows will download the TrueType outline fonts to that printer whenever necessary (and if an alternative isn't available, PostScript printers will substitute their built-in fonts, if appropriate). If your printer doesn't support downloaded outline fonts, TrueType will construct a bitmap of the font and send the bitmap to the printer. Either way, TrueType fonts are printed to the best of the printer's ability.

Because TrueType is so transparent, you may not even be aware of its controls. From the Control Panel, choose Fonts. Then click on the TrueType button in the Fonts dialog box (see Figure 8-21).

Do not collect $200

Changes made in the TrueType dialog box (see Figure 8-21) do not take immediate effect. You must restart Windows before they become evident. If you make a change in this dialog, Windows will ask if you want to restart. Be sure you have saved all your documents before you answer.

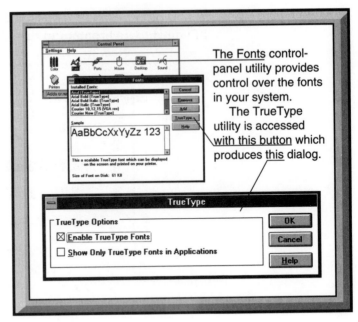

The Fonts control-panel utility provides control over the fonts in your system.

The TrueType utility is accessed with this button which produces this dialog.

Figure 8-21: You may not even be aware of the TrueType controls your system offers.

Note that the TrueType dialog box allows you to turn off all other fonts, or to turn off TrueType itself. Why might you want to turn off TrueType? Read on.

Adobe Type Manager

Over a year before TrueType appeared in Windows 3.1, Adobe introduced its scalable type manager, *Adobe Type Manager* (ATM). ATM is essentially identical in performance to TrueType: fast and transparent. Like TrueType, it also prints beautifully on just about any printer. It's not free, however. Though it's included free of charge with some applications (though never with Microsoft applications—remember, Adobe and Microsoft aren't the best of friends), you usually pay a nominal charge. ATM and TrueType are competitors.

ATM has its own control panel; its icon usually appears in the Utilities window (see Figure 8-22). The ATM window is similar to Windows's Fonts dialog box: it allows you to add and delete ATM fonts, and turn ATM on or off.

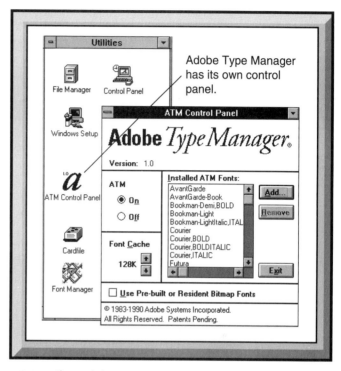

Figure 8-22: The Adobe Type Manager window lets you enable or disable the utility, set its memory usage and select ATM fonts.

Bring your checkbook

Unfortunately, buying ATM isn't usually enough. ATM arrives with Times, Helvetica, Symbol and Courier; but if you want fonts that are built into most PostScript printers— Avant Garde, Palatino, Bookman, Schoolbook and the Zapfs—you will have to buy Adobe Plus Pack. Plus Pack and ATM together cost about $200.

As is the case with TrueType, if you make any changes in the ATM window, you must restart Windows. Again, be sure you've saved your documents before you do.

Though ATM and Plus Pack aren't cheap, they are fully compatible with PostScript printers and PostScript fonts. This is not the case with TrueType (remember, PostScript printers will substitute their built-in fonts when they encounter TrueType fonts in a document). In other words, you should always use ATM when you're printing with a PostScript printer, even if that printer is off site.

Facelift

You can make the same argument for Facelift, the scalable type manager from Bitstream. Through its recent association with a number of prestigious European type foundries, Bitstream has overcome its image as a supplier of bitmapped fonts, and now offers hundreds of elegant outline font designs. If you're fond of Bitstream fonts, you should use Facelift for their onscreen presentation.

Caveats

You have little reason for not using a scalable type management system. The alternative—bitmapped screen fonts—is as antiquated as a vacuum tube and about as useful.

Because one of Windows's primary benefits is WYSIWYG, why hamper it with bitmapped screen fonts?

One answer to that question is memory. All scalable font managers require a modest (a relative term) chunk of memory in order to accomplish their task. A minimum of 128k is required; they all prefer more. If your system has 4mb of RAM or more, the memory required by a type manager probably won't be much of a sacrifice.

There's another answer: speed. Font managers scale and rasterize fonts in the background, and that work takes time. Time, too, is relative: on a 386 25Mhz system, you'll observe delays. The delays recede on a 386 33Mhz system and are generally unnoticeable on 486 systems.

If you can afford the memory and speed isn't a problem, which one should you use? If you're printing on a PostScript device, use Adobe Type Manager. If the majority of your fonts are Bitstream, use Facelift. Otherwise, use TrueType. It's free after all, and you probably already have it.

The important message is *use a type manager*. Without one, you will never be able to format type properly onscreen (formatting display type in particular, with its finicky leading and kerning demands, is a chore without a type manager). You also won't see all the fonts within a family (Windows may just lean characters over for italics or make them fatter

The Hatfields & the McCoys

Though I endorse the use of scalable type managers, I don't endorse using more than one at a time. Though you can do it, you're squandering memory and compromising the speed of your system. Occasional conflicts arise as well: these type managers are competing utilities after all; there's little reason for them to be buddies.

for bold). And you'll never develop an affinity for the jaggies. In desktop publishing, type managers are a necessity.

INSTALLING FONTS

Bitmapped or outline, screen or printer, all fonts have to be installed. Unless Windows knows about a font, it will never appear on Word's font list. Unless fonts are built into your printer, their definitions will have to be available for downloading. If you are using a scalable type manager, it needs local outline font definitions, even for fonts built into the printer.

Installing TrueType Fonts

You install TrueType fonts using the Control Panel's Fonts utility. Refer to Figure 8-23 as I describe the process:

✔ Open the Control Panel (which is probably in your Main window) by double-clicking on its icon.

✔ Double-click on the Fonts icon. The Fonts window will open (top of Figure 8-23).

✔ Click on the Add button. The Add Fonts window will open (center of Figure 8-23).

✔ Select the drive and directory where your new font is stored.

✔ Select the font by clicking on its name. Note that you may select all the listed fonts by clicking on the Select All button. You may also select multiple fonts with the Shift key.

✔ Click on the OK button. The Add Fonts window will disappear, exposing the Fonts window. Your new font name(s) will appear here when the installation process completes (bottom of Figure 8-23).

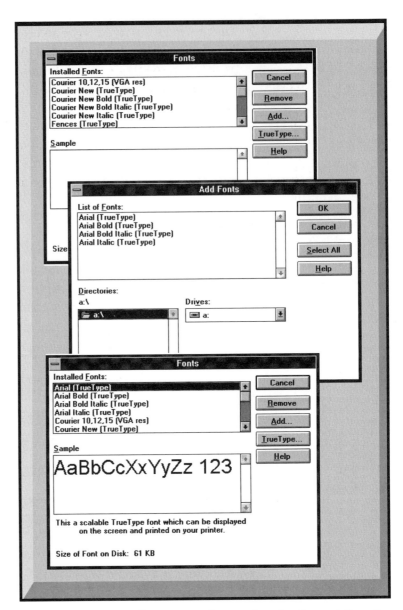

Figure 8-23: You install TrueType fonts using the Control Panel's Fonts utility.

For every font you select, two files are added to your \WINDOWS\SYSTEM subdirectory. The outline definitions reside in a .TTF file; the font metrics are stored in an .FOT file. Both files are binary format; neither can be opened with a text

Don't have a cow, man

Though I indicated that .FOT TrueType font metrics files cannot be opened using a text utility, Word can do it. Tell Word to look for all files (*.*) in your \WINDOWS\SYSTEM subdirectory and then open (as text only) any of the Arial .FOT files. Some text will be visible among the binary garbage on the screen. Written at the height of the Simpsons TV craze, early releases of these files contained bovine-related quotes attributed to a certain cynical antagonist starring in that show.

utility. Windows must have access to both files in order for a TrueType font to work properly. All installed fonts will also be listed in the [FONTS] section of WIN.INI.

While Figure 8-23 is still at hand, you might note that the Fonts utility also provides an option for removing fonts as well. This option also allows you to remove fonts from your font list or your disk. This capability is especially convenient when you want to delete unused bitmapped fonts from your disk and recover the space they occupy.

Installing PostScript Fonts

PostScript fonts are available from scores of vendors, and each font ships with its own installation utility (Adobe's is pictured in Figure 8-24). Though the operation of these utilities is described in the manuals accompanying the fonts, a few notes warrant mention.

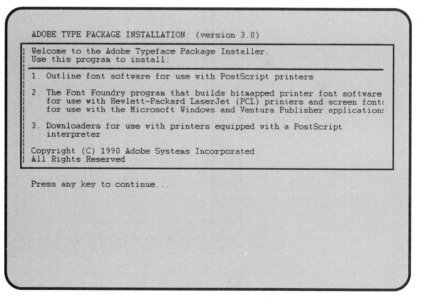

Figure 8-24: Adobe's installation program for PostScript fonts is DOS-based and almost completely automatic.

✔ You should install and select a PostScript printer driver in Word (File menu, Print, Printer option) before you add PostScript fonts.

✔ A section will be added to your WIN.INI file (under the printer's name: [Linotronic 630,FILE], for instance), which will list all the names and locations of the various PostScript font files. This section must match for all installed PostScript printers listed in WIN.INI.

✔ PostScript fonts are usually installed in their own directory (\PSFONTS). At least two files will be created per font: .PFB files (the font outlines) and .PFM files (font metrics). Both of these files are in a binary format.

✔ If you're using Adobe Type Manager, a third file (.AFM) will be created for each installed font. This file contains the font metrics for onscreen display. It's ASCII text that Word can open.

✔ As I write this book, Adobe's installation program offers no provision for removing PostScript fonts once they're installed. PostScript font deletion is a complex process that involves modifying WIN.INI and the \PSFONTS directory. It's not recommended for people of delicate constitution.

Messing around with system files—which is what font files are—is always perilous. Even if you never touch the things, read font installation manuals thoroughly before modifying your Windows system.

WINDOWS'S PRINT MANAGER

A concept that evades many Windows users is that the Print Manager is an *application*, just like Word or Paintbrush. When you print a document from another Windows application, the application passes the printer, font and file information to the Print Manager, which then controls printing the document in the background.

Background printing is requisite to desktop publishing. Desktop-published documents tend to be long and complex, and they can take a long time to print. With the Print Manager, you can return to work long before the document emerges from the printer, secure in the knowledge that the task is in good hands. Indeed, the Print Manager lets you know if it encounters any problems, regardless of what you're doing at the time.

Though Windows activates the Print Manager when Windows is first installed, it may have been turned off. To reactivate the Print Manager, choose the Printers utility from the Control Panel. The Printers window offers a check box in the lower-left corner (see Figure 8-25). You should turn it on.

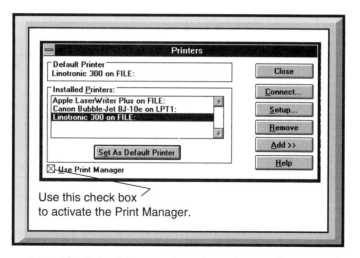

Figure 8-25: The Print Manager is activated using the Control Panel's Printers utility.

After you've turned it on, the Print Manager rarely requires attention. It opens whenever Word (or any other application) prints a document and closes when printing has concluded.

Shuffling Priorities

There is only one unavoidable delay—one that occurs while Word sends the document to the Print Manager. Because this part of the printing operation takes place entirely on the hard disk, it doesn't take long. Once the Printing indicator finishes (in the status bar at the bottom of the Word screen), you're free to do other things.

Those "other things" can include printing additional documents. Open the document that's to be printed next, choose Print (again) from the File menu, and OK the dialog. You can follow these steps for as many documents as you like (within reason—see the sidebar).

Normally, the Print Manager prioritizes multiple documents in the order they were received. You can change this priority, however. Here's how:

✔ Activate the Print Manager by either double-clicking on its icon on the desktop, or switching to it from the Task List (press Ctrl-Esc). Its window appears (see Figure 8-26).

✔ Reorder the queue by dragging document lines. For instance, if you were in a hurry to print WIN.INI (the third-priority document in Figure 8-26), you could promote it to second-priority status by dragging it above the line representing NEWORDER.DOC.

Clogging up the works

The Print Manager accomplishes its task by building files in your printer's format, temporarily storing them on your hard disk and feeding them to the printer as it's ready to accept them. These temporary files, however, can be quite large. In other words, leave plenty of room on your hard disk. If you don't, the Print Manager will clog up and you'll be called upon to mediate.

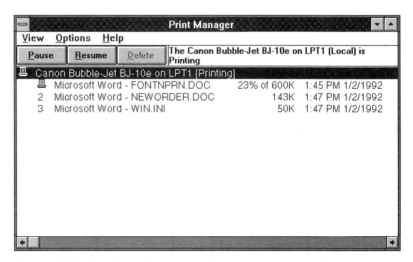

Figure 8-26: The Print Manager window lets you configure the utility to your liking and reorder the queue of documents waiting to be printed.

The menu options available in the Print Manager window allow you to assign priority to the Print Manager itself and control the messages it displays. You should get acquainted with this utility. Read its Help file. It won't take long.

Printing Multiple Documents

The Print Manager is hardly limited to printing multiple Word documents. After the Printing message leaves the screen, you can leave Word (by minimizing or exiting), load another application and print a document from there.

If you have a number of documents to print from one application or many, you may print them directly from the desktop. You can print multiple documents by using the File Manager and dragging the document icons to the Print Manager's icon, just as you would if you were to copy a file. Alternatively, select a document and then choose Print from the File Manager's File menu. No matter how you issue the command, the Print Manager will start the appropriate application, open the document to be printed, issue the print command, print the document and then close the application before moving on to the next task. This feature is especially convenient when you have a lot of printing to do and don't want the bother of running every application that's involved.

THE CONTEMPORARY ALCHEMISTS

The joint issues of fonts and printing are intricate and eternal. Our mania for typeset-quality output has placed a strain on our systems, our budgets and our comprehension. Whereas programs like Word somehow become more replete and simultaneously easier to use, fonts and printers lurk in the shadows, cooperating begrudgingly while they wait for another inopportune moment to confound us with quandaries and enigmas.

We are, nonetheless, the ones who must supply the illumination. Our challenge is to turn the poverty of word processing into the wealth of desktop publishing. Our tools are fonts and printers. The futility of the task is often overwhelming, painful and occasionally—once in a great while—successful.

That's more than we can say for the alchemists.

9 *AutoFormat, Wizards & Templates*

With Word for Windows Version 2.0, Microsoft discovered the "wall"—the point at which users reached their capacity for features. Microsoft interviewed some of us and discovered that what we wanted more than anything else was ease of use. Word's feature set was prodigious but daunting. "Give us a hand," we said. "We're mired in opportunity." Microsoft responded with Version 6.0, and the primary changes facilitate ease of use.

Perhaps most significantly, these changes include AutoFormat, wizards (a feature name which, interestingly, Microsoft doesn't capitalize) and tremendously-improved templates. This chapter addresses these changes.

AUTOFORMAT

I was reading about a new Mercedes-Benz model the other day. Typical of luxury cars, everything is powered: doors, locks, antenna, trunk release and seat. In fact, the seat contains a memory: when you open one of the front doors, the seat slides all the way back for easy exit and entry. After you sit down, the seat returns to one of three memorized positions, adjusting its fore/aft, tilt and lumbar adjustments to your preferred settings.

Maybe someone at Microsoft drives a Mercedes, because Word offers a similar feature: *AutoFormat*. Let's admit it: most of the design work we do with Word is repetitive. Though we may prepare new designs now and then, most of our work involves documents we've prepared before: memos, letters, faxes—that kind of stuff.

Which is why Word offers templates. Templates contain all of the formatting information we need to prepare documents we've designed before. Used regularly, templates can save hours of preparation time.

But we still have to apply the styles and format the bullets and type the em dashes and use the ten-key pad to enter annoying little tidbits such as the copyright (©) symbol or registered (®) symbol. Wouldn't it be nice if we could just push a button and Word would do it all for us?

Which, of course, is what AutoFormat does. Specifically, it does the following:

✔ Assigns a style to each paragraph, with an option to alter a style previously assigned.

✔ Removes extra paragraph marks.

✔ Replaces indents inserted with the Space bar or the Tab key with proper paragraph indents.

✔ Inserts true bullet characters in place of asterisks and hyphens, or similar characters that may have been used to denote bulleted lists.

✔ Replaces (C), (R) and (TM) with ©, ® and ™.

Perhaps the best way to explain this feature is to walk you through a typical AutoFormatting session. We begin with a typical memo (see Figure 9-1).

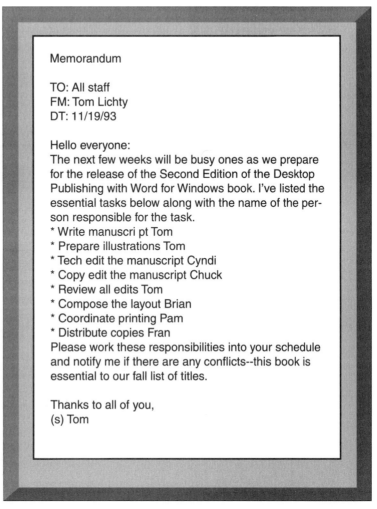

Memorandum

TO: All staff
FM: Tom Lichty
DT: 11/19/93

Hello everyone:
The next few weeks will be busy ones as we prepare
for the release of the Second Edition of the Desktop
Publishing with Word for Windows book. I've listed the
essential tasks below along with the name of the per-
son responsible for the task.
* Write manuscri pt Tom
* Prepare illustrations Tom
* Tech edit the manuscript Cyndi
* Copy edit the manuscript Chuck
* Review all edits Tom
* Compose the layout Brian
* Coordinate printing Pam
* Distribute copies Fran
Please work these responsibilities into your schedule
and notify me if there are any conflicts--this book is
essential to our fall list of titles.

Thanks to all of you,
(s) Tom

Figure 9-1: Without any formatting, this memo seems flat and
lifeless—a perfect candidate for Word's AutoFormat command.

With the document open in Word, I choose the Format
menu's AutoFormat command (see Figure 9-2) and choose
OK to close the first AutoFormat dialog box.

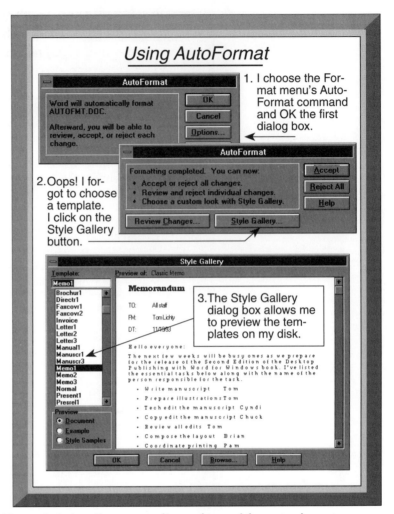

Figure 9-2: AutoFormat applies styles and formats characters quickly and without my intervention.

Figure 9-2 describes an all too typical AutoFormat scenario: the document has been prepared with the Normal template in effect. It's really not a problem, however, because the AutoFormat command offers the option of applying a template to the document after the command has run its course (see step 2 in Figure 9-2).

After you select an appropriate template from the Style Gallery, click OK and then click on the Accept button in Figure 9-2's second dialog box, Word reformats the document, leaving the finished product displayed onscreen (see Figure 9-3).

Memorandum

TO: All staff
FM: Tom Lichty
DT: 11/19/93

Hello everyone:
The next few weeks will be busy ones as we prepare for the release of the Second Edition of the Desktop Publishing with Word for Windows book. I've listed the essential tasks below along with the name of the person responsible for the task.

- Write manuscript.................. Tom
- Prepare illustrations.............. Tom
- Tech edit the manuscript.... Cyndi
- Copy edit the manuscript... Chuck
- Review all edits..................... Tom
- Compose the layout............. Brian
- Coordinate printing.............. Pam
- Distribute copies.................. Fran

Please work these responsibilities into your schedule and notify me if there are any conflicts—this book is essential to our fall list of titles.

Thanks to all of you,
(s) Tom

Figure 9-3: The finished document, with formatting courtesy of the AutoFormat command.

Like the seats in a Mercedes, the AutoFormat command offers customization controls suitable for every occasion. Look them over for yourself by choosing Options from the Tools menu, then clicking on the AutoFormat tab (Figure 9-4).

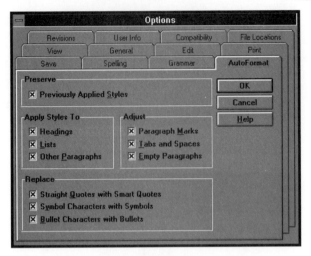

Figure 9-4: The AutoFormat command has formatted the bullets, applied new styles, emphasized the heading and even changed the double-hyphen into an em dash.

AutoFormat won't do *everything* for you—if you look carefully you'll see that I had to adjust the tabs manually in Figure 9-3's bulleted list—but it can relieve formatting of much of its tedium. In fact, if you apply selected styles as you construct the document, you have the option to leave them untouched. Alternatively, you can tweak the styles that AutoFormat applies (as I did with Figure 9-3's bullets) any way you wish after the command has concluded.

My preferred strategy looks something like this:

✔ Start a new document by choosing New from the File menu.

✔ Select the appropriate template from the New dialog box.

✔ Compose the document normally, applying styles only when they're not body text, bullets or headings. Precede bulleted paragraphs with an asterisk or a hyphen, and indicate special characters by placing them inside of parentheses: (C), for example, will convert to a copyright symbol. Don't worry about publisher's quotation marks either: AutoFormat takes care of those too.

✔ Spell check the document after you finish entering text.

✔ Choose AutoFormat from the Format menu, change its configuration if you wish (by clicking on the AutoFormat dialog box's Options button—see the top window in Figure 9-2), then click OK.

✔ Review AutoFormat's changes if you wish (use the Review Changes button pictured in the second window in Figure 9-2), accepting or rejecting them selectively.

✔ Click the Accept button and admire the work you didn't have to perform.

The AutoFormat command is one of those little features that can vastly improve your productivity whenever you prepare routine documents, and because routine documents comprise the majority of your work, the productivity improvement is significant.

If you're rewarded with a raise for your increased productivity and efficiency, be sure to buy the Mercedes with the magic seats.

WIZARDS

A couple years ago, a friend of mine bought a bread machine with her income tax refund money. She told me how she loves the taste of homemade bread, but she simply didn't have the time to make it properly the old-fashioned way. She also admitted to the pang of guilt she feels whenever she refers to her bread as "homemade." On the other hand, by now she's made at least a hundred loaves of bread by doing nothing more than dumping in the ingredients and pressing the Start button and they've all turned out perfectly.

Such is the magic of *wizards*. A wizard is a kind of mini program that creates and formats a document for you. All you have to do is select the one you want to use, answer a few questions, enter your text and, in essence, press the Start button. The document will turn out perfectly every time.

Word supplies nine different wizards that create and format different kinds of documents. You will see the following documents provided in the form of wizards among the list of templates when you select New from the File menu (see Figure 9-5).

- ✔ Meeting agenda
- ✔ Award certificate
- ✔ Calendar
- ✔ Fax cover sheet
- ✔ Letter
- ✔ Memo
- ✔ Newsletter
- ✔ Legal pleading
- ✔ Résumé

Another wizard assists in creating and formatting a table.

Figure 9-5: Word's wizards are among the list of templates in the New dialog box.

If you're on a tight timeline or otherwise need some assistance completing some work, but you still want the professional look of a job well done, consider using a wizard. (See Figure 9-6.)

Wizard Name	Features	Styles available
Agenda Wizard	Meeting agenda, including date, time, location, topics, attendees	Boxes, Modern, Standard
Award Wizard	Awards certificate in landscape or portrait, fancy borders, custom wording, names	Formal, Modern, Decorative, Jazzy
Calendar Wizard	Calendar in weeks, months or years; can include logo	Boxes & Borders, Banner, Modern, Jazzy
Fax Wizard	Creates fax cover sheet providing space for all pertinent information and message	Contemporary, Modern, Jazzy
Letter Wizard	Creates a business or personal letter; options of using pre-written letter and including envelope	Classic, Contemporary, Typewriter
Memo Wizard	Creates a memo with heading and separate distribution list, if desired	Classic, Contemporary, Typewriter
Newslttr Wizard	Creates a newsletter with up to four columns, newsletter name in display type, can be 2-sided, and be any length	Classic, Modern, Jazzy
Pleading Wizard	Creates a legal pleading with options for page layout, lines on either side of page, line and page numbers	n/a
Resume Wizard	Creates a résumé organized in your choice of entry-level, chronological, functional or professional style; can include pre-written cover letter	Classic, Contemporary, Elegant
Table Wizard	Creates and formats a table; provided headings can contain days, months, quarters, years, numbers in any alignment	Six different styles of borders and shading

Figure 9-6: This list of wizards and their features leaves little to be desired.

Using a Wizard

Now let's learn how to use a wizard. Do you want to create a résumé, for example? Let's look at the wizard-assisted process of document creation, step-by-step:

✔ From the File menu, choose New.

✔ In the New dialog box, locate and select the Resume Wizard.

✔ Make sure the Document (rather than Template) option is selected, then click on the OK button (see Figure 9-7).

Figure 9-7: In the New dialog box, select the wizard you want, make sure Document is selected, and click OK to begin your journey.

✔ The first Resume Wizard dialog box provides four types of résumés from which you can choose (see Figure 9-8). For this example, we'll use the Entry-level type résumé. Click on your choice, then click on the Next> button.

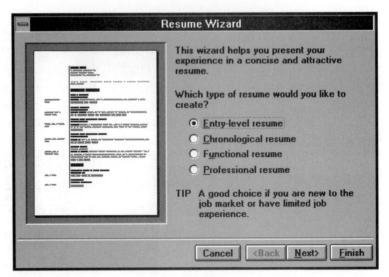

Figure 9-8: In the first Resume Wizard dialog box, make your selection from the four types of resumes.

✔ The second Resume Wizard dialog box (see Figure 9-9) receives the name and address of the person you're creating the résumé for. Tab from text box to text box, completing each, and then click on the Next> button.

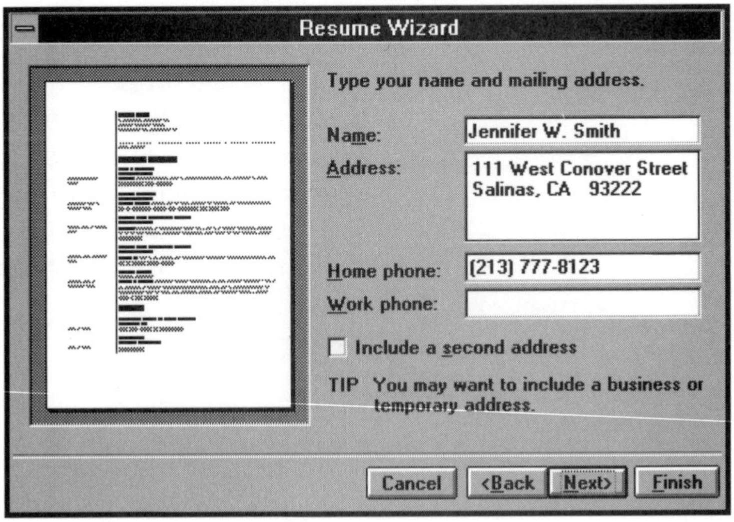

Figure 9-9: In the second Resume Wizard dialog box, enter name, address and phone number(s) that should appear on the résumé.

✔ The third Resume Wizard dialog box suggests including nine heading options in your résumé. Click to clear the marked boxes of any headings you don't want (see Figure 9-10). In this résumé, I will clear "Awards received," "Languages" and "Hobbies." When you're finished, click on the Next> button.

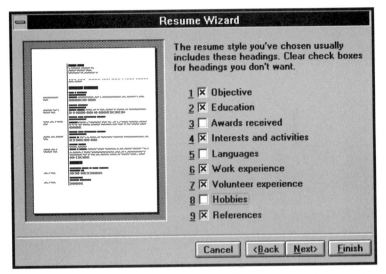

Figure 9-10: To remove any regular headings from a résumé, clear the appropriate box in this third Resume Wizard dialog box.

✔ The fourth Resume Wizard dialog box (see Figure 9-11) displays a list of nine more headings that are sometimes used in résumés. Click on any you want to include in your résumé, and click on the Next> button when you're ready to continue. Our résumé won't include any other headings.

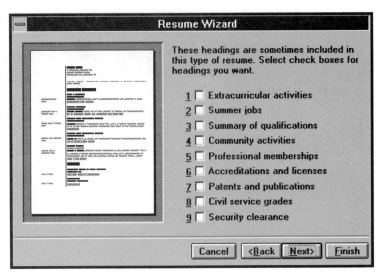

Figure 9-11: To add additional headings, select them from this fourth Resume Wizard dialog box.

✔ You have yet another opportunity to add your own headings and rearrange them in the fifth and sixth Resume Wizard dialog boxes, respectively (see Figure 9-12). To add new headings, type them in the text box, then click on the Add button after you add each heading. To rearrange the order in the sixth box, click to select the heading and then click on the Move Up or Move Down button accordingly. When you're finished with each dialog box, continue to the next one by clicking on the Next> button.

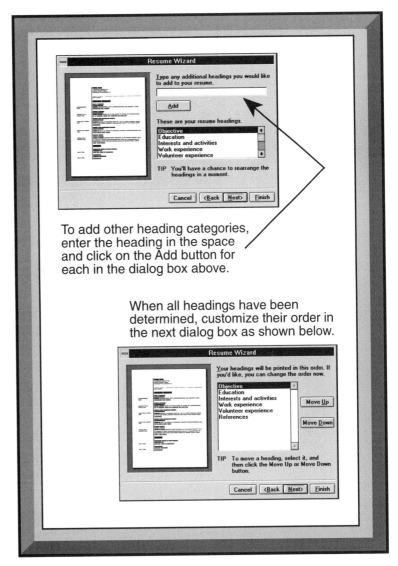

Figure 9-12: You have several chances to include headings provided by the wizard as well as add your own and then rearrange their order.

✔ In the next dialog box, choose the style of résumé you want, either Classic, Contemporary or Elegant. We will use Contemporary for the résumé in this exercise.

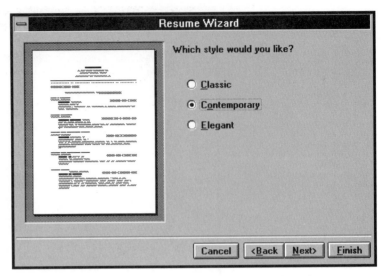

Figure 9-13: The sample changes to reflect which style résumé you select in this dialog box.

✔ The last dialog box (see Figure 9-14) gives you the options of creating a cover letter, displaying help or simply displaying the résumé as you enter its body text. We'll keep the last option. The Next> button is dimmed indicating there are no more questions. Click on the Finish button to get to the document.

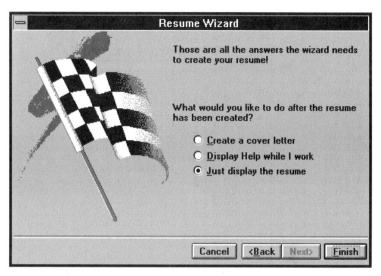

Figure 9-14: This Resume Wizard dialog box signifies the completed process of the wizard. After you reach this point you are on your own to finish up with the specific text.

Modifying documents created with wizards

Wizards are programmed to include some fairly sophisticated formatting in the documents they create. As you are customizing a wizard-created document, be sure to display the paragraph marks, spaces and tabs by clicking on the Show/Hide ¶ button on the Standard toolbar. This way you won't accidentally delete something you couldn't see.

✔ Now we're ready for the document itself, and our wizard journey is over. Edit the résumé like you would edit any other document, typing in the text you want. When you are finished, save, name and print it (see Figure 9-15).

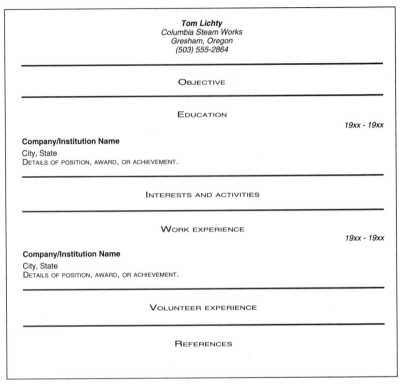

Figure 9-15: The résumé document is ready for you to add the specifics to it.

Wizards take you one step at a time, requesting one answer after another to a list of questions, and finally producing an almost complete product with minimal help from you. All of Word's wizards are like that.

Now that I think about it, bread machines are that way too. The analogy is a good one. The problem with bread machines is that they produce a distinctly-shaped loaf. Anyone with a half-teaspoon of cooking experience can spot a loaf of bread-machine bread from across the kitchen. And anyone who has used Word can spot wizard-produced documents with similar acuity. They may look good, but they all look the same. If you're going to make bread for the kids' sandwiches, use the machine; but if you're going to enter your recipe at the county fair, you'd better do it yourself.

TEMPLATES

If wizards are the bread machines of document construction, templates are the cookbook. Here we have much more opportunity to express our ingenuity. Like recipes, templates offer infinite potential for personalization: they include all of the ingredients and methods, that, if followed religiously, result in a competent finished document. But if you've a mind to add a pinch of this and a dollop of that, well, the template will never discourage the potential.

Templates Defined

Don't be intimidated

Don't let macros scare you off. True, they can be complicated and require the knowledge of programming in Word Basic; but the most common form of macro is a simple string of stored keystrokes, ready for playback as required. If you encounter a series of commands that you have to issue altogether too frequently, choose Macro from the Tools menu, click the button marked Record, assign your macro a keystroke (or a toolbar button, or a position on a menu— or all three), and record your efforts.

The next time you encounter the need to issue that annoying series of commands, all you have to do is run the macro.

Templates are the last of our three automated methods of creating and formatting documents. All documents are associated with one template or another. If you don't specify a template, Word assigns the Normal template to your document. A template controls some significant formatting functions in your document. Specifically, templates include their own set of styles, section formatting, customized toolbars and menus, AutoText, macros, and any text and graphics that should always be included in that document. They work like a document that is already set up, just waiting to be typed in.

Word ships with many templates for documents ranging from academic papers to fax cover sheets. Some of them are quite elaborate, involving macros and fields far beyond most of our comprehension. Where wizards are completely automated, templates follow suit without quite so many bells and whistles, and perhaps the most powerful aspect of templates is the ability to create your own from scratch for any type of document, with complete customization.

Suppose that you're responsible for processing your company's semi-annual report. It's usually 25–30 pages in length. It contains a dozen or so styles, a number of tables and charts with captions, more than a single column and more than a single side. Even though you create this document only twice a year, it's a complex document and you don't want to start from scratch each time. What to do? Design a template and use it each time.

Template Attributes

Not only can templates include formatting and text, but they also can include a whole host of attributes that create, in essence, a unique document environment. Some of these attributes permanently belong to a template and therefore can only be altered in the template itself. Others are part of the template, but can be altered in the document currently being processed without affecting the template itself.

These attributes include styles, macros and even toolbars (see Figure 9-16).

Attribute	Level affected by formatting	Manner related to template
AutoText	Template	Part of template and cannot be altered specifically for individual document
Macros	Template	Part of template and cannot be altered specifically for individual document
Customized menus	Template	Part of template and cannot be altered specifically for individual document
Toolbars	Template	Part of template and cannot be altered specifically for individual document
Styles	Document	Part of template, but can be altered specifically for individual document; choice of whether these alterations should become part of template
Section formatting: margins headers/footers page numbers page size page orientation printer source columns line numbers vertical alignment foot/endnotes	Document	Part of template, but can be altered specifically for individual document; can't be added to template through the document
Text and graphics	Document	Part of template, but can be altered specifically for individual document; can't be added to template through the document

Figure 9-16: The list of attributes that may be incorporated in a template leaves little to be desired.

The Zoom Button

Macros and toolbars!!? Think of the potential: you can create an environment where not only the appearance of the document is available for change, but so is the environment itself.

Perhaps an example is in order. Consider the Standard toolbar. Word offers scores more buttons than the Standard toolbar can accommodate. Accordingly, you can add buttons to your toolbars whenever you please—and remove those that you don't require. Perhaps best of all, you can make these changes part of a template.

There's one toolbar button that no desktop publisher should be without. It's not a part of the default button set, but it will do wonders for your productivity. That button is the Zoom button. Refer to Figure 9-17 as I show you how to create it.

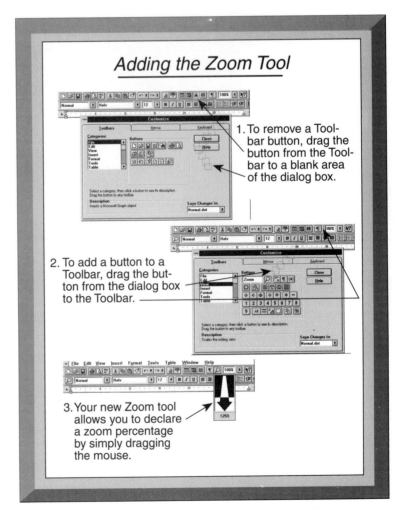

Figure 9-17: Adding and removing buttons from toolbars is as simple as clicking and dragging.

✔ Be sure the toolbar you intend to modify is showing. For the purpose of this exercise, modify the Standard toolbar.

✔ From the Tools menu, choose Customize.

✔ Click the Toolbars tab, if necessary, to activate the Toolbars dialog box.

✔ On the Standard toolbar, find a button you don't use and remove it. I'm an Excel user, so I have little need for the Microsoft Graph button. To remove a button, drag it to a blank area within the dialog box.

✔ Click View in the Categories list at the left of the dialog. A bevy of buttons will appear. Drag the Zoom button (the one with a picture of a magnifying glass on it) to the Standard toolbar. Be sure to drag it not only to the toolbar of your choice, but also the *location* of your choice on that toolbar.

✔ Click the Customize-Toolbars dialog box's Close button.

The Zoom tool will now reside on your Standard toolbar. Try using it: press on it (don't just click), then drag the mouse down until you have declared the degree of magnification (or reduction) you desire. When you release the mouse, Word will zoom accordingly. Using this tool beats typing a custom zoom percentage into the Zoom text box, and it's incredibly gratifying.

The power you'll feel when you first customize a toolbar is heady. Use it to your advantage: remove all of the buttons you don't use and add those that suit your style. Add the toolbar changes to your template and you've created a uniquely customized environment, tailored to your needs.

The Normal Template

Before we consider creating custom templates, let's discuss the templates that ship with Word. As previously mentioned, all documents have a specific template associated with them. Even if you haven't used a wizard or template, your documents have been based on a template named Normal. Documents created with wizards are typically based on the Normal template, but have other formatting characteristics added to them during the wizard production process.

The Normal template contains the defaults of the Word program. Unless altered, the defaults include the following:

- ✔ 8.5- by 11-inch letter-size paper
- ✔ Portrait orientation
- ✔ Times font
- ✔ 10-point size
- ✔ 1-inch top and bottom margins
- ✔ 1.25-inch left and right margins
- ✔ Single-line spacing
- ✔ Left alignment
- ✔ English language
- ✔ The Standard toolbar, menus and key commands

You should alter the Normal template to have all your new documents include a particular format. If, for example, you work for a law firm, you may work solely with legal-size paper. Rather than altering the page size in every single document, change that formatting only once in the Normal template (Normal.dot), and each new document will automatically have the correct page size.

Even when working in a document attached to a template other than Normal, creating macros and AutoText entries, and customizing toolbars, menus, or key commands, the respective dialog boxes all include the option of also saving the changes to the Normal template, not just the current template. When they're saved to Normal.dot, macros and AutoText entries are available globally, regardless of what template you're currently using.

Other Supplied Templates

In addition to Normal.dot, Word supplies 27 more templates. These templates could be categorized into three groups: Design, Production and Academic/Career.

Category: Template	Features	Families available
Design:		
Brochure	3-panel, 2-fold, landscape	Classic
Directory	2-column, cover page avail.	Classic
Presentation	for overhead transparencies	Classic
Production:		
Fax cover sheet	can include picture (logo, art)	Classic, Contemporary
Letter and memo	for business or personal use	Classic, Contemporary, Typewriter
Press release	mostly double-space layout	Classic, Contemporary, Typewriter
Invoice, purchase order, time sheet (weektime)	primarily for use as fill-in business forms	n/a
Report	can include tables of contents, authorities, figures; list of illustrations, dividers, index	Classic, Contemporary, Typewriter
Academic/career:		
Manuscript	books, plays, stories, movies, articles	Classic, Typewriter
Résumé	three résumé formats	Classic, Contemporary, Elegant
Manual	facing pages layout, styles for cover page, title page, dividers; tables of contents, authorities, figures; index	Classic
Thesis	features from Manual template, plus styles for notes, glossary, bibliography or reference	Classic

Figure 9-18: Word's supplied templates can be categorized into three groups.

What does that template do?

Ever wonder what a template is supposed to do, but just never had the time it takes to explore your question completely? Now you can see what the developers of the template intended by viewing an example using it in the Style Gallery option on the Format menu. Within that dialog box, choose to Preview an Example, then select any template you want and, voilà, Word displays sample text formatted with that template's styles.

You'll notice the Families Available column in Figure 9-18. All but four of the supplied templates have characteristics from one of four different families. Several documents intended to work together will look consistent if they originate from the same family. For example, if you wanted to include a résumé along with a manuscript to your publisher, you might create both documents using their Classic-style templates. The template names are followed by numbers in parentheses indicating which family they are from: Classic (1), Contemporary (2), Typewriter (3) and Elegant (4).

Creating a Document Based on a Template

The procedures for using templates and wizards to create a document are the same. Most templates stop short of the process of questions that wizards are so fond of, but otherwise the similarities between wizards and templates are more profound than the differences. The template creates a new unnamed document with formatting attributes characteristic to that template. From there, it is up to you to enter the text, apply the styles, and otherwise format the document.

The precise procedure for creating a document with a template follows.

Buttons use default
For every button on the Standard toolbar, there is an equivalent menu command. The first button issues the File New command. Because Normal is selected by default, using the button to create a new document also automatically attaches the Normal template. This characteristic holds true with all Standard toolbar buttons.

✔ From the File menu, choose New.

✔ In the New dialog box, click to select the template desired (see Figure 9-19).

✔ Make sure the Document option (rather than Template option) is selected. (Note that selecting the Template option is the way to create a new template, and that new templates can be created from existing templates.)

✔ Finally, click OK. Almost instantaneously a new document will appear on your screen with features resulting from the chosen template. Modify as desired, save changes, and name the new document.

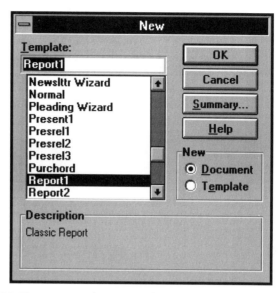

Figure 9-19: To create a document based on a template, select the template and make sure that Document is selected in the New dialog box.

Changing the Template Attached

When a document is created with a template, the template is attached to that document. Changing to a different template is a simple process of choosing Templates from the File menu, attaching the new template and clicking OK.

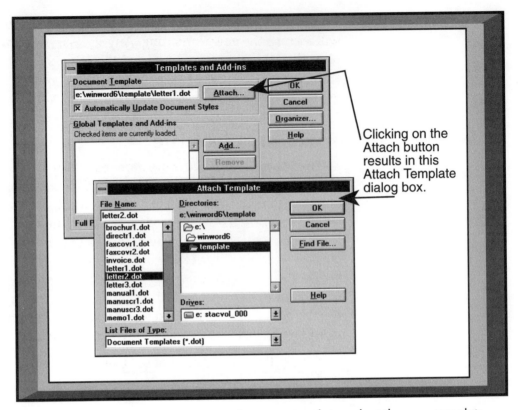

Figure 9-20: To attach a new template, select the new template from the Attach Template dialog box.

Don't forget:
Remember that style names are case sensitive; therefore if the template you are using has a style called *Caption* and you attach a different template that has a style called *caption*, your document will end up with both styles.

When you attach a different template, all text and formatting remain unchanged. Notice, however, the check box labeled "Automatically Update Document Styles" in the Templates and Add-ins dialog box (see Figure 9-20). If during the process of switching templates, you specified that the document styles be updated and if any of the styles used from the previous template have the same name as styles in the new template, those styles will be updated to reflect the formatting in the new template. All text with updated styles will assume the new formatting. Any styles in the new template that didn't previously exist in the document will be added to the document when the template is attached. Existing styles not in the template will remain the same.

Customizing a Template

In truth, templates are nothing more than Word documents, and can be edited as such. Simply open the template like any other document, make any changes you want, and save the template. Any document based on the template prior to the alterations will not change any of the document-level attributes as shown in the table of Template Attributes in Figure 9-16. Again, if in the File-Templates and Add-ins dialog box you selected Automatically Update Document Styles, any revised styles will be updated when you open the document.

Following are the steps for modifying a template.

✔ From the File menu, choose Open.

✔ Select Document Templates in the List Files of Type box (see Figure 9-21).

✔ In the File Name box, type or select the name of the template you want to modify, and then click OK.

Can't find your templates?

Although you can alter the locations that Word looks for templates, it first checks the WINWORD\TEMPLATE directory by default. If you created a template and stored it someplace else, either modify your template location in the Tools-Options-File Locations tab or enter the full path name for your template in the New dialog box.

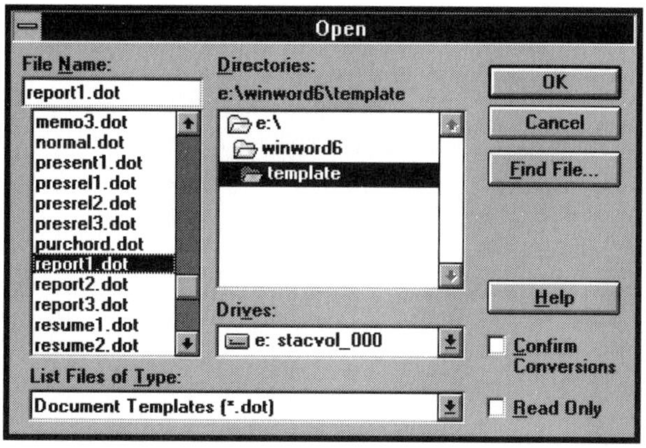

Figure 9-21: To open a template, make sure Document Templates is selected in the List Files of Type box.

Marking the book

Within any particular document, you can modify the styles offered by a template. You optionally can apply the modifications to the template as well. The template is very much like a cookbook recipe: if you want to modify it a bit, go ahead. If you don't make a mark in the book, the modification will apply only to the dish you're cooking at the moment.

On the other hand, if you want all subsequent documents based on a template to embody changes made to the current document, pull down the Format menu and choose Style. Click on the Organizer button in the Style dialog box and copy any style into the template. This process is like marking the cookbook: changes will appear in all subsequent renditions of the recipe if the cookbook itself is changed. It's your choice.

✔ Edit and format the template just like a Word document, including:

   ✔ Adding and deleting text or graphics

   ✔ Applying and changing font and paragraph formatting

   ✔ Changing page layout and other section formatting

   ✔ Creating and modifying styles

   ✔ Modifying shortcut keys, toolbars and menus

   ✔ Defining and changing AutoText entries

   ✔ Creating and changing macros

   ✔ Copying, renaming and deleting template items with the Organizer

✔ When you're finished, save the changes and close the template. The next document you create with the template will reveal all the changes you made.

Organizing Template Attributes

In Chapter 6, "Styles," I mentioned that in addition to renaming and deleting styles, you can also copy styles from one document or template to another. In addition to Styles, the Organizer dialog box also includes tabs for AutoText, Toolbars and Macros (see the bottom window in Figure 9-22). These items can be renamed, deleted and copied, but only from template to template.

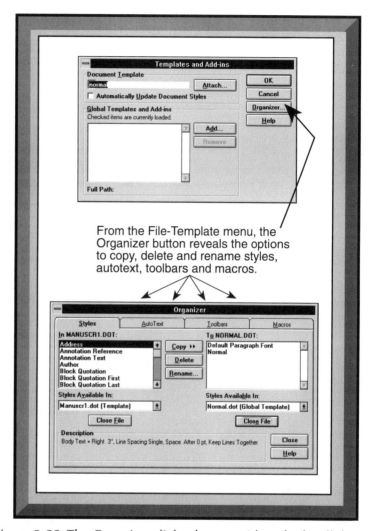

Figure 9-22: The Organizer dialog box provides tabs for all the template attributes that can be copied, deleted or renamed.

Chapter 6 demonstrated getting to the Organizer dialog box through the Style menu. You can access the Organizer from the File-Templates and Add-ins menu as well. Using either approach, proceed as follows:

✔ Select the tab that provides the items with which you want to work. Notice that Word displays the items available to the active document and its attached template as well as those items in the Normal template.

Make your efforts count

Transferring styles between documents and templates is easily misunderstood. It's all too easy to modify a document style and forget to modify your template. The problem also works in reverse: template style changes are not automatically incorporated into dependent documents; you must copy them or have them automatically updated as discussed in this section.

This lack of automation implies that while you have the flexibility of independent formatting among documents, you're also responsible for keeping your templates and documents synchronized when necessary. If you aren't attentive, anarchy breaks out. Templates and documents each find their own paths. No matter how carefully you planned your style strategy, negligence renders your efforts ineffectual.

✔ To change templates or documents, click on the Close File button below the appropriate list. Then click on the Open File button. Select the new template or document and click OK.

✔ To rename something, select it and click on the Rename button. To copy or delete items, select as many as you want (use Ctrl or Shift to select more than one), and then click on the Copy or Delete button. If you copy toolbars that are assigned with macros, you must also copy those macros.

✔ When you're finished, click on the Close button.

Creating a New Template

You can use two methods to create new templates. The first method is to create a template from scratch, meaning you construct every part of the template new or copy it from an existing template. The second method is to create a template from an existing document or template. If you've already created a template or document and the new template will have many of the same characteristics, the latter method can save processing.

Creating a Template From Scratch

Creating a template from scratch is precisely the same as creating a document from scratch. The only difference is choosing the Template button (instead of the Document button) in the File-New dialog box (see the top window in Figure 9-23). When you're ready to save the template, you will notice the Save File as Type box reflects Document Template rather than the usual Word Document option. This means the template will have a .DOT extension attached instead of the usual .DOC extension. And, if saved into the Templates subdirectory, the new template will automatically become an option in the Template list when you subsequently select the File-New option.

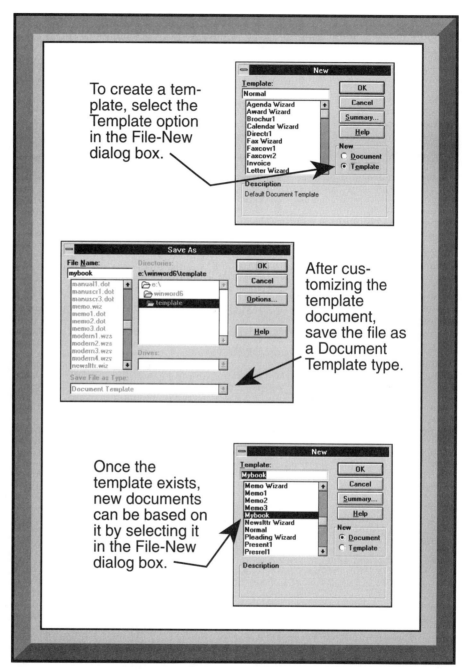

To create a template, select the Template option in the File-New dialog box.

After customizing the template document, save the file as a Document Template type.

Once the template exists, new documents can be based on it by selecting it in the File-New dialog box.

Figure 9-23: A template is created when you choose the Document Template format to save it in.

Creating a Template From Another Document or Template

There are many advantages to creating a document from another document or template, the most significant being the amount of time that is saved from not repeating something already done. If just about any quantity of template attributes already exist, you benefit from using them. You can delete or modify the remaining attributes as necessary.

To use another document or template, follow these steps:

✔ From the File menu, choose Open.

✔ If the item to use is a document, select the document name from the File Name box and click OK. If the item to use is a template, display the list of templates by selecting Document Templates in the List Files of Type box, and then click OK (see Figure 9-24).

Taking advantage of wizard characteristics

Why not take advantage of all the characteristics in a wizard? They're easily adapted into a template by using the wizard to create a document and then modifying the document and saving it as a template as explained here in the text. See: being creative isn't difficult.

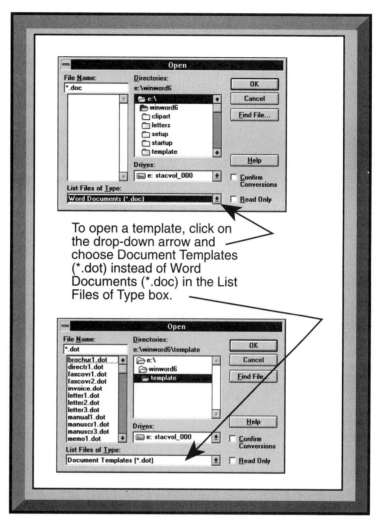

Figure 9-24: To open a template file, choose Document Templates instead of Word Documents from the List Files of Type box.

✔ From the File menu, immediately choose Save As and give the template a new name, saving it as a template. Make sure you save the template with a new name before making any changes, so you don't accidentally forget and save over the old template or document.

✔ Make the desired changes, including:

  ✔ Adding and deleting text or graphics

  ✔ Applying and changing font and paragraph formatting

  ✔ Changing page layout and other section formatting

  ✔ Creating and modifying styles

  ✔ Modifying shortcut keys, toolbars and menus

  ✔ Defining and changing AutoText entries

  ✔ Creating and changing macros

  ✔ Copying, renaming and deleting template items with the Organizer

✔ When you're finished creating the template, choose Save from the File menu.

THE LAST WORD

Perhaps Microsoft should have named this release of the software "the Last Word," rather than Word for Windows Version 6.0. There really isn't much left for it to do, after all, and there's little opportunity to improve upon its ease of use. I suppose we'll look back on Version 6.0 someday and remark upon its immaturity. "Can you imagine," we'll say. "You actually had to *type!*" That's about the only improvement that remains.

Whether or not Microsoft has, we have certainly reached our Last Word. Word is resplendent with desktop-publishing features; now it's up to you to make use of them. At this point, desktop publishing with Word for Windows shouldn't be difficult and it most certainly will be adventuresome. Perhaps best of all, you'll probably have as much fun as a mouse in malt. Go ahead: nobody's looking.

Appendix

THE *ANSI* CHARACTER SET

The American Standard Code for Information Interchange (ASCII) assigns a numeric value to every character—alphabetic, numeric or punctuation—that can be entered from a standard keyboard. Even a few others such as paragraph breaks and tabs are defined by the ASCII set.

The ANSI (American National Standards Institute) set adds another 128 characters to those offered by ASCII, including foreign characters, publishers' quotes, em dashes, fractions and others of specific interest to the desktop publisher.

Word accommodates the ANSI set via the 10-key pad. To enter any of these characters, hold down the Alt key and type the four-digit code that appears beside the character in the table below. When you release Alt, the character will appear.

Though this table is provided as a convenience, remember that Word offers the same information whenever you choose Symbol from the Format menu. The Symbols tab offers all of the ASCII *and* ANSI characters for every TrueType font installed in your system, and the Special Characters tab offers a convenient method of entering the most frequently-used ANSI characters, including quotation marks; special spaces and hyphens; and the copyright, trademark, and registered symbols.

0145 ....'	0182 ....¶	0219 ....Û
0146 ....'	0183 .... ·	0220 ....Ü
0147 ....''	0184 ....¸	0221 ....Ý
0148 ....''	0185 ....¹	0222 ....Þ
0149 ....°	0186 ....º	0223 ....ß
0150 ....–	0187 ....»	0224 ....à
0151 ....—	0188 ....¼	0225 ....á
0152 ....~	0189 ....½	0226 ....â
0153 ....™	0190 ....´	0227 ....ã
0154	0191 ....¿	0228 ....ä
0155 ....›	0192 ....À	0229 ....å
0156 ....œ	0193 ....Á	0230 ....æ
0157	0194 ....Â	0231 ....ç
0158	0195 ....Ã	0232 ....è
0159 ....Ÿ	0196 ....Ä	0233 ....é
0160	0197 ....Å	0234 ....ê
0161 ....¡	0198 ....Æ	0235 ....ë
0162 ....¢	0199 ....Ç	0236 ....ì
0163 ....£	0200 ....È	0237 ....í
0164 ....¤	0201 ....É	0238 ....î
0165 ....¥	0202 ....Ê	0239 ....ï
0166 ....¦	0203 ....Ë	0240 ....ð
0167 ....§	0204 ....Ì	0241 ....ñ
0168 ....¨	0205 ....Í	0242 ....ò
0169 ....©	0206 ....Î	0243 ....ó
0170 ....ª	0207 ....Ï	0244 ....ô
0171 ....«	0208 ....Ð	0245 ....õ
0172 ....¬	0209 ....Ñ	0246 ....ö
0173 ....-	0210 ....Ò	0247 ....÷
0174 ....®	0211 ....Ó	0248 ....ø
0175 ....¯	0212 ....Ô	0249 ....ù
0176 ....°	0213 ....Õ	0250 ....ú
0177 ....±	0214 ....Ö	0251 ....û
0178 ....²	0215	0252 ....ü
0179 ....³	0216 ....Ø	0253 ....ý
0180 ....´	0217 ....Ù	0254 ....þ
0181 ....µ	0218 ....Ú	0255 ....ÿ

Glossary

A

Ascender
The stem of a lowercase letter that rises above the main body. Examples include *b*, *d*, *f* and *l*.

B

Bad break
In composition, starting a column or page with a widow; or ending a column or page with an orphan. Word automatically corrects bad breaks. *See also* Widow *and* Orphan.

Baseline
The figurative line that runs along the "base" of a line of text. The better this line is defined (serifs help), the easier it is to read the text.

Baseline alignment
The alignment of the baselines of adjoining columns of text. It's also an important consideration for facing pages, where it should be maintained across the gutter.

Bézier

A complex line segment composed of the line itself and as many as four points: a starting point, ending point and up to two control points, to which the line is "magnetically" attracted. The resulting curve resembles a French curve. The Windows metafile format converts Bézier curves into multiple line segments; the PostScript metafile format retains them. *See also* Metafile *and* PostScript.

Bit

A contraction of BInary digiT, the basic unit of digital information.

Bitmaps

Graphic or textual images produced by a pattern of individual dots, or "bits." Photographic and freehand graphics are often bitmapped. In this context, bitmapped is synonymous with raster. *See also* Vector *and* Object.

Bleed

A printed image that extends beyond the trim edge to the edge of the page.

Blurb

A short capitulation of the subject matter of a document, usually placed on the title page near the headline.

Body type

A type used for the text of a printed piece, as distinguished from the heading. Body type is usually 12 points in size or smaller. *See also* Text. *Contrast with* Display type.

Boldface type

A heavier weight type than the regular or roman style of a typeface.

Border

A free-standing box or a box drawn around an element. Word's Border menu provides fairly elaborate control over the appearance of borders.

Byte

A unit of digital information, equivalent to one character of eight bits. In the vernacular, a byte is the amount of memory (RAM or disk) required to store one keystroke.

C

Camera-ready

Final copy ready to be photographed with a graphic-arts camera.

Caps and small caps

Two sizes of capital letters made in one size of type, commonly used in most roman typefaces. *See also* Small caps.

Color separation

In photography, the process of separating color originals into the primary printing color components in negative or positive form.

Condensed type

A narrow or slender style of a typeface. Word cannot distort letterforms this way; Microsoft Draw and WordArt can. (*Note:* Word uses this term to describe type with reduced spacing between characters. *See* Spacing.)

Continuous tone

Gradient tones from white to black, created of dots. Continuous-tone images are photographic; computers simulate gray using a halftone or dithering process. *Contrast with* Halftone *and* Dither.

Crop

Eliminates unwanted portions of a graphic or page. Word crops graphics when you drag on a handle while pressing the Shift key.

D

Descender

The part of a lowercase letter that extends below the baseline. Examples include *g*, *j* and *p*.

Display type

Type used for headlines, subheads, pull-quotes and page elements other than text. Generally, display type is defined as type set in sizes larger than 12 points. *Contrast with* Body type.

Dither

The reproduction of continuous-tone artwork, such as a photograph, by grouping clusters of dots (at the printer) or pixels (for the screen). *See also* Halftone. *Contrast with* Continuous tone.

Drop cap

The initial letter of a paragraph that drops below the baseline of the first line of text to a lower line. Text often wraps around a drop cap. *See also* Initial capital.

Dummy

A preliminary layout showing the positions of illustrations and text as they are to appear in final printed form.

E

Em
In composition, a unit of measurement exactly as wide as the uppercase *M* in a given font.

Embedded object
In Windows, an object that contains a reference to the application that created it. Typically, the original application is revealed by double-clicking on the object. *See* Linked object.

En
One-half the width of an em (*see* Em), often used to describe the width of a space.

Expanded type
Type modified to be wider than normal. (***Note:*** Word uses this term to describe type with increased spacing between characters. *See* Spacing.)

F

Family
In typography, a family of type usually includes roman (regular), italic, bold and bold-italic fonts.

Flush-left and flush-right
Type set up to align at the left (or right) edge of a column. This text is flush-left (also called align left). Justified type is set flush-left and flush-right. *Contrast with* Justify.

Flush paragraph
A paragraph set with no indention.

Folio

Information (date, chapter title, page number, etc.) set at top, bottom or side of a page. Folios often feature rules and borders—even graphics—and may contain several lines.

Font

A complete assortment of letters, numbers and punctuation of a given size and style of a typeface.

G

Gutter

The vertical space or inner margin between a printed area and the end of a page or between facing pages. This term also can refer to the area between adjoining columns of a layout.

H

Halftone

The reproduction of continuous-tone artwork (such as a photograph) through a crossline screen that converts the image into dots of various sizes. Some scanning software simulates halftones by dithering. *See also* Dither *and* Continuous tone.

Handle

Small black squares surrounding a selected object. Objects may be distorted, sized and cropped in Word by dragging on these handles.

I

Initial capital
Distinctive graphical or typographical treatment applied to the initial character of an article or paragraph. *See also* Drop cap.

Italic
The style of letters that slant, in distinction from upright or roman letters. Often used for emphasis within text, italics are usually an entirely separate font from their roman derivatives. *See also* Oblique.

J

Jump
An article that begins on one page of a document and continues on another (usually not sequential) page. Jump page references usually appear at the bottom of the origin column and at the top of the column in which the story continues.

Justify
Uniform alignment of all lines of text. Justified text lines are the same length, producing smooth left and right margins. *Contrast with* Flush-left and flush-right.

K

Kerning
The process of removing space between pairs of characters so that they appear closer together. *Contrast with* Letter spacing *and* Spacing.

Kiss
The process of kerning characters until they barely touch, or kiss. *Compare with* TNT.

L

Leader
Rows of dashes or dots used to guide the eye across the page. Leaders, typically referred to as tab leaders, are used in tabular work.

Leading
The distance from the top of one line of type to the next, usually measured in points. Word sets leading with the line spacing section of the Format-Paragraph dialog box.

Letter spacing
The process of adding space between pairs of characters so that they appear farther apart. Letter spacing is the opposite of kerning. *Contrast with* Spacing.

Line art
Graphics composed of pure black and pure white, with no gray or color. *Contrast with* Halftone.

Line spacing
See Leading.

Linked object
In Windows, an object that contains a reference to the original file on disk. If that file is changed, the linked object changes also. *See also* Embedded object.

Lowercase
The small letters in type, as distinguished from capital letters. *Contrast with* Uppercase.

M

M
Abbreviation for quantities of 1,000 sheets of paper. Do not confuse with *em.*

Metafile
A graphics file format containing multiple types of graphics and text. The metafile format indigenous to the Windows environment is the Windows MetaFile, or .WMF format. It includes both raster and vector graphics, and text.

Moiré
The uneven and usually undesirable pattern caused by incorrect screen angles of overprinting halftones. Moiré patterns also develop when certain bitmapped (raster) images are reduced or enlarged.

O

Object
In graphics, the term used to describe graphic images composed of lines, arcs, ellipses and rectangles—the so-called "objects" of object-oriented graphics. Draw is an object editor. *See also* Vector. *Contrast with* Raster *or* Bitmaps.

Oblique
In typography, a form of italic character, essentially the regular character "leaned over." While most roman type families feature true italics, many sans-serif families use obliques. *See also* Italic.

Orphan

The first line of a paragraph appearing at the bottom of a page or column. *Contrast with* Widow.

P

Pica

Unit of measurement used principally in typesetting. One pica equals 1/6 inch, or 12 points. Word can be set to the pica system of measurement using the Options-Tools-General command sequence.

Point

Unit of measurement, used primarily for designating type sizes and leading. As used today, the point is equal to 1/72 inch.

PostScript

A proprietary metafile format, published by Adobe Corporation. PostScript is a page-description language, particularly rich in typographical and textual features: rotated and distorted type is supported, as are graduated fills, bitmaps of various resolution, and Beziér curves. The Windows environment is entirely supporting of PostScript. *See also* Beziér *and* Metafile.

Pull-quote

A quotation "pulled" from the body of a document and given special graphical or typographical treatment to set it apart from the body and attract the reader's attention.

R

Race

In typography, a broad category of type that includes numerous families with common characteristics. Sans-serif is a race, as is roman.

Ragged-left and ragged-right

Type set with an even left or right margin and an uneven or ragged right or left margin. Also known as align-left or align-right. The most common alignment scheme involving uneven margins is flush-left/ragged-right. *See also* Flush-left and flush-right. *Contrast with* Justify.

Raster

Graphic or textual images produced by a pattern of individual dots. Photographic and hand-drawn graphics are often scanned as raster images. In this context, raster is synonymous with bitmapped. *Contrast with* Vector *or* Object.

Roman

A race of type characterized by the use of serifs and a marked contrast between thick and thin strokes. Times is a roman typeface. The term also describes the "normal" font in a family of fonts. Times Roman is the "normal" font in the Times family, which includes Times Bold, Times Italic and Times Bold-Italic. *See also* Bold *and* Italic.

Rule

In design, a line that prints. The word *line* refers to a non-printing element in this context. *See also* Border.

Runaround

Type set to wrap around a graphic or other design element (also called wrapped text).

S

Sans-serif
Typeface designs without serifs, the finishing strokes at the ends of letters. *See also* Serif.

Scaling
Reducing or enlarging an image to fit a specific area. Word scales graphics when you use the Format-Picture command sequence.

Scanner
A device that systematically scans images and converts them into electrical signals that can be used by a computer. *See also* Raster *and* Bitmaps.

Serif
The short crosslines at the end of the main stem of some letter forms. Times has serifs, unlike Helvetica, a sans-serif typeface. *See also* Sans-serif.

Sidebar
Parenthetical text affiliated with adjacent body text. Sidebars are usually given distinctive graphical or textual treatment to set them apart from the main text.

Small caps
An alphabet of small capital letters, approximately 20 percent smaller than normal uppercase letters. They're often used with larger capital letters. *See* Caps and small caps.

Spacing
The uniform addition or removal of space between words and/or characters in body text or display type treatments. Word sets spacing in the Format-Font dialog box.

T

Text
The body matter of a page, as distinguished from the display type. *Contrast with* Display type.

TNT ("Tight Not Touching")
The process of setting type so tight that characters almost, but don't quite, touch. *Compare with* Kiss.

U

Uppercase
In typography, uppercase letters are capitals. When type was set by hand, individual stamps of type were stored in a case that was placed on an inclined surface (not unlike a music stand) for convenient access. Since capital letters weren't used as often as lowercase letters, the capitals were placed at the top of the case (the upper case), reserving the lower half for non-capital letters.

V

Vector
In graphics, a vector image is one composed of graphical primitives: rectangles, ellipses, arcs and lines. More elaborate vector-base formats provide options for complex fills and curves. Vector graphics may be enlarged or reduced without loss of quality. *See also* Object. *Contrast with* Raster.

W

Widow

The last line of a paragraph appearing at the top of a page or column. Widows can be mistaken for heads or subheads and are thus considered bad form. *Contrast with* Orphan.

X

X-height

The height of the body of the lowercase x in a particular size and font. The term is typically used to describe the height of all lowercase characters, exclusive of ascenders and descenders. *See* Baseline, Ascender *and* Descender.

Bibliography

Books

Biggs, John R. *Basic Typography*. New York: Watson-Guptill, 1968 (out of print).

Black, Roger. *Desktop Design Power*. New York: Bantam Books, 1991.

Brown, Alex. *In Print: Text and Type in the Age of Desktop Publishing*. New York: Watson-Guptill, 1989.

Bruno, Michael H., ed. *Pocket Pal: A Graphic Arts Production Handbook*, 14th edition. Memphis, TN: International Paper Company, 1989.

Burke, Clifford. *Type From the Desktop: Designing with Type and Your Computer*. Chapel Hill, N.C.: Ventana Press, 1990.

Craig, James. *Designing with Type: A Basic Course in Typography*, revised edition. New York: Watson-Guptill, 1980.

Crane, Mark W., Pierce, Joseph R., and Holzgang, David A. *LaserJet Companion*. Redmond, WA: Microsoft Press, 1991.

Crane, Mark W. *Word for Windows Companion*. Redmond, WA: Microsoft Press, 1990.

Dorn, Raymond. *How to Design & Improve Magazine Layouts*, 2nd edition. Chicago: Nelson-Hall, 1986.

Dover Publications, Inc. 180 Varick St., New York, NY 10014. (Clip-art books.)

Feiring, Roy A. "The Neoclassic Printing Movement, 1890–1940." Master's thesis, University of Oregon, 1976.

Hurlburt, Allen. *Layout: The Design of the Printed Page.* New York: Watson-Guptill, 1977 (out of print).

Hurlburt, Allen. *Publication Design.* New York: Watson-Guptill, 1971 (out of print).

Lichty, Thomas W. *Design Principles for Desktop Publishers.* Glenview, IL: Scott Foresman, 1988.

Nelson, Roy Paul. *Publication Design*, 5th edition. Dubuque, IA: William C. Brown, 1991.

Parker, Roger C. *Looking Good in Print*, 3rd edition. Chapel Hill, NC: Ventana Press, 1993.

Stone, Sumner. *On Stone: The Art and Use of Typography on the Personal Computer.* San Francisco: Chronicle Books, 1991.

Strunk, William, Jr., and White, E.B. *Elements of Style*, 3rd edition. New York: Macmillan, 1979.

White, Jan V. *Editing by Design*, 2nd edition. New York: R. R. Bowker, 1982.

White, Jan V. *Designing for Magazines*, 2nd edition. New York: R. R. Bowker, 1982.

White, Jan V. *Mastering Graphics.* New York: R. R. Bowker, 1983.

Wilde, Richard, and Wilde, Judith. *Visual Literacy: A Conceptual Approach to Solving Graphic Problems.* New York: Watson-Guptill, 1991.

Manuals

Windows Version 3.0 User's Guide. Redmond, WA: Microsoft, 1990.

Windows Version 3.1 User's Guide. Redmond, WA: Microsoft, 1992.

Microsoft Word for Windows User's Guide. Redmond, WA: Microsoft, 1993.

Periodicals

Aldus Magazine. Aldus Corp, 411 First Avenue South, Seattle, WA 98104. Bimonthly.

Communication Arts. Coyne and Blanchard, 410 Sherman Oaks, Palo Alto, CA 94303. Eight issues/year.

Desktop Communications. 2 Hammarskjold Plaza, New York, NY 10017. Bimonthly.

Font & Function, The Adobe Type Catalog. Adobe Systems, P.O. Box 7900, Mountain View, CA 94039-7900. Thrice yearly.

Print: America's Graphic Design Magazine. RC Publications, 6400 Goldsboro Road, Bethesda, MD 20817. Bimonthly.

Publish. PCW Communications, 501 Second Street, San Francisco, CA 94107. Monthly.

U&lc. International Typographic Corporation, 2 Hammarskjold Plaza, New York, NY 10017. Bimonthly.

Index

COLOPHON

This book was produced on two PC compatibles, 386 & 486, and a Macintosh Quadra 700, all using PageMaker 5.0. Proofs were printed on a LaserWriter NT II, and electronic files were output directly to film using a Linotype L330.

This book is set in two typefaces. The body type is Palatino. Sidebars and display type are Optima.

From Ventana Press...

More Companions For Creative Computing

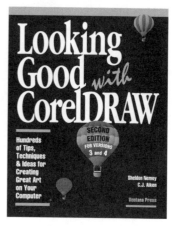

Available from bookstores or Ventana Press. Immediate shipment guaranteed. Your money returned if not satisfied. To order or for more information contact:

Ventana Press, PO Box 2468, Chapel Hill, NC 27515
800/743-5369 (U.S. orders only)   919/942-0220   Fax 919/942-1140

The Windows Shareware 500
$39.95
417 pages, illustrated
ISBN: 1-56604-045-0
Whether you're a shareware veteran or skeptic, this book is required reading. The only comprehensive guide to 500 of the best Windows shareware programs. Comes with four disks.

Word for Windows Design Companion, Second Edition
$21.95
473 pages, illustrated
ISBN: 1-56604-075-2
Learn the basics of good design with step-by-step instructions. Filled with innovative design advice and creative examples for getting the most from your Word investment.

Looking Good With CorelDRAW!, Second Edition
$27.95
328 pages, illustrated
ISBN: 1-56604-061-2
Guidelines and suggestions are given on how to best take advantage of CorelDRAW's powerful new desktop publishing features for Version 4.

Windows, Word & Excel Office Companion, Second Edition
$21.95
600 pages, illustrated
ISBN: 1-56604-083-3
Your Microsoft business bible. This three-in-one reference is organized as a quick course in each program. Chapters contain valuable information on basic commands and features, plus helpful tutorials, tips and shortcuts.

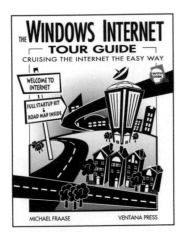

Voodoo Windows
$19.95
282 pages, illustrated
ISBN: 1-56604-005-1
A unique resource, *Voodoo Windows* bypasses the technical information found in many Windows books to bring you an abundance of never-before-published tips, tricks and shortcuts for maximum Windows productivity. A one-of-a-kind reference for beginners and experienced users alike.

The Windows Internet Tour Guide
$24.95
275 pages, illustrated
ISBN: 1-56604-081-7
Push your PC to cruising speed on the Internet! Comes complete with software that converts the Internet to an easy graphic interface, along with free trial service and step-by-step instructions.

The Official America Online for Windows Membership Kit & Tour Guide
$34.95
402 pages, illustrated
ISBN: 1-56604-013-2
This book/disk set includes the AOL starter disk, 10 free hours of online time for new and current members, a free month's membership plus your official AOL "tour guide."

the
Ventana Press

Desktop Design Series

To order these and other Ventana Press titles, use the form in the back of this book or contact your local bookstore or computer store. Full money-back guarantee!

Return order form to:
Ventana Press, PO Box 2468, Chapel Hill, NC 27515
☎919/942-0220; Fax 919/942-1140

Can't wait? Call toll-free, 800/743-5369 (U.S. only)!

Looking Good in Print, Third Edition
$24.95
424 pages, illustrated
ISBN: 1-56604-047-7
With over 200,000 copies in print, **Looking Good in Print** is looking even better, with a new chapter on working with color, plus new sections on photography and scanning. For use with any software or hardware, this desktop design bible has become the standard among novice and experienced desktop publishers alike.

The Makeover Book: 101 Design Solutions for Desktop Publishing
$17.95
282 pages, illustrated
ISBN: 0-940087-20-0
"Before-and-after" desktop publishing examples demonstrate how basic design revisions can dramatically improve a document.

Advertising From the Desktop
$24.95
464 pages, illustrated
ISBN: 1-56604-064-7
Advertising From the Desktop offers unmatched design advice and helpful how-to instructions for creating persuasive ads. This book is an idea-packed resource for improving the look and effect of your ads.

Newsletters From the Desktop
$23.95
306 pages, illustrated
ISBN: 0-940087-40-5
Now the millions of desktop publishers who produce newsletters can learn how to dramatically improve the design of their publications.

The Presentation Design Book, Second Edition
$24.95
320 pages, illustrated
ISBN: 1-56604-014-0
The Presentation Design Book is filled with thoughtful advice and instructive examples for creating presentation visuals that have the power to communicate and persuade. For use with any software or hardware.

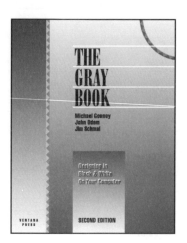

The Gray Book, Second Edition
$24.95
272 pages, illustrated
ISBN: 1-56604-073-6
This "idea gallery" for desktop publishers offers a lavish variety of the most interesting black, white and gray graphics effects that can be achieved with laser printers, scanners and high-resolution output devices.

T O ORDER additional copies of *Desktop Publishing With Word for Windows, Second Edition,* or any other Ventana Press title, please fill out this order form and return it to us for quick shipment.

	Quantity		Price		Total
Advertising From the Desktop	_____	x	$24.95	=	$_____
Desktop Publishing With Word for Windows, 2nd Edition	_____	x	$21.95	=	$_____
The Gray Book, 2nd Edition	_____	x	$24.95	=	$_____
Looking Good in Print, 3rd Edition	_____	x	$24.95	=	$_____
Looking Good With CorelDRAW!, 2nd Edition	_____	x	$27.95	=	$_____
The Makeover Book	_____	x	$17.95	=	$_____
Newsletters From the Desktop	_____	x	$23.95	=	$_____
The Official America Online for Windows Membership Kit & Tour Guide	_____	x	$34.95	=	$_____
The Windows Internet Tour Guide	_____	x	$24.95	=	$_____
Presentation Design Book, 2nd Edition	_____	x	$24.95	=	$_____
Type From the Desktop	_____	x	$23.95	=	$_____
Voodoo DOS, 2nd Edition	_____	x	$19.95	=	$_____
Voodoo Windows	_____	x	$19.95	=	$_____
The Windows Shareware 500	_____	x	$39.95	=	$_____
Windows, Word & Excel Office Companion, 2nd Edition	_____	x	$21.95	=	$_____
Word for Windows Design Companion, 2nd Edition	_____	x	$21.95	=	$_____

Shipping: Please add $4.50/first book, $1.35/book thereafter; $8.25/book "two-day air," $2.25/book thereafter. For Canada, add $6.50/book. = $_____

Send C.O.D. (add $4.50 to shipping charges) = $_____

North Carolina residents add 6% sales tax = $_____

Total = $_____

Name_____

Company_____

Address (No PO Box)_____

City_____ State_____ Zip _____

Daytime Telephone _____

___ Payment enclosed ___VISA ___MC   Acc't # _____

Expiration Date_____ Interbank # _____

Signature _____

Please mail or fax to: **Ventana Press, PO Box 2468, Chapel Hill, NC 27515**
☎ **919/942-0220, FAX: 919/942-1140**

CAN'T WAIT? CALL TOLL-FREE ☎ 800/743-5369 (U.S. only)!